CREATIVE DWELLING
Empathy and Clarity in God and Self

American Academy of Religion
Academy Series

edited by
Barbara A. Holdrege

Number 98

CREATIVE DWELLING
Empathy and Clarity in God and Self

by
Lucinda A. Stark Huffaker

Lucinda A. Stark Huffaker

CREATIVE DWELLING
Empathy and Clarity in God and Self

Scholars Press
Atlanta, Georgia

CREATIVE DWELLING
Empathy and Clarity in God and Self

by
Lucinda A. Stark Huffaker

Copyright © 1998 by the American Academy of Religion

All rights reserved. No part of this work may be reproduced or transmitted in any form or by any means, electronic or mechanical, including photocopying and recording, or by means of any information storage or retrieval system, except as may be expressly permitted by the 1976 Copyright Act or in writing from the publisher. Requests for permission should be addressed in writing to the Rights and Permissions Office, Scholars Press, P.O. Box 15399, Atlanta, GA 30333-0399, USA.

Library of Congress Cataloging in Publication Data
Huffaker, Lucinda A. Stark.
    Creative dwelling : empathy and clarity in God and self / Lucinda A. Stark Huffaker.
       p. cm. — (American Academy of Religion academy series ; no. 98)
    Includes bibliographical references and index.
    ISBN 0-7885-0329-4 (pbk. : alk. paper)
    1. Process theology. 2. Feminist psychology. 3. Self.
I. Title. II. Series.
BT83.6.H84 1998
230'.046—dc21   98-44463
                                                        CIP

Printed in the United States of America
on acid-free paper

CONTENTS

PREFACE vii

INTRODUCTION ix

1. IN SEARCH OF SELF: *A Feminist Dilemma* 1

    The Normalcy of Men
    Feminist Epistemology and the Modern/Postmodern Debate
    Parameters and Particularities
    Two Aspects of Women's Experiences of Self
    Theological "Eavesdropping"
    "Whiteheadian Feminism"

2. THE NATURE OF CREATIVITY 17

    Creativity in Theological Contexts
    Psychological Investigations of Creativity
    Whitehead's Portrayal of Creativity
    Summary

3. CREATIVITY AS COMPASSION: *Empathic Attunement to the World* 45

    Empathy's Role in Psychological Development
    A Process Perspective on Empathy
    Theological Interpretations of Empathy

4. CREATIVITY AS COMPOSITION: *Clarity Through Complexity and Contrast* 83

    Clarity and Selfhood
    Clarity in Women's Psychological Development
    Clarity in Process Thought
    Theological Implications

5. DWELLING: *An Experiment with Metaphor* 119
    The Power of Metaphor
    The Developmental Journey
    Dwelling as a Place
    Self as a Dwelling
    Dwelling as a Practice
    Self-Emergence Through Dwelling
    Conclusion

6. CONCLUSION: *Postlude as Prelude* 147

BIBLIOGRAPHY 159

INDEX 175

PREFACE

I like to think of writing as conversation, something ongoing and communal. Writing as conversation reminds me that the discussion is in process, has multiple voices, and relies on relationships. Participation in a conversation requires the presence and contribution of others. The "final word" on a topic is neither expected nor desired. Instead, comments build on one another and voices test and add to each other. It has fostered my own creativity to approach my writing as conversation. I often refer to "our discussion" as though my reader sits with me, probing my comments with "Yes, but..."s and "What about...?"s. I hope there will also be many "Oh, that's so true...!"s. I try to connect my ideas with other parts of the conversation and leave room to encourage others to speak, especially those who have ordinarily been silenced.

Of course, there are several problems with this metaphor. Writing is much more permanent and static than conversation. Authors move on to new perspectives, different interests, even ideological reversals, while their texts solidify a moment in their thought. And there is no assurance, as in conversation, that those to whom one's writing is addressed will ever hear and respond!

Nevertheless, this book enters a conversation about the self and about feminism and about God. Why this conversation? It is a conversation that has shaped my life, and many others' also. It is interdisciplinary because there are no boundaries to the creative improvisation that gives life meaning. It is about connection and process, change and continuity, achieving and resting. Born from my own resistance to others' well-intended advice about relationships, this conversation is about confirming choices and discerning healthy connections. Whether this conversation will engage others—that is the large unknown. However, I think that readers across several disciplines and vocations will find the conversation intriguing and helpful: psychologists and theologians, ministers and college professors, lay women and feminists, mothers and sons.

I owe a debt of gratitude to the people who read drafts of this book, and especially to those women who read pieces and said that it was important, that it said something they needed to hear, that it described and confirmed their experience. I am also grateful to Larry Graham, who was midwife to the creative labor of writing, and to Del Brown, Barbara Holdrege, Raymond Williams and others who laid a path for its publishing by Scholars Press. I have appreciated the insightful suggestions and generosity of Catherine Keller, William Placher, and many, many others. Perhaps I am most grateful to my family, who (in this ongoing conversation) keep me honest and love me regardless.

INTRODUCTION

I am a weaver—both literally and metaphorically. I delight in blending yarns of various textures and colors into patterns on my loom, watching the fabric emerge in a new coherence. If I have chosen well, the strands of yarn are transformed through the process into cloth that is both beautiful and structurally sound. Quite similarly, I have found it sustaining both intellectually and spiritually to bring together ideas, images, and observations from several arenas of life and interweave them to yield new insights. Weaving these connections into personally meaningful designs is a task I consider fundamental to personal and social transformation because it is the new connections that break through our complacency to create an impact upon the older underlying fabric of our meaning framework. Unless the disparate strands of new ideas wield the influence of becoming warp and weft, the existing fabric of our presuppositions prevents us from accepting or incorporating new information. When we recognize relationships between and among new ideas and our experiences, the ideas start to make sense in ways that transform the patterns of our worldviews: our attitudes, values, language, behaviors, and eventually, our societies.

In spite of decades of study and argument about the influence of gender in the fields of philosophy, psychology, and theology, views of the human self that are rooted in the old, underlying fabric of the normative male experience have been resistant to change. In this book I weave together particular strands in process theology and feminist psychology to provide a new understanding of the human person that confronts patriarchal values still entrenched in our society. Both of these theoretical standpoints emphasize the fundamental role that relational connections play in the constitution of self and world.[1] When they are brought into dialogue, their correlations and contrasts form a pattern whose vividness sharpens our questions of each and creates a new fabric to dislodge the old material of the isolated self and its entourage of values. Process theology becomes a means of clarifying and extending the influence of feminist insights while feminist psychology critiques certain aspects of process theology. That is, process thought strengthens feminist claims about the value of women's investment in relationships, and it advances their dialogue with other modes of inquiry, extending the influence of their psychological insights. At the same time, the emerging fabric of meaning also corrects certain excesses in process thought that overemphasize inexhaustible novelty and perpetual striving.

Creativity forms the dominant thread that orders the discussion. It is a concept that helps mediate disciplinary boundaries like those between theology and psychology because of its shared meaning: it connotes a human and divine openness to the world that issues forth in a unique and beautiful synthesis. Creativity provides a conceptual framework for feminist models of self that coordinates their various emphases while making them more coherent, extensive, and powerful.

The two facets of selfhood that provide the psychological focus for the conversation are drawn from the new paradigm of women's psychological development being advanced by the Stone Center for Developmental Services and Studies, among others.[2] *Empathy* as a crucial feature of human emergence and *clarity of self* as it is achieved through increasing complexity and contrast have been the focus of Stone Center theorist Judith Jordan. Her work provides the foundation from which I venture across a wide domain of related literature on the psychology of women, personality development, empathy, and identity formation in order to establish the qualities and dynamics of healthy human connections. The central theological voice is drawn from the process thought of Alfred North Whitehead and his interpreters, especially those feminist theologians like Marjorie Suchocki and Rita Brock who filter Whitehead's schema through clear feminist commitments. My choice of process philosophy is neither arbitrary nor ultimate but demonstrates a type of interdisciplinary conversation that both discloses the vast webbing of our worldviews and is fundamental to its transformation. A third major contributor to the dialogue is feminist theologian Catherine Keller, whose method of excavating the ideological, mythological, and sociosystemic connections between psychology and theological anthropology has been the guiding vision for this project. In addition to these three source strands, the project's texture is enriched by engaging numerous experts and representatives of the research and opinions brought to bear on each topic (for example, creativity, empathy, multiple roles, transcendence, dwelling, and so on) as the argument progresses.[3] The underrepresented voices of particular ethnic, class, and gay/lesbian groups contribute an additional dimension wherever they have sustained related conversations.

The challenge of moderating such a multifarious discussion lies in generating a pattern that guides the reader through the connections to some forward-looking conclusions without (1) losing the design through fragmentation or (2) trivializing it by overstating obvious similarities and not allowing space for the reader's own contributive connections. With this task in mind, I begin by contextualizing the problem of constructing more adequate and inclusive models of human selfhood within feminist and modern/postmodern debates about epistemology and the perspectival nature of truth (Chapter 1). I then use the criteria suggested by these debates to outline the scope and limitations of the present project, including the importance and method of theological reflection upon these changing views of human nature, and the problems and potential of using process thought as a conceptual framework.

Chapter 2 introduces the focusing concept of creativity and explores its traditional and contemporary usage in theology. Psychological understandings of creativity are analyzed to demonstrate how the concept bridges the two disciplines with common associations. Then I discuss and critique creativity as it is represented in Whitehead's schema and link it with important themes that were evident in theological and psychological usages. These themes continue to reverberate through the remaining chapters as I rely repeatedly on creativity to organize the discussion of self-emergence through relationships.

Chapters 3 and 4 examine the dynamics of empathy and clarity of self in women's psychological development. In each chapter, I point out significant departures from traditional developmental models and show how these are supported by correlations with specific process formulations about the nature of reality. Theological reflection upon these two aspects of selfhood conclude the chapters, providing fresh perspectives on such topics as the divine and human natures, sin, sanctification, immanence, transcendence, and spirituality.

Here we shift in order to enliven the conceptual discussion with an exploration of "dwelling" as a metaphor that illumines concrete examples of creativity in the activities which have occupied women for centuries (Chapter 5). As an alternative metaphor to the popular one of "journey," "dwelling" is used in an iconoclastic and visionary way to portray the aspects of selfhood delineated in this manuscript. Finally, I offer some very preliminary suggestions for extending the connections into other domains like education and public policy (Chapter 6).

The categories and analyses of process thought provide a suitable and timely framework for conceptualizing the facets of selfhood that are being uncovered and emphasized in feminist theories of psychological development. By reflecting on the theological implications that attend these reformulations, I hope to advance the discussion that seeks understandings of God and human selfhood that more adequately reflect and affirm the diversity of human experience.

NOTES

1. Process philosophy and theology that is based on Alfred North Whitehead's philosophy of organism are not the only schemas or conceptual frameworks that support the relational aspects of people and environments. I have chosen them for reasons that will be set forth in Chapter 1 and amplified in the chapters that follow, but I would welcome and encourage other conversation partners that can shed light on our wrestling with the liminalities of selfhood.

2. The Stone Center is located at Wellesley College, Wellesley, Mass., where it hosts workshops and colloquia devoted to collaborative theory-building about the dynamics of self-constituting relationships as they are manifested in women's experiences. The Center publishes the works-in-progress of researchers, teachers, and therapists who critique traditional psychologies and psychotherapies and propose an alternative psychological system based on radical relationality. Many of the works-in-progress that I have cited in this book have since been more conveniently collected in two volumes: Judith V. Jordan, Alexandra G. Kaplan, Jean Baker Miller, and Irene Stiver, *Women's Growth in Connection: Writings from the Stone Center* (New York: Guilford Press, 1991); and Judith V. Jordan, ed., *Women's Growth in Diversity: More Writings from the Stone Center* (New York: Guilford Press, 1997).

3. It is impossible to present each of these views in full here, but I believe the examples do not misrepresent or "prooftext" these delegates in the dialogue.

ONE

IN SEARCH OF SELF

A Feminist Dilemma

The feminist[1] critique of traditional theories of personality within psychology has been vociferous and persistent over the past twenty years. Feminist analysis charged that the traditional or mainstream psychological models of human development and maturity were not only based on generalizations from (white) male subjects, but also formulated according to the methods and values of a dominant and dominating group in a white patriarchal society, facilitating social control of minority and subordinate groups at least by convenience if not by design.

The Normalcy of Men

Women have argued that traditional theories based on the male as the normative human do not reflect the experiences of women and, in fact, falsify our own self-images and psychological development. Such theories could hardly provide a balanced or adequate description of human personhood. So feminists in psychology began to reexamine the particular ways that women failed to fit existing models of human health and well-being in order to uncover what was missing in the traditional accounts of human selfhood.

When psychologists began to study women's lives and experiences to construct more adequate models of the human person, two things became apparent: (1) much of women's experience had been ignored by the male agenda, and (2) it was impossible to fit the information from women's lives into the existing language and categories of male science.

The "problem" or difference in women's development was quickly located in their experience of relationships. Pioneers like Jean Baker Miller, Nancy Chodorow, and Carol Gilligan observed that women's sense of identity and self-esteem were rooted in their relationships. This made them more "dependent," "attached," or "connected" with others than were their "normative" male counterparts, and these characteristics were in conflict with regnant models of maturity based on individuality and autonomy. Ruthellen Josselson summarizes this conundrum:

> While most developmental theories, from Freud until fairly recently, purported to be universal theories, it is becoming increasingly clear that these theories illuminate phenomenology unique to men. Again, it is the development-as-separation model that founders and falls. Development is seen to move toward increasing autonomy, culminating in the image of the corporate president, the man at the top, who runs his own show, beholden to no one, independent, self-actualizing. Women, because they attain less clearly bounded selfhood, caught up as they are in caring for and responding to others, are seen implicitly if not explicitly to be somehow less mature.[2]

The disparity is deeper, however, than simply not measuring up to male standards of healthy adult functioning. More comprehensive analyses revealed that characteristics and qualities associated with women's high investment in relationships apparently serve important functions in—and develop as a result of—a society where gender inequality predetermines social role expectations. Paradoxically, female characteristics that have been neglected or devalued are the very sorts of relational qualities, quintessentially human, that covertly sustain men in their postures of separateness and self-sufficiency. In her analysis of the complementarity of dominants and subordinates in our society, Jean Baker Miller argued that, as subordinates, "women have developed the foundations of extremely valuable psychological qualities" which are redemptive as a balance in areas of male inferiority (relationship, nurturing, emotional responsiveness, and so on).[3]

Differences between men and women that can be attributed to gender inequality and social location have alerted feminists to the magnitude of the effects of oppression in the environment upon personality development and mental health.[4] Traditional personality theories have been judged inadequate and simplistic in their treatment of the complex contextual factors influencing individuals in their particular, concrete situations. Instead, androcentric models that strive to describe the normative human strip away "any meaningful context including gender, race, ethnicity and culture, sexual orientation, and interpersonal connections."[5] The result is that external criteria of health and maturity are imposed without exposing the relativity of those criteria to a specific gender/class/race perspective.

Mistakes were made in understanding personhood because a dominant group, those holding the power of definition and knowledge, universalized as normative the experiences and values of that group—white males. It becomes apparent that the dynamics of power relations cannot be removed from our theories of personality; indeed, questions of power are primary to our representations of healthy personhood and the way they are utilized. Not just male supremacy, but the multidimensional effects of social and economic structures, cultural symbols, and religious language and ritual are examples of the diverse arenas of power that contribute to our self-understandings.

Feminist Epistemology and the Modern/Postmodern Debate

These nested families of observations and challenges push feminist critiques deeper than the androcentric and individualistic models of psychological development and functioning. Feminists also question research methods and mainstream epistemological approaches within the social sciences that represent the single, dominant perspective of Enlightenment metaphysics as the sole avenue to truth. Michelle Fine and Susan Merle Gordon have written that feminist psychologists "challenge the authoritative position of the researcher; unsettle claims about objectivity, bias and truth; and confuse intentionally the accepted segregation of social theory, method, and politics."[6] These challenges are directed toward the very philosophical foundations of the modern scientific method and its definition of knowledge. They are part of the postmodern deconstruction of the Cartesian opposition between the knowing subject and a known object that hypothesizes an Archimedean point from which the all-encompassing truth can be discerned and abstracted.

Feminists have engaged these epistemological questions within the broader context of the modern/postmodern dispute about the nature of reality and its consequent reexamination of western understandings of self. In this debate feminists have found themselves in the "anomalous position" of arguing the merits and errors of both sides.[7] Some feminists cite appreciatively the postmodern challenge to the fundamental dichotomies of Enlightenment thought, particularly that of masculine/feminine and subject/object. They say that such categories result in the privileging of one pole over the other, for example, the assumption that "only men can be subjects, and hence, knowers."[8] Postmodernism's insistence on the interpretive nature of all knowledge strengthens feminists' critiques of the masculinist bias of rationalism and supports the commitment to hearing the voices of diverse perspectives and many truths. The linking of knowledge and power exposes the historical patterns that have shaped our understandings of human selfhood and opens the door to feminist reconstructions of psychology.[9]

However, other feminists are suspicious of the postmodern move to overcome dualism and relativize all knowledge by rejecting both subject and object as essential categories. They charge that the deconstruction of the subject removes agency and the basis for political action in pursuit of equality. Feminists who adhere to inherent differences between men and women, exalt the virtues of women's nature, and advocate a "feminist epistemology" to replace the masculinist one see postmodernism undermining a subjectivity that women and minorities have just begun to discover. They feel that, as one more "stronghold of the fathers," postmodernism has too conveniently decentered a subject just as women are beginning to define themselves as agents.[10]

Finally, feminists like Nancy Frankenberry alert us to the tendency in certain postmodern methodologies to "elide or deny the category of lived experience" that is the starting point for feminist theory. Instead, these relativistic trends underscore the linguistic constitution of experience to the extent that language as one of the mediators of our experience becomes language as the sole determiner of all relations with the environment.[11]

Without getting lost in the quagmire of analytical categories or paralyzed by riding the fence in the modern/postmodern debate, our conversation will benefit from an awareness of the issues being discussed. Indeed, sensitivity to the various critiques being proffered actually reflects a feminist commitment to contextualizing inquiry, in this case, within the present intellectual environment. Sandra Harding has written insightfully that feminist theorizing must necessarily stretch, reinterpret, and borrow from traditional discourses while recognizing that categories and revisions will be characterized by instability. She counsels that "we should learn how to regard the instabilities themselves as valuable resources" as we continue to detect androcentrisms and struggle to include "the absent, the invisible, [and] the silenced" in our theorizing.[12]

Reconsidering the nature and importance of the self as a knowing, experiencing subject is central to feminist attempts to reconstruct more adequate and accurate images of personhood. The modern/postmodern debate heightens our awareness of certain dangers to avoid in feminist theory-building, while suggesting some necessary parameters.

Parameters and Particularities
Reaping the Benefits of Postmodern Critiques

Postmodern analysis offers feminism a way to guard against "the tendency to construct theory that generalizes from the experiences of Western, white, middle-class women."[13] The appeal to women's experience as a privileged source of knowledge must be qualified by the recognition of the diversity among women and the role that power plays in interpreting reality and defining truth.[14] Improved models of human being and becoming must include ways to value and incorporate differences rather than to ignore or pathologize them. They must deal with the social construction of self whereby social roles and linguistic categories act as primary sources of identity. All of these reflect an integration of contextual factors into a complex interactional or "thick" description of personhood.[15]

Another parameter is suggested by the postmodern rejection of foundationalism and essentialism that cautions us against hasty glorification of "feminine virtues" like nurturing, empathy, and connection. Upon closer examination, many of these characteristics may turn out to be particular to the socialization of white women in

American culture. "I have been socialized to connect across difference in order to provide the 'cement of society,'" writes Susan Thistlethwaite, who argues that we perpetuate white racism by rendering the differences of culture and race invisible in our eagerness to exalt relationality.[16] We must struggle to sort out the social embeddedness of our proclivities.

Claims of innate female qualities reify a dichotomy that the postmodern stance discerns as the root of oppression, for these are also the characteristics and skills developed in accordance with women's functional existence as subordinates in a hierarchical system of domination. These dynamics are further complicated by western women's concurrent identities as both oppressed and oppressor. Feminists must continue to explore whether these "feminine" characteristics are integral to women's identities and contribute to a more wholistic view of humanity or are dysfunctional and symbiotic means of survival in an oppressive environment.

A postmodern stance also prevents us from seeking a single, overarching theory or model of "the self" that is somehow universally applicable. Such metanarratives of a single unitary truth are rejected; it will require multiple theories and perspectives to describe the complexity of human being/becoming.[17] Margaret Gentry likens the priority given to coherence in traditional ("modern") scientific theory to a jigsaw puzzle: researchers and theory builders search for the missing pieces of a single, coherent truth, each working on their own particular compartment that will "enter the picture seamlessly in the end."[18] In contrast, new models of self, informed by feminist analysis and method, will be more like a quilt, which Gentry describes as a cooperative venture of individual perspectives and styles whose overall pattern is still emerging. "No one knows what a feminist psychology will look like any more than we know what equality in a post-patriarchal world will look like. We are beginning to piece the separate parts together—to explore the kinds of stitching to use in connecting the pieces and how to place the separate pieces into the pattern."[19]

Given these postmodern parameters and the inevitable particularities of my own perspective, self and selfhood will be taken in this manuscript to refer to that convergence of awareness that a person recognizes as his or her uniqueness and particularity among all persons, and actually all of life. While it is fluid and emergent rather than static, selfhood nevertheless represents a continuity that distinguishes a particular person's experience and movement through time and space from others who intersect and participate in that movement for a while.

Two Aspects of Women's Experiences of Self

Two particular "pieces of the pattern" of human selfhood that have emerged as significant in women's psychological development form the focus for this work. The first piece is the human experience of connection that is made possible by our ability to empathize with another. Empathy is appreciatively perceiving the psychological state, including some combination of thoughts, emotions, and desires, of another. The experience of empathy and the development of empathic skills are thought to be key elements in the consolidation of the self by some feminist scholars. In fact, empathy as a fundamental ingredient in mutual relationships has become important in disciplines as diverse as anthropology, physics, art, and metaphysics because of the significance of empathy for any effort to bridge differences in perspective. Hence, postmodern assertions that "reality is multiple and we construct our own realities" mean that "empathy becomes the fundamental way of knowing across diverse personal realities...a fundamental way of meeting another person from a different experiential reality."[20]

The second aspect of women's psychological development to be explored is what Judith Jordan has called "clarity in connection."[21] The phrase refers to the ability to integrate complex experiences of oneself within a web of relationships into a coherent and focused sense of self-identity. Jordan's notion of "clarity" recognizes that the self is not a single, monolithic entity which interacts with its external world. Instead, we experience ourselves as multiple feelings, attitudes, and behaviors, and these are often conflicting and ambiguous. We are many selves that must be orchestrated into coherence, an ongoing process that we recognize as our identity. Studies in the psychology of women that have examined the interplay of multiple roles and relationships with women's sense of self give some insight into the timely mechanics of managing complexity without dissolving into fragmentation.

Both of these aspects of women's development have been customarily viewed as emotional weaknesses that fall short of mature psychological functioning but which are, nevertheless, characteristic of women. Consequently, reconsideration of these aspects in a more positive light must be carefully distinguished as an attempt to correct an imbalance in personality theory rather than glorifying a "feminine essence." Hence my discussion is less about "gender differences" than about new constructions of the self. The former can quickly be marginalized to avoid the latter, because the latter involves fundamental challenges to traditional ideology and method.[22] The characteristics of human subjectivity, always at the center of psychological inquiry, must shift dramatically to accommodate feminist and postmodern insights into the dynamic, multiple, yet coherent and agential self.[23]

Theological "Eavesdropping"

The particularity of this study is further defined by my treatment of theological issues regarding selfhood. As new theories and models of the self emerge, theologians are called to reflect on contemporary understandings within the broader context of our human quest for ultimate meaning. Bringing psychological models into dialogue with theological concepts fulfills another commitment that feminist theorizing shares with a postmodern stance, and that is a refusal to investigate experience according to discreet categories or disciplines. The link between psychology and theology is an essential contribution to understanding personhood wholistically.[24]

Exploring the implications of new models of self for our understandings of God and the divine-human relation is crucial if theology is to be a relevant and adequate resource for contemporary life. Sallie McFague writes that "theologies that are credible and persuasive, that make sense to people living at a particular time, are ones that take seriously the public portrayal of reality current in their day."[25] However McFague goes on to say that the relationship of theology to science is not one of a new scientific foundationalism. Rather, she suggests that it is one of "'eavesdropping': theologians should listen to what the scientists are telling us about reality, and use it as an important resource for reformulating doctrines concerning God and the world."[26] By "eavesdropping" theologians can benefit from ways that science resonates with faith as well as ways that science illumines and transforms faith. On the other hand, theological reflection brings to the foreground some implicit presuppositions in our theorizing while it also provides a language of meaning to enliven our evolving visions of reality.

The relationship of religious worldviews to the politics of gender has been powerfully demonstrated and critiqued by feminist theologians.[27] Among these, Catherine Keller in particular deconstructs the symbiotic relationship between patriarchal religion, sexism, and traditional models of the self as separate and autonomous. Keller demonstrates how, by making separation both the means and the end of selfhood, our civilization has built and maintains the enormous structure of sexism/patriarchy. A framework of myth, religion, philosophy, and psychology conspires to give homage to the male norm of autonomous selfhood. My work builds on Keller's initial constructions of an alternative model in which she makes "interpretive use" of Alfred North Whitehead's process philosophy "to articulate something like a feminist ontology of self."[28]

Keller's experiment steers clear of the extremes of a self that is lost to engulfing connections and a self that is completely isolated by its self-sufficient separation. She proposes a third option, a "connective self" that is constituted by its relationships without compromising its "focused individuality." She is able to traverse this minefield of contradiction by her choice of process philosophy to articulate a logically coherent view of individuals constituted by their connections. It is a self that is both free *and* dependent, fully individual *and* fully related.

"Whiteheadian Feminism"
An Oxymoron?

My discussion expands on Keller's appropriation of Whitehead's process philosophy by drawing on Whitehead and his theological interpreters to explore in greater depth two particular aspects of selfhood. Empathy and clarity in connection, like relationality and individuality in Keller's work, might seem to be incongruous qualities, but process thought again provides a logically coherent way to say "both/and." Elaborating the discussion through process theological categories suggests ways to rethink our understanding of the divine nature by applying some of the correctives that we have found necessary for our models of human wholeness.

Points of Agreement

Process thought has been appropriated in varying degrees by a number of feminist writers who have appreciated the conceptual grounding that process philosophy gives to their experience.[29] They have found that it resonates with the feminist view of reality as essentially subjective, social, and processive while it also recognizes the limitations that persons' contexts place on their freedom and creativity. Process philosophy locates its starting point in human experience, as does feminist theorizing (but with the latter stipulating it as *women's* experience). Both perspectives reject a dualistic and hierarchical worldview in favor of one that sees an organic whole, "weighted toward a mutual enhancement" of its interrelated events.[30] Both see concrete particularity as prior to abstraction but do not belittle the importance of the latter for clarity of thought and communication. Process theology has been useful in revisioning the divine in images more congruent with feminist interpretations, expressing in novel ways the character of the relationship of persons, God, and world. Openness and mutuality are the hallmarks of these relationships, and divine attributes as well as human virtues have been reinterpreted to reflect this important difference from orthodox doctrine.

Process thought, especially as it has been given expression by contemporary empirical theologians, is particularly appropriate for this discussion because of its ability to explain the "elemental and organic togetherness of the experiencing subject and the experienced environment."[31] That is, the self is understood to be both a subject for itself and an object contributing to other subjects. Or, as Marjorie Suchocki elegantly puts it, "Through relationships, one continuously adds to the completion of others through the completion of oneself."[32] Process terminology illuminates the subtle mechanics of how the self can emerge as a unique identity from and through its connections rather than by severing those connections in search of autonomy.

Process thought also demonstrates how diversity contributes to the ideal of beauty. Through its summary concept of creativity and its use of aesthetic criteria like harmony, intensity, contrast, and complexity, process thought explains that beauty embodies a *complex unity*, a "harmonized complexity, a multiplicity that holds together."[33] Process empiricist Nancy Frankenberry argues that explaining experience in terms of "an aesthetic matrix rather than as a rational structure" provides a way to value diversity and contrast as qualitative components of religious experience.[34] Such an aesthetic matrix is similarly helpful in explaining and valuing women's struggles to include variety while maintaining clarity in connection.

These several aspects of process thought offer a language and analytic categories that help illumine the complex dynamics of emerging selfhood. Process theology places categories of religious experience and speculation in dialogue with our new "self"-understanding in an endeavor to establish coherence and integrity among our shifting perspectives. I have chosen creativity as the focal point of my appropriation of process thought because creativity, as Whitehead's ultimate category, encompasses the key notions of process philosophy while naming the activity by which the being/becoming self is actualized. Creativity acknowledges external influences on the socially constructed self without succumbing to total determinism. At the same time, creativity is intuitively appropriate as a description of our self-composition.[35]

Some Feminist Critiques

There are, however, important and valid criticisms of using process thought to ground feminist theorizing about the self. These can be presented in two general categories. The first group of criticisms and precautions reflects the general concern about feminist appropriation of pre-existing theories that employ "the master's tools." For example, Mary Daly, while she writes appreciatively of the potential of process thought for feminist revisioning, also warns against the hidden patriarchal values inherent in theories that "do not explicitly move out of patriarchal space."[36] Feminists require a specifically political agenda committed to social action for justice. Grand metaphysical schemas like Whitehead's are too abstract, some insist, glossing over the concrete particularities of human life that inform and motivate our social action.[37] Indeed, postmodern critiques cast doubt on the tenability of *any* all-encompassing theory that neglects its sociohistorical method in favor of metaphysical issues.[38]

A second group of criticisms of process thought echo these warnings about its patriarchal roots, but they are directed at concepts particular to the process perspective that conflict with feminist priorities. For example, Susan Thistlethwaite, in her critique of how white feminism has dealt with difference, warns against the consonance some women feel with process thought as a theory of connectedness. She argues that the process emphasis on connection and harmony masks white patriarchal values that operate to blind us to injustice based on cultural and racial difference. Thistlethwaite sees the longing for connection as a trap for white women, who have been "socialized to harmony" as part of our seduction into "uncritical acceptance of white-assumed privilege."[39] Hence differences, she argues, especially those which define our positions within patriarchy, are more primary than connections made at some higher level of rational synthesis (like that of process thought). For Thistlethwaite, concrete *differences* are the fundamental resources for an effective social criticism.

Another pointed criticism concerns the hierarchical features of Whitehead's philosophy. Nancy Howell has examined the process notion of a "hierarchy of value" and concludes that it perpetuates the patriarchal pyramid of domination.[40] Hierarchical values also encourage a certain progressivism that neglects the merit of stability and security. Howell further critiques Whitehead's limitation on the possibility of intersubjective relationships because it would seem to make our interpersonal connections only superficial. Nevertheless, Howell concludes that these problematic points in process thought can be revised so that process philosophy could serve as a basis for a feminist theory of relations.[41]

Living with the Tensions

These challenges to process thought are significant. Any appropriation should be a critical one that exercises a hermeneutic of suspicion about potential points of overlap between process and feminist concepts. However, I believe with feminists like Nancy Howell that there is merit in pursuing the usefulness of process philosophy and theology as a conceptual framework for feminist theorizing. Not only

In Search of Self 13

is the schema, in its empirical and feminist revisions, starting to appear larger and more broad-minded than the historicized man who conceived it, but self-consciously building on prior theorizing also protects us from the error of "the view from nowhere," a free-floating claim to adequacy no better than some Archimedean point. Any contribution to theory-building will, however, be a "playful, regional description"[42] rather than a claim about metaphysical or ontological truth. I identify with Bernard Loomer's phrasing of the more tentative, pragmatic strain in Whitehead:

> Suffice it to say that I am attempting to do theologically what Whitehead suggested should be done philosophically, namely, to take a set of ideas, the best that one has, and unflinchingly to explore experience with the aid of those ideas. To do so "unflinchingly" suggests the quality of courage that is required in this venture, especially when the inquiry takes place in unfamiliar and traditionally forbidden territory, and when the tentative conclusions may appear to be so at odds with what has been accepted as true and adequate and helpful for so long....I assume that courage and tentativity, along with humility, are inherent qualities of faith.[43]

What follows, then, is a critical dialogue between feminist psychology and process theology around the topics of creativity, empathy, and clarity in connection. The discussion attempts to hold in tension the weaknesses and strengths of both partners in the conversation and the particularity of the author's perspective with the multiplicity of alternative views. The aim is not to resolve all tensions, antagonisms, and contradictions in the encounter, but to advance more useful, less distorted ways to think about the human self.[44]

To summarize, this discussion is situated among feminist attempts to construct more adequate models of human selfhood that correct for gender biases in traditional renditions of human development. These feminist concerns are themselves contextualized by epistemological questions that are a significant part of the modern/postmodern debate about the nature and accessibility of truth and reality. In accordance with concerns raised by postmodern critiques, I will present a particular facet of human selfhood side by side with correlative notions in process thought to demonstrate the viability of creativity as a conceptual framework that enhances feminist descriptions and contributes to the cooperative venture. A critical and self-reflective appropriation of process theology will provide the testing ground for relating the insights gained to the categories of ultimacy that so powerfully influence human thought and behavior. Creativity is the conceptual thread that connects the psychological, philosophical, and theological arenas of the discussion by its unique attributes, which are identified in the next chapter.

NOTES

1. I am using "feminist" to refer to a group of perspectives that advocate the full humanity of women, realizing that there are many feminisms. At the same time, "feminist" as a universalizing term has its own history of oppression through erasure of race, class, and sexual orientation. These issues of particularity are acknowledged to be in tension with every attempt to describe the experiences of women as a group throughout this manuscript. See Imelda Whelehan, *Modern Feminist Thought: From the Second Wave to 'Post-Feminism'* (New York: New York University Press, 1995), 207.

2. Ruthellen Josselson, "The Embedded Self: I and Thou Revisited," in *Self, Ego, and Identity: Integrative Approaches*, ed. Daniel K. Lapsley and F. Clark Power (New York: Springer-Verlag, 1988), 92.

3. Jean Baker Miller, *Toward a New Psychology of Women* (Boston: Beacon Press, 1976), 26.

4. Lenore E. A. Walker, "Foreword," in *Personality and Psychopathology: Feminist Reappraisals*, ed. Laura S. Brown and Mary Ballou (New York: Guilford Press, 1992), viii.

5. Ibid.

6. Michelle Fine and Susan Merle Gordon, "Feminist Transformations of/Despite Psychology," in *Gender and Thought: Psychological Perspectives*, ed. by Mary Crawford and Margaret Gentry (New York: Springer-Verlag, 1989), 159.

7. Susan J. Hekman, who deems this debate "the principal intellectual issue of our time" and "central to feminism," outlines the reasons underlying feminism's ambiguity toward postmodernism and makes her argument for the compatibility of the two positions in *Gender and Knowledge: Elements of a Postmodern Feminism* (Boston: Northeastern University Press, 1990), 7. Her argument is revisited, with commentary from other feminist theorists, in a special issue of *Signs* 22, no.2 (Winter 1997).

8. Ibid., 9.

9. Hekman discusses Michel Foucault's contributions in this regard. See especially pp. 17–21, 68–73.

10. Whelehan, 199, 201. See also the essays in *Feminism/Postmodernism*, ed. by Linda J. Nicholson (New York: Routledge, 1990). Nicholson's introduction summarizes the tensions between the feminist and postmodern stances.

11. Nancy K. Frankenberry, "Pragmatism, Truth, and Objectivity," *Soundings* 74, nos. 3–4 (Fall/Winter 1991): 517, 519.

12. Sandra Harding, "The Instability of the Analytical Categories of Feminist Theory," *Signs* 11, no. 4 (1986): 664, 648. More recently, Linda Nicholson has helpfully identified the necessarily tentative character of our theorizing as

"epistemic humility." Linda Nicholson, "Feminism and the Politics of Postmodernism," in *Feminism and Postmodernism*, ed. by Margaret Ferguson and Jennifer Wicke (Durham, N.C.: Duke University Press, 1994), 69–85.

13. Linda Nicholson, introduction to *Feminism/Postmodernism*, 5.

14. Sheila Greeve Davaney, "The Limits of the Appeal to Women's Experience," in *Shaping New Visions: Gender and Values in American Culture*, ed. by Clarissa W. Atkinson, Constance H. Buchanan, and Margaret R. Miles (Ann Arbor: UMI Research Press, 1987), 31–49. See also Mary McClintock Fulkerson, *Changing the Subject: Women's Discourses and Feminist Theology* (Minneapolis: Fortress Press, 1994).

15. "Thick" description refers to various appropriations of Clifford Geertz's original use of the term with regard to ethnography and the interpretation of cultures. See Clifford Geertz, "Thick Description: Toward an Interpretive Theory of Culture," in *The Interpretation of Culture*, ed. by Clifford Geertz (New York: Basic Books, 1973); and William Dean, *History Making History* (Albany: State University of New York Press, 1988), 13.

16. Susan Brooks Thistlethwaite, *Sex, Race, and God: Christian Feminism in Black and White* (New York: Crossroad, 1989), 89. Ironically, white feminists' eagerness to celebrate our human connections initially enabled us to ignore significant differences among women like race, class, and sexual orientation, effectively erasing the most formative experiences of the majority of women.

17. Hekman, 11–12.

18. Margaret Gentry, "Feminist Perspectives on Gender and Thought: Paradox and Potential," in *Gender and Thought: Psychological Perspectives*, ed. Mary Crawford and Margaret Gentry (New York: Springer-Verlag, 1989), 4.

19. Ibid, 5.

20. Arthur C. Bohart and Leslie S. Greenbert, "Empathy and Psychotherapy: An Introductory Overview," in *Empathy Reconsidered: New Directions in Psychotherapy*, ed. Arthur C. Bohart and Leslie S. Greenbert (Washington, D.C.: American Psychological Association, 1997), 12. See also Mark H. Davis, *Empathy: A Social Psychological Approach* (Boulder, Colo.: Westview Press, 1996), 221.

21. Judith V. Jordan, *Clarity in Connection: Empathic Knowing, Desire and Sexuality*, Work in Progress, no. 29 (Wellesley, Mass.: Stone Center, 1987).

22. Fine and Gordon, 3.

23. For more detail about the path and positions of feminist psychology, see Jill G. Morawski, *Practicing Feminisms, Reconstructing Psychology: Notes on a Liminal Science* (Ann Arbor, Mich.: University of Michigan Press, 1994).

24. James W. Jones writes that our relationship to the sacred resonates with the relationships that constitute our sense of self. James W. Jones, *Contemporary Psychoanalysis and Religion* (New Haven: Yale University Press, 1991), 65–66. Jones is one among many who attest to the mutual influence of psychological and religious self-understandings. For other examples, see Romney M. Moseley, *Becoming a Self Before God* (Nashville: Abingdon, 1991); Ana-Maria Rizzuto, *The Birth of the Living God* (Chicago: University of Chicago Press, 1979); Caroll Saussy, *God Images and Self Esteem* (Louisville, Ky.: Westminster/John Knox Press, 1991); and Gail Lynn Unterberger, *Through the Lens of Feminist Psychology and Feminist Theology* (Ann Arbor: University Microfilms International, 1990).

25. Sallie McFague, "Cosmology and Christianity: Implications of the Common Creation Story for Theology," in *Theology at the End of Modernity*, ed. Sheila Greeve Davaney (Philadelphia: Trinity Press International, 1991), 26.

26. Ibid., 24.

27. Mary Daly considered the basic question about God to be the key to the radical potential of the women's movement itself. See Mary Daly, *Beyond God the Father: Toward a Philosophy of Women's Liberation* (Boston: Beacon Press, 1973), 28–29. Others writing on this topic would include the authors contributing to *Womanspirit Rising: A Feminist Reader in Religion*, ed. Carol P. Christ and Judith Plaskow (San Francisco: Harper & Row, 1979, 1992).

28. Catherine Keller, *From a Broken Web: Separation, Sexism, and Self* (Boston: Beacon Press, 1986), 5.

29. Several examples are found in the essays in *Feminism and Process Thought*, ed. Sheila Greeve Davaney (New York: Edwin Mellen Press, 1981); also, Mary C. Grey, *Towards a Christian Feminist Spirituality of Redemption as Mutuality in Relation* (Ann Arbor: University Microfilms International, 1987); and Nancy R. Howell, "A Feminist Theory of Relations," Ph.D. diss., Claremont Graduate School, 1991.

30. Marjorie Suchocki, "Openness and Mutuality in Process Thought and Feminist Action," in *Feminism and Process Thought*, ed. Sheila Greeve Davaney (New York: Edwin Mellen Press, 1981), 63.

31. Nancy Frankenberry, *Religion and Radical Empiricism* (Albany: State University of New York Press, 1987), 84.

32. Suchocki, "Openness and Mutuality," 63.

33. Keller, *From a Broken Web*, 190.

34. Frankenberry, *Religion and Radical Empiricism*, 110.

35. I realize that my choice of creativity and a process framework is first of all existential rather than theoretical. Process categories, terms, and descriptions *fit* my experience. With Marjorie Suchocki I confess, "The process conceptuality has revitalized my worship of God, and illumined my relationships." Suchocki, "Openness and Mutuality," 81.

36. Daly, *Beyond God the Father*, 189. Also, Sandra Harding, "Instability," 645–48. Daly's warning would also relate to criticisms of process thought's elitist unintelligibility.

37. Carter Heyward, "The Radicalization of Christian Feminism Among White U.S. Women," *Journal of Feminist Studies in Religion* 1, no. 1 (1985): 110. Also, Thistlethwaite, *Sex, Race, and God*, 87–88.

38. Dean, *History Making History*, 66.

39. Thistlethwaite, *Sex, Race, and God*, 23, 91. Thomas H. Graves offers a similar critique in "A Critique of Process Theodicy from an African Perspective," *Process Studies* 17, no. 2 (Summer 1988): 103–11.

40. Nancy R. Howell, "The Promise of a Process Theory of Relations," *Process Studies* 17, no. 2 (Summer 1988): 85–86.

41. Ibid.

42. Delwin Brown, personal communication, August 1993.

43. Bernard Loomer, "The Size of God," in *The Size of God: Bernard Loomer's Theology in Context*, ed. by William Dean and Larry E. Axel (Macon, Ga.: Mercer University Press, 1987), 23.

44. Sandra Harding opts for this approach in her discussion of feminism and science. Sandra Harding, *Whose Science? Whose Knowledge? Thinking from Women's Lives* (Ithaca, N.Y.: Cornell University Press, 1991), xi.

TWO

THE NATURE OF CREATIVITY

The idea of creativity has wide appeal because it is associated with originality and imagination as they are manifested in the great achievements of humanity.[1] Artists, inventors, and scientists embody the qualities of creativity that give rise to (and are often identified with) social progress. Creativity is the ability to blend familiar, diverse materials together to produce something completely new. It is the composition of extraordinary novelty from ordinary and available ingredients. Creativity is especially appropriate as a concept that grounds our exploration of selfhood because it captures the complex, variegated, fluid yet agential quality of identity that feminist and postmodern stances affirm. Employing creativity allows us to explore selfhood as an improvisational process.

However, the concept is much too rich to reduce to a sentence definition. Exploring its nuances in theological usage and psychological research amplifies our understanding and introduces specific characteristics that will link creativity with empathy and clarity of selfhood as they are discussed in later chapters. Focusing on the particular analysis of creativity found in process philosophy and theology will help clarify what is distinctive about the present approach while establishing some important continuities with more traditional treatments of creativity.

Creativity in Theological Contexts

> In the beginning, God created the heavens and the earth. (Genesis 1:1)

Christianity, along with virtually every other ancient and modern religious faith, has mythic creation stories that explain how the world came to be.[2] In most of these stories creation of the world is the expression of the creative nature of a divine being. "The heavens are telling the glory of God; and the firmament proclaims his handiwork." (Psalm 19:1) The beauty and wonder of the natural world are a testimony to the greatness and goodness of the supreme Creator, God's original act of creation on display. And the divine creativity is manifested anew in every sunrise, spring flower, and new baby.

Divine and Human Creativity in Tension

> Then God said, "Let us make humankind in our image, according to our likeness." (Genesis 1:26)

That humans are also creative can be viewed as one expression of the image of God (*imago dei*) by which humans mirror aspects of the divine nature. Human creativity, implicit in the *imago dei*, is a gift that summons us to responsible participation in creating the new order of life that is the Kingdom of God. Our creativity is our call to reshape our lives and reconstruct our worlds, creating new value where there was indifference, contempt, or loss.[3]

Human creativity requires a measure of human freedom and autonomy, without which there would be no personal agency to fulfill our responsibilities in creative transformation. Creation is an expression of one's freedom because it involves a liberation from the determined. That is, creation brings something new and therefore undetermined into being.[4] Creativity involves breaking free from what is dictated and exercising choice about what new thing will come to be. It is this aspect of intentionality in creativity that rescues the notion from a vague, romanticized feeling. Creativity is spontaneity "combined with intentionality, purposing, resolve."[5]

If human creative self-expression is to be more than mere abstraction, it would seem to exist in tension with God's ability as Creator to effect whatever God wills. What is the relationship of human freedom to divine providence, of human to divine creativity? In his *Systematic Theology*, Paul Tillich's answer is that human creativity is derivative from the divine creativity and, therefore, of a different order that is not as perfect or powerful. God's power of creation is characterized by needing neither materials (*ex nihilo*) nor assistance (*a se*).[6]

According to this view, creativity that brings into being that which had no being is strictly reserved for God. It follows, then, that human creativity is better described as discovery or transformation, because what humans actually create is new syntheses out of given material. Only God, as the Ground of Being, demonstrates the power of originating being. "God creates man; he gives man the power of transforming himself and his world. Man can transform only what is given to him. God is primarily and essentially creative; man is secondarily and existentially creative."[7]

Tillich's clear and precise distinction between divine and human creativity is one way theologians have articulated the disparity between the divine and human natures. It emphasizes the separation between humans and God. For those who assert God's absolute freedom and power, it is important that God's creativity be unconstrained by the characteristics of pre-existing facts. Therefore, God creates whatever God wills. In contrast, human creativity is understood to be limited by its materials and context, a testimony to the ontological gap between God and humans. That gap is accentuated to a greater degree by some theologians than others, depending on their doctrinal priorities.[8] In process theology, God's creativity, like ours, bears the limits of historical context, so the distinction between human and divine is stated differently. In the next chapters we shall ponder the effects of such boundary disputes.

Context is indisputably a very important qualifier of human freedom and creativity. Past experiences as well as present conditions determine the natural and spiritual "raw materials" from which humans create. The unequal distribution of power and resources in our culture has promoted creative agency in some persons at the expense of others. Brown reminds us that "ideologies of the privileged classes carefully ignore" the constraints that our material environment places on creative self-expression, lest we be forced to admit that our privilege is bought by others' deprivation.[9] Creativity is always "contextual" in that it is conditioned or limited by multiple influences from history and the environment. Nevertheless, by definition, creativity is not completely determined by the framework of context but always introduces some margin of novelty, even though it may be quite small.[10]

Another distinction made between human and divine creativity is human creativity's potential for evil. If creativity is demonstrated simply by bringing something new into being, then evaluating the result of creation introduces issues of morality and ethics. God's creation, by definition in Genesis 1, is good. Human creation, on the other hand, can be terribly evil, in fact or potential. Certainly nuclear power and weapons are manifestations of human creativity, as is the technological wizardry that converts rainforests into farmland. Even Hitler's plan for world dominance by the Aryan race could fit the criteria for creativity. Besides bearing the mark of human creativity, these examples also introduced the potential for mass destruction. The doctrine of the *imago dei* contains the seeds of human sin as well as human dignity. "Only a creature who bears the image of God and is capable of loving God and his neighbour can 'sin' in the Christian sense of that word," writes Daniel Day Williams. "The history of love and the history of sin are the same history."[11] The power of creation is morally neutral; what we humans in our contextual freedom choose to create—what we do with our creativity—is a decision that determines our orientation to the will of God.

Rethinking Creativity's Theological Usefulness

As humans, we not only create external objects, we also create ourselves. We construct our experience. Social theorist Gus di Zerega has written:

> Human consciousness is irreducibly creative because it does not passively experience its outlook, but takes a stance with regard to it. It creates a perspective on the world, a perspective that molds but does not fully determine experience. The self creates a world—but is itself created in return.[12]

We are always changing: our appearance, our feelings, our opinions. We take the raw data provided by our senses, memories, and emotions and construct our unitary experience of the present moment. We take the diverse information provided by our ongoing experience and synthesize it into a cohesive self-identity. "Thou hast created me creator of myself," Jules Lequier has written.[13] Acknowledging this created or constructive character of human knowing has been a central tenet of postmodern perspectives. Recognizing the heterogeneity of experience and the partial and perspectival nature of our constructed knowledge compels us to seek out the voices that have not been heard for a more adequate understanding of our shared reality. Creation and creativity are among the notions that have been reworked and reclaimed by theologians seeking to give expression to the experiences of oppressed and heretofore unheard peoples.

Among liberation theologians, for example, creation and creativity have both negative and positive connotations.[14] In Genesis, creation is depicted as subduing chaos and establishing order. God established the order of day and night, land and sea, and animals reproducing after their kind. Adam, mirroring the divine nature, continued this creative ordering by naming the animals. "To name something, in the Hebrew view, is to give that thing its essence, to order it, to give it a place in the nature of things....Adam was to create an order, a system of meanings, out of nothing, so to speak."[15]

Yet order, to those who are oppressed, has too often been the oppressor's justification for quelling resistance. That is, "order" is a euphemism for "tyranny." The "created order," as it was applied in Thomistic theology, has justified hierarchies of domination and oppression. The "created order" was the status quo and, ironically, the very antithesis of creativity. "To exist, humanly, is to name the world," wrote Paulo Freire.[16] The power to create, or to name one's world, has been withheld from those whose contextual limitations are the creations of the dominant culture.

In addition, Latin American liberation theologians are suspicious of theological discourse on creation that misses the sense of emergency and concrete particularity of the lives of oppressed people. To extol the beauties of creation in the midst of lives sacrificed to injustice can be theologically irrelevant and irreverent. "To speak of trees...is a kind of silence about injustice."[17]

Nevertheless, creation and creativity have been positively reinterpreted and appropriated by liberation theologians who emphasize the hope of creative power and transformation. As an expression of the new coming into being from nothing, creation offers the possibility of a totally different type of existence and a new world. Creation in this view is not establishing order over chaos, where "order" is used to validate dominance and oppression. Creation is a manifestation of power (and it may require a little chaos). The God who stands in solidarity with the oppressed will exercise God's power to create a new and more just world.

Creativity viewed as transformative power has also been an important theme for feminist writers and theologians like Audre Lorde, Carter Heyward, Rita Brock, and Mary Daly, who associate creativity with erotic power. However, erotic power is not God's omnipotence setting aright the world's injustices. Erotic power is a power we share with God that rises from within us when we nurture our deepest knowledge and feelings.[18] This interior power is the very source of our creativity. Feminists/womanists propose erotic, creative power as the antithesis of patriarchal power that seeks to dominate and control through coercive, hierarchical patterns.

Reenvisioning the creative power of the erotic is an expression of feminists' affirmation of our embodiment. It is a rejection of the mind/body dualism that has denigrated women for their association with bodily feelings and sexuality. "The erotic is the flow of our senses, the movement of our sensuality, in which we experience our bodies' power and desire to connect with others."[19] Erotic power both produces and is enhanced by our creativity. It is the lifeforce that connects us with others in our world and empowers us through those connections. Erotic power is creative power, and this power is our experience of the divine presence in the world.[20]

In certain contemporary approaches to spirituality, creativity is also associated with the experience of God's presence. Most notable is perhaps Matthew Fox's "creation spirituality," which links human creativity as a moral virtue with God's creation in the natural world. Fox identifies the *via creativa* as the third of four paths of the spiritual journey. In this third path, experiences of the *via positiva* (awe and delight) and the *via negativa* (darkness and letting go) are combined and "something is born of dark and light—what [Meister] Eckhart called 'breakthrough.'"[21] Fox considers creativity to be the fundamental law of the universe (including the human psyche), and he envisions the dawning of a new spiritual era where creativity is the principle virtue that humans encourage in individuals and communities.[22] Creativity should replace obedience, which Fox believes has been the primary moral virtue since the Newtonian era and has served the patriarchal impulse to control.[23]

David Griffin also identifies this tension between obedience and creativity in spirituality, but he has located their beginnings during the Reformation and Renaissance, respectively, and he maintains that their clashes and compromises shaped the emergence of the modern worldview.[24] Griffin observes that the spirituality of obedience won dominance in the church, unfortunately, placing it in opposition to the spirit of creativity admired in the sciences and the arts. As a process thinker, Griffin views creativity as the ultimate reality; hence he advocates a spirituality of creativity that reflects "the fundamental religious drive of human beings...to be in harmony with the ultimate power of the universe."[25] Thus to be religious means to be creative rather than to be obedient; this makes obedience a consequence of the religious life rather than its goal. Griffin, like Fox, identifies creativity as a spiritual path that attunes us to the Holy Spirit of Creativity that pursues God's work in the world.

That creativity also characterizes women's experiences of spirituality has been demonstrated by Maria Harris in her description of women's spirituality as a "dance of the spirit."[26] Harris' sequence of seven steps of the spiritual dance resemble the steps of the creative process as it is described by psychologists. "Creating" is also one particular step in the dance that focuses on creativity as the daily activity of forming one's life into a work of art. Harris uses the metaphor of birthing to depict how creativity arises from inner resources and inspiration. As a result, spirituality can be interpreted as allowing the inner music to take form in our lives so that we communicate our connection to "the deep undercurrent that forms the rhythm of the universe itself."[27] In each of these contemporary descriptions of spirituality, creativity is understood to be the best expression for aligning one's life with God's greatest intentions for goodness in the universe.

Summary

Creativity plays a significant role in Christian theology because we humans are thought to bear the image of our Creator God. Difficulty arises, however, when we try to articulate the distinction between divine and human creativity, for human creativity must be limited in some way that is not true for God's creative activity. Even so, contextual creativity expresses some degree of self-determination.

Creativity's transformative power has been reinterpreted and revitalized to reflect important aspects of liberation and feminist perspectives. It has also been appropriated as a new and more promising way to describe a spirituality that is congruent with contemporary scientific and feminist worldviews. In these contexts, creativity has richer connotations than simply novelty that has value, or bringing something new into being. Its theological context reveals creativity's interconnection with issues of freedom and power, the hope of transformation, and the discovery and affirmation of life's connections. As we shall see, these themes are also particularly relevant to emerging conceptions of women's experiences of selfhood.

Psychological Investigations of Creativity

While theological treatments of creativity describe its various roles in our frameworks of meaning, it is psychology that has applied the tools of science to systematically study its manifestations in human behavior. These studies of creativity can be clustered as exhibiting four different perspectives on this complex phenomenon:

1. The creative product
2. Characteristics of creative people
3. The creative process
4. Methods for stimulating creativity[28]

Research conducted according to the above agendas bears the mark of creativity's modern association with exceptional, heroic human achievements. Creativity as a type of genius, a notion that betrays its roots in the idealized individuality of "great men," is not the focus of the present discussion of creativity and human selfhood. However, certain theoretical consistencies and experimental results from this research complement our later discussion by helping to articulate the character of creativity, even though our interest is in the more democratic form rather than creative genius. Reflecting on theory in light of relevant empirical data provides an additional test for the adequacy of our conclusions.

Evaluating the Creative Product

Naturally, contemplating the product of creative genius is an activity that is more prevalent in the field of aesthetics than in psychology. Nevertheless, every field's investigation of creativity must consider what criteria will be used to evaluate the data. How do we determine whether something or someone is creative? How is "creative" to be defined and what methods can be used to measure it? Although there is certainly no universally accepted operational definition of creativity, there does seem to be some consensus that the primary evidence for creativity is originality and value.[29] Neither of these components is sufficient in itself. Originality must demonstrate its positive value by being relevant, intelligible, and effective, and what is valued must be something novel, not having existed before.

It can be argued that a Bach fugue, the discovery of DNA, and a chef's Bernaise sauce are all the products of a creative mind and process. Yet we value these items differently according to our particular contextual criteria.[30] Although value judgments are subjective, at times even arbitrary, value or merit is still a significant qualification placed on sheer originality or novelty, a testimony to the social character of the creative product.

Societal standards for creativity will reflect the biases of the ruling group. Those who control power and resources usually recognize and reward for its aesthetic appeal that which reflects and reinforces the dominant culture's values. Hence, in western culture, (white) men have been "responsible for far more artistic and scientific works generally deemed 'great.'"[31] Women and persons of color are underrepresented on lists of geniuses and great creative achievements that have traditionally been regarded as a (white) male prerogative. Only part of this absence is due to their historically restricted access to educational and artistic resources. Significantly, the creativity of society's subordinates is not recognized by narrow, externally imposed evaluations, remnants of a fading modern worldview that are being challenged for their grandiosity and presumptuousness. Rediscovering and placing value in the historical lives, literature, and art of women and a variety of ethnic communities is empowering these groups as they explore identities that are not parasitic on their relation to the dominant culture.

Creative People

Personality characteristics that seem correlated with exceptional creative productivity in a person have been of particular interest to research psychologists. In other words, what are creative people like? What do they have in common? Research strategies dealing with creative people hypothesize that discovering certain constellations of personality characteristics will provide clues about the nature of creativity, its origins, and methods for cultivating it.[32]

Three qualities of exceptionally creative people are particularly relevant to our discussion of the creative activity of emerging selfhood. The first of these qualities is an increased awareness of, or openness to the world.[33] In depth psychologies this is considered to be a greater openness to the free flow of primary process images from the unconscious. That is, one's internal censor, which is responsible for adapting desires and behavior to the expectations of the external world, allows more freedom for various images to rise to consciousness. Psychologists who study cognition and perception focus on the censorship that affects external perceptions. Openness to the world suggests more thorough observational skills that "take in" more of the environment in a heightened sensitivity. One interpretation suggests that this facilitates "divergent thinking," which allows creative people to explore a wider variety of alternatives before closing off their options.[34] Premature evaluation because of established habits or what psychologists call "set" has been found to inhibit creativity. Instead, creative people demonstrate flexibility in their thinking and a spirit of open-mindedness, although this is often tempered by a conviction about their views that gives them strength to go against the tide. Autonomy of judgment is an important attribute for those who introduce novelty into culture.[35] So, while openness is essential for creativity, integrity cannot be sacrificed.

It is possible for openness and integrity to coexist in the creative person because of a second quality. Creative people seem to have an exceptional tolerance for tension and ambiguity. Research shows that creative people are comfortable with areas of uncertainty and the unknown. They are capable of holding and comparing many ideas at once, and as a consequence they have more complex lives and see a more complex universe.[36]

Feeling comfortable with ambiguity is probably related to a third quality, and that is a creative person's ability to make connections between otherwise disparate phenomena. Arthur Koestler speaks of "bisociation" as this juxtaposition of previously unrelated ideas that results in the novel synthesis or solution. Arieti calls it a "magic synthesis" of primary and secondary thinking processes. Jung writes of the "transcendent function" that brings about a healing union of opposites in the psyche. Still others refer to a transcendence of fundamental dualities like subject and object or thinking and feeling in order to bring the creative vision to fulfillment.[37]

There is an old saying: some people build walls while others build bridges. Apparently, extremely creative people can build bridges where most of us see walls. Researchers have found that creative people are not only extraordinarily open, sensitive, and receptive to their worlds of experience, but they are also able to respond constructively with new ways of seeing beyond its fragmentation. These are characteristics that we will be glad to find democratized by new perspectives on women's psychological development.

The Creative Process

Another aspect of creativity that is well represented in the psychological literature is the creative process, its structure, and the psychological states attending it. The creative process is commonly identified by four stages: preparation, incubation, illumination, and verification.[38] Certain characteristics of these four stages are pertinent to our discussion of emerging selfhood.

The first step, *preparation*, includes gathering background information and skills that will be used in the process. These provide the ingredients for what becomes the question, and one would imagine that the more open one is to one's world, the richer will be the questions that emerge. Preparation culminates in a rift or gap in knowledge or understanding, a breach in what presently exists. This rift takes the form of a problem demanding attention, a "nut that needs to be cracked."[39] The previous equilibrium is disturbed in some way that requires resolution. For our discussion, the salient observation is that creativity begins with a break with the past, but it is also dependent on the foundation laid by that past for the character of future possibilities.

Incubation is the intermediary step during which possible solutions are generated and considered. Various pieces of information collected during the preparation phase "simmer like the ingredients in a stew"[40] until the solution emerges as an original creation. However, intentionality and plain hard work may also be required to analyze, generate, and test potential solutions until the correct one emerges. Frustration, blind alleys, and dry spells may characterize this stage. Conscious effort and unconscious processes are probably both involved in this experience of patient and persistent "scanning" for the breakthrough.

During incubation, conflicting, contradictory stimuli are brought together and combined in new and unforeseen ways. The characteristics of creative persons discussed above correlate well with the work of this stage: they are comfortable with ambiguity and contrast, they see connections where others do not, and they generate unusual combinations. It is this role of contrast and synthesis in the production of novelty that is significant for our discussion. And, while conscious intentionality is a factor, there is certainly a lot of important activity occurring outside of consciousness as well.

Many consider the third phase, or *illumination*, to be the trademark of the creative process.[41] It is certainly the most dramatic and well known. Illumination or inspiration describes the seemingly sudden and spontaneous realization of the solution to the problem. All of the energy tied up in the incubation phase is released in this "Eureka" experience of insight. It cannot be forced or programmed; it seems almost whimsical in its sudden appearance. If, as Abra suggests, incubation is like the gestation of a child in the womb, illumination is the moment of birth, the goal of the process, the realization of a totally new actuality.[42] Arieti coined the term "endocept" for this new creation that presses the creator for its incarnation in an external medium.[43] "It is a Holy Grail floating just out of reach, a siren to the creator's tortured Odysseus."[44] It becomes a lure for the creator's persistence through the final stage of representation to the public world.

This final important stage is called *verification*. In addition to being given representation, the new solution must be tested, integrated into the context that produced it, and communicated to others. The insight becomes public where it will be evaluated. If it is found to be relevant and effective, it will contribute to and enrich the preparation stage for others' creative activity.

These last two steps of the creative process highlight the importance of the lure to resolution and the desire and significance of sharing the product with others. Both of these themes will be found in expanded form in process thought.

Fostering Creativity

Especially relevant for an analysis of gender and creativity is the role of environmental factors in stimulating or limiting creativity and, by extension, self-development. For example, one sociocultural factor that Arieti has identified as characteristic of a "creativogenic society" is exposure to different and even contrasting lifestyles and cultures, accompanied by a tolerance and interest in differing views.[45] Stated simply, the presence and acceptance of diversity seems to nurture creativity. Or, applying some of the data discussed above, it makes sense that "openness to the world" combined with a stimulating environment would provide the richest ingredients for "incubation." This observation would seem to counter the ideal of a melting-pot homogeneity in society.

Another factor appears just as obvious and has been just as profoundly ignored. Creative self-expression is dependent upon the availability of sufficient physical and cultural support, as well as free access to cultural media. Hence psychologists reiterate theologians' observations regarding the contextual limits of creativity. Arieti points out that these factors have been denied to women and oppressed minorities throughout history, accounting for their more limited contribution to white male culture. As early as 1929, Virginia Woolf reflected on the contextual factors limiting women's creativity in *A Room of One's Own*.[46]

Sex differences in creativity have most often been attributed to limitations in women's education, vocational opportunities, financial security, and other similar environmental factors that are beginning to change. However, some investigators see more serious deterrents to creative achievement ingrained in women's psychological makeup. Rhona Ochse argues that women's relational focus impedes creativity because "a strong need for social intimacy and the strong motivation to create pull in different directions."[47] Ochse cites researchers who believe single-minded dedication is the most salient characteristic of creative people, and this would naturally seem to conflict with women's multiple social roles and relational commitments.

After studying the lives of three famous women poets for clues to "the psychological circumstances of female creativity,"[48] Paula Bennett also deduces that relationships obstruct creativity. Bennett determines that anger fuels these women's creativity, and from her psychoanalytic viewpoint, anger is borne from the work of separation—from one's mother, from oppressive cultural stereotypes that mothers embody, and from one's past compliance with those roles. Bennett concludes that separation is essential for the creative side of life to emerge. For her, separation and solitude are the key ingredients that stimulate creativity.

These two viewpoints set creativity in opposition to relational commitments, directly contradicting my argument that creativity describes women's self-constitution in relationships. I believe that the authors make the mistake of evaluating the circumstances that foster creativity using the criteria of a male-dominated culture. In other words, they find what they look for. Why, we might ask, choose single-mindedness rather than openness and the enjoyment of ambiguity as the most salient characteristic of creative people? Ironically, Bennett observes that the women poets she studied were ambiguous about their need for separation. An example she cites from poet Adrienne Rich's life demonstrates Rich's longing for a means to bring the "energy of relation" and the "energy of creation" into harmony.[49] Bennett concludes that the difficult work of separation, which she argues is necessary for self-empowerment and creative expression, *can be done, given a safe context for bonding.*[50] That is, I would point out, it is the sustaining connection within another relationship, rather than separation, that enables the renegotiation of existing relationships. And there is other research of artistic expression that calls into question "the image of artist as a solitary soul, pushing away others in order to create."[51] Creativity, as I will argue in the next chapters, is enhanced by the rich texture of our multiple connections.

What we learn from these opposing interpretations of women's creativity is that gender differences in creative achievement are more complex than equal opportunity. Environmental support and psychosocial influences, along with access to the power to name what is creative, are all significant agents in determining whether creativity will be actualized.

Creative Living

While most psychological study has treated creativity as something rare and extraordinary, the language of creativity and the creative process has also been used in more egalitarian ways to talk about human personhood in general. Some theorists speak of living itself as a creative endeavor and connect creativity with the religious dimension of human experience. Representative of this perspective would be humanistic and existential psychologists like Abraham Maslow, Rollo May, Eric Fromm, and Carl Rogers, who use creativity to characterize a particular way of living—"spontaneous, perceptually fresh, and uninhibited"—that identifies the self-actualizing, life-engaging individual.[52] These writers see creativity as a propensity to make meaningful connections in one's experience and with the world. Not surprisingly, this method of encounter with the world is believed to be characterized by openness, empathy, and courage in order to overcome the barriers between us. Creative life decisions and creative products like art become analogous in that both contribute to our experiences of life's coherence and meaning.

Life itself embodies creativity, according to educational theorists who use the creative process as a comprehensive model for the reinterpretation of human development. For example, James Loder argues that the creative process outlines the "logic of transformation" or the "grammar" that forms the underlying structure for all human knowing.[53] Loder believes that this same patterned process operates at every level of life in the dynamics of biological maturation, and it is replicated in theories of psychological development and Christian sanctification.

Deeply ingrained as the "guiding pattern of the human spirit,"[54] the creative or transformational process is thought to serve as a prototype that is then transposed to the level of intentional conscious behavior in artistic and scientific creativity. Loder identifies other transpositions of "transformational logic" as operating in therapy and in spiritual healing through symbol and myth.[55] The dynamics of the creative process constitute the "primary reality," and for Loder, even the movement of God's Holy Spirit follows this format for the transformation of human lives.[56]

Loder's account has several things in common with my own endeavor: (1) it views creativity as a fundamental dynamic inherent in all levels of reality, (2) it relates creativity to existing theories of human psychological development, and (3) it explores creativity and developing selfhood within a theological framework. However, I differ with Loder in several areas. First, Loder writes from a psychoanalytic stance that does not reflect an awareness of the influences of gender and does not respond to feminist critiques and revisions. That is, his conceptualization is heavily dependent upon the traditional model of separation as central to ego development. The problem is compounded by its extension into the theological language of sin and salvation, where sin is represented by traditional categories rooted in male experiences of egocentrism and alienation. Second, Loder's perspective ignores postmodern issues of the perspectival nature of truth claims and anti-substantialist descriptions of selfhood as I identified them in Chapter 1. Finally, Loder locates his discussion within the Reformed theological tradition that declares a radical separation between God and humans, based on original sin, so that God's presence is spoken of as one that is "convicting" as much or more than it is "affirming." Such a theological stance has not been helpful in understanding how women incorporate the sacred in their lives.

Nevertheless, Loder's model sets the stage for process views of creativity. Loder sees creativity extending downward from human experience to more fundamental levels of reality and upward to describe the character and activity of a transcendent reality. Such a continuum parallels the link that process thought makes between the activity of human experience and the wider reality represented by nature and metaphysics. Psychology's investigations of creativity provide an empirical link between our existential experiences of creativity and the philosophical use of creativity as a conceptual framework for women's experiences of self.

Whitehead's Portrayal of Creativity

In the process or organic philosophy of Alfred North Whitehead,[57] creativity is the metaphysical ultimate that characterizes every real entity. It is not reserved for God or humans; instead, everything that exists embodies or manifests creativity. So central is creativity to Whitehead's cosmology that Charles Hartshorne thought Whitehead's analysis of creativity might be his greatest contribution to American philosophy.[58]

Creativity in Concrescence and Transition

According to Whitehead, reality is made up of droplets of experience, or occasions of experience. They are the "primary actual units of which the temporal world is composed."[59] Creativity is the ultimate generic activity that gives rise to each of these individual occasions. One could say that each moment of existence is a work of art. An occasion, the most basic unit of reality, describes both the process and the outcome of a decision (cf. *painting* as a verb and *painting* as a noun). Like the intentionality and decision referred to in earlier parts of this chapter, it is the occasion's decision that synthesizes diverse elements from the past into a new and unique unity. Whitehead identifies this new unity with subjective experience. Hence experience is constructed of these occasions, or actual entities, and each actual entity is an act or process of self-creation.

"Concrescence" is the word Whitehead coined to identify the momentary process by which a new actual entity constitutes itself from the data of its particular context, or antecedent actualities. Concrescence is "the production of novel togetherness."[60] The inner aspect of this novel self-creation is feeling, or what Whitehead called "prehending" because it is how the entity experiences or "takes in" other entities. Feelings or prehensions describe how other occasions of experience contribute to its character. We are related—not through concrete substance—but affectively, because "the basis of experience is emotional."[61]

But creativity is not to be found solely in a single entity's satisfaction of self-becoming. "A subject is not just something in and for itself."[62] The philosophical problem of the one and the many is solved in creativity, where "the many become one, and are increased by one."[63] The diverse "many" become one complex unity of feeling and then perish as an immediate experience. Meanwhile, the unique character and actuality of that one entity contribute to the potential richness of all future occasions. The world is "increased by one." Whitehead referred to this manifestation of creativity as "transition." We might think of concrescence and transition as representing our experiences of simultaneously living for ourselves and living for others. Whitehead reminds us that the distinction exists only in abstraction.

Whitehead's analysis of creativity relies on the relational nature of reality: as subjects, actual entities are constituted by their internal relations with antecedent entities, and as objects, actual entities contribute to or have impact upon the becoming of future occasions. This shifting perspective between experiencing subject and contributing object, between concrescence and transition, is the rhythm of the universal creative process,[64] and consequently, as we shall see, the rhythm of emerging selfhood.

Creativity and Novelty

Whitehead associated creativity with the origination of novelty, just as psychologists do. "The word Creativity expresses the notion that each event is a process issuing in novelty,"[65] and "creativity is the principle of *novelty*."[66] In Whitehead's writing, however, there seem to be two different conceptions of novelty. In one sense, novelty requires the actualization of something not previously present in potential. That is, an entirely or absolutely new ingredient has been added to the "mix" from which actuality emerges. Whitehead believed that this type of novelty, which we might distinguish as *generative novelty*, is made possible by God's intervention or participation in every moment of creation. Each occasion begins with God's contribution of particular feelings (the initial aim) to its potential ending or satisfaction.[67] "God is the organ of novelty....Apart from the intervention of God, there could be nothing new in the world....The novel feelings derived from God are the foundations of progress."[68]

However, Whitehead also speaks of novelty in a different way as that achieved by an actual entity's individual and unique merging of components from their "disjunctive diversity" into a "concrete togetherness." That is, the simple reconfiguration of feelings that were previously present but are felt from *this* actual entity's perspective (the subjective form) is also authentic novelty, one that we might distinguish as *constructive novelty*. "The subjective form is the immediate novelty; it is how *that* subject is feeling that objective datum."[69] It is the creation of something new from existing materials, the "emergent synthesis of a previous multiplicity."[70] In this sense, novelty is an inevitable outcome of every act of self-creation in a way that is distinguishable from God's introduction of novel possibilities in the initial aim. "An actual occasion is a novel entity diverse from any entity in the 'many' which it unifies....Thus the 'production of novel togetherness' is the ultimate notion embodied in the term concrescence."[71]

Thus Whitehead seems to use novelty as the fingerprint of creativity in two ways. One, which I have called generative novelty, is novelty introduced by God in an action reserved for God (that is, the initial aim). The other, or constructive novelty, is novelty produced by each entity as it composes its own identity. Constructive novelty is the result of generic creative activity by which every actual entity synthesizes multiple feelings into a unity of satisfaction.[72]

"Internalizing" Creativity

Whitehead's various illustrations of creativity and novelty exist separately only in abstraction, as Whitehead repeatedly reminded his readers. So concrescence and transition, the initial aim and satisfaction, cannot be said to happen in any kind of order or with any type of priority except as we stretch them out in abstraction for explanation and analysis. Nevertheless, the abstractions reveal an imbalance in emphases in process thought that may reflect what John Cobb has called its "almost exclusively masculine...style and tone."[73]

The imbalance grows from Whitehead's proposal of two ways to talk about God's relation to creation. God's consequent nature describes God's prehension or feeling of every droplet of experience in its entirety. Nothing is lost to God's experience. God is always with us (Immanuel). God's primordial nature names the activity by which God evaluates (or decides, or judges) those feelings and from them creates the best possibility for beauty and goodness. It is how God transforms our mistakes to possibilities, our weaknesses to strengths. Obviously, both aspects of the divine nature are essential to our understanding of God's love.

Generative novelty, which is associated with the primordial nature of God, receives more attention and esteem in Whitehead's writing. Generative novelty is the key factor in adventure, advance, progress, and intensification. In stark contrast, concrescence that does not appropriate (that is, positively prehend or feel) the novelty that is made possible or introduced by God is described as "boredom," "repetition," "static," or "habit," even though genuine creativity is embodied in what is necessarily a novel synthesis.

The greater value given generative novelty in Whitehead and his interpreters has helped perpetuate certain patriarchal applications and limited the potential of process thought as a postmodern philosophic alternative. For example, Pete Gunter has observed the need for "a transmutation in the concept of creativity itself" in order to convert its expansionist connotations to more ecological or conserving ones.[74] Gunter argues that "human creativity must grow beyond its adolescent expansive expansionist phase and become more internalized" if we are to resolve the conflict between creativity and ecology.[75] Creativity that centers on unique, individualized expression and stresses social progress conflicts with ecological goals that balance individual fulfillment with conserving natural systems and cultural life. "The continual search for ever more creative forms of thinking and expression may further undermine our collective ability to live in a sustainable relationship with an already overstressed environment."[76]

Generative novelty seems to reflect such expansionist and progressivist tendencies because it carries connotations of perpetual striving for "more" and "better." Constructive novelty, on the other hand, may contain some options for an alternative, more "internalized" and ecological interpretation of creativity. Constructive novelty conserves the past and promotes stability. It is the source of the universe's concreteness because it explains the continuity we experience as material objects. In our everyday experience, it is the creative activity of "making special" what is otherwise ordinary.[77]

Whereas generative novelty is associated with God's primordial nature, constructive novelty might be best associated with God's consequent nature, which Whitehead beautifully describes as "the weaving of God's physical feelings upon his primordial concepts."[78] According to Whitehead, the ever-concrescing God harmonizes or "weaves" physical prehensions (God's feelings) of the evolving universe with the ideas and possibilities being formulated in the primordial nature.[79] God shares this characteristic of constructive novelty (that is, self-creation) with every concrescing droplet of reality. The consequent nature of God is God as fully actual or real.

God's consequent nature receives much less attention in Whitehead's writing than does the primordial nature.[80] God's conse-

The Nature of Creativity

quent nature, which John Cobb has said "appears gynandrous,"[81] involves experience that has been culturally associated with attributes of women: receptive, physical, derivative, incomplete, determined, finite, conserving, and patient.[82] Without reifying these as "feminine" characteristics, we can still ponder how these qualities might help us envision and value a more "internalized" creativity.

These aspects of creativity in process thought are suggestive of untapped depths of meaning in Whitehead's schema and, perhaps, some concrete implications that have been neglected (and others that need correcting) because of the patriarchal cultural context of the development of process thought. At the same time, the rich and detailed analysis that Whitehead makes of creativity as a metaphysical ultimate lays a foundation for a fresh consideration of human selfhood from the perspective of women's experiences of relatedness. The two ventures will complement each other as our discussion progresses.

Summary

The phenomenon of creativity has a fertile and variegated history of research and usage across many disciplines, but in all of them creativity has been valued as an ideal to which we aspire, a quality that manifests the best of human capabilities. Theologically, it is a divine attribute that is shared, in limited measure, by those created in God's image. In psychology as well as the other arts and sciences, creativity is expressed through a patterned process by which we courageously free ourselves from the strictures of the past to give birth to something new. In what may be its most powerful application, however, creativity has been identified with the motion of life and ultimately reality itself. Human selfhood, according to this last appropriation, becomes an ongoing creative synthesis of experiences, memories, relationships, and expectations into a more or less cohesive personal identity.

When its notions are expanded and tested by previously unacknowledged arenas of experience, process thought's conceptualization of creativity contributes profoundly to the understanding of creativity as our self-constituting endeavor. Whitehead provides an analysis of creativity that helps us understand how a unique identity is constituted by, and emerges from, a complex world of relationships. He developed a language that can articulate how persons are connected while maintaining the integrity of their differences. While the language can be technical and abstruse, it elucidates the very dynamics that feminists have identified in women's development of a relational sense of self.

The theological, psychological, and philosophical treatments of creativity considered above supplement the brief definition that introduced this chapter with related disputations, empirical data, and technical analysis. They furnish the overall project with a richly textured background from which to draw characteristics that will link the theological and psychological arenas of discussion. Just as Chapter 1 contextualized the present conversation within a more comprehensive problem about the qualities of postmodern selfhood, so does Chapter 2 situate its responding thesis within current disciplinary perspectives on the proposed solution. Specific attributes of creativity that cross the boundaries of these disciplines, like openness, value, power, contrast, and ambiguity, help articulate the dynamics of relational selfhood that we will now explore.

NOTES

1. The discussion that follows is based on the modern understanding of creativity and creative genius that has dominated the arts and sciences in the west. That this is a relatively recent and local, as well as ahistorical and ethnocentric view is demonstrated by Morris Berman, who contrasts it with an alternative, more democratic version like that found in nonwestern cultures or medieval art. Morris Berman, "The Two Faces of Creativity," Chapter 10 in *Coming to Our Senses: Body and Spirit in the Hidden History of the West* (New York: Simon and Schuster, 1989). Nevertheless, creativity's western characterizations form the backdrop against which the present exploration of selfhood is undertaken. My discussion will be a critical appropriation of modern western creativity that seeks to reframe and expand the concept beyond the neurotic, conflict-laden model of the individual creative genius to what C. A. Bowers describes as a more ecologically responsible form of creativity that is "contextual and expressive of the interdependence that characterizes" the larger biotic and social community. C. A. Bowers, *Educating for an Ecologically Sustainable Culture* (Albany: State University of New York Press, 1995), 72.

2. Edward Farley, *Divine Empathy: A Theology of God* (Minneapolis: Fortress Press, 1996), 238. Marie-Louise von Franz discusses various types of creation myths in *Patterns of Creativity Mirrored in Creation Myths* (Zurich: Spring Publications, 1978, 1975, 1972). Sallie McFague uses the "big bang" scientific creation story to formulate a postmodern theological anthropology ("Cosmology and Christianity," 31–38).

3. Daniel Day Williams, *The Spirit and the Forms of Love* (New York: Harper & Row, 1968; reprint, Lanham, Md.: University Press of America, 1981), 140.

4. Beverly Wildung Harrison calls freedom "the power of creativity" that is actualized when people have agency to co-create their world. See *Our Right to Choose: Toward a New Ethic of Abortion* (Boston: Beacon Press, 1983), 96–109.

5. Delwin Brown, *To Set At Liberty: Christian Faith and Human Freedom* (Maryknoll, N.Y.: Orbis Books, 1981), 32. The decision-making aspects of creation will be my focus in Chapter 4.

6. Paul Tillich, *Systematic Theology, Vol. 1* (Chicago: University of Chicago Press, 1951), 252–56.

7. Tillich, 256. I have chosen to retain Tillich's use of masculine pronouns to highlight the gendered perspective of this argument.

8. Lewis S. Ford contrasts Tillich's and Whitehead's views on creativity and ontological continuity in "Tillich, Whitehead and Creativity," in *Paul Tillich on Creativity*, ed. Jacquelyn Ann K. Kegley (Lanham, Md.: University Press of America, 1989), 121–30.

9. Brown, *To Set At Liberty*, 33. Brown discusses the interplay of creativity and context as the polar elements of freedom on pp. 31–36.

10. Larry Kent Graham expands Brown's discussion of "contextual creativity" to express the tension between freedom for transformation and limitations imposed by persons' life circumstances that one encounters in the ministry of care. See *Care of Persons, Care of Worlds: A Psychosystems Approach to Pastoral Care and Counseling* (Nashville: Abingdon Press, 1992), especially pp. 180–202.

11. Daniel Day Williams, 141–42.

12. Gus di Zerega, "Empathy, Society, Nature, and the Relational Self: Deep Ecology and Liberal Modernity," *Social Theory and Practice* 21, no. 2 (Summer 1995): 248.

13. Quoted in Charles Hartshorne, *Creative Synthesis and Philosophic Method* (La Salle, Ill.: Open Court Publishing, 1970), xi. Hartshorne makes extensive use of the example of human experience to illustrate creative synthesis in this book and numerous articles.

14. Vitor Westhelle, "Creation Motifs in the Search for a Vital Space: A Latin American Perspective," in *Lift Every Voice: Constructing Christian Theologies from the Underside*, ed. Susan Brooks Thistlethwaite and Mary Potter Engel (San Francisco: Harper, 1990), 128–40.

15. Brown, *To Set At Liberty*, 9.

16. Paulo Freire, *Pedagogy of the Oppressed* (New York: Seabury, 1974), 76. See also Daly, *Beyond God the Father*, 8.

17. Bertold Brecht, quoted in Westhelle, 130.

18. Audre Lorde, "Uses of the Erotic: The Erotic as Power," in *Sister Outsider* (Freedom, Calif.: The Crossing Press, 1984), 53–59.

19. Carter Heyward, *Touching Our Strength: The Erotic as Power and the Love of God* (San Francisco: Harper & Row, 1989), 187.

20. Rita Brock, *Journeys by Heart: A Christology of Erotic Power* (New York: Crossroad, 1991), 46. Also, Heyward, *Touching Our Strength*, 99.

21. Matthew Fox, "Creation Spirituality: A Personal Retrospective," *Listening* 24, no. 2 (1989): 116–36. See also Matthew Fox, *Original Blessing* (Santa Fe: Bear & Company, 1983). In Fox's model, we see the customary association of creativity with combining different, even conflicting, elements to produce something new.

22. Matthew Fox, *The Coming of the Cosmic Christ* (San Francisco: Harper & Row, 1988), 19–21, 199–211. Fox's ideas show much affinity with process thought at several points. See his essay, "A Mystical Cosmology: Toward a Postmodern Spirituality," in *Sacred Interconnections: Postmodern Spirituality, Political Economy, and Art*, ed. David Ray Griffin (Albany, N.Y.: State University of New York Press, 1990), 15–34.

23. Fox, *The Coming of the Cosmic Christ*, 202.

24. David Ray Griffin, *God and Religion in the Postmodern World: Essays in Postmodern Theology* (Albany: State University of New York Press, 1989), 29–30.

25. David Ray Griffin, "Creativity In Post-Modern Religion," in *Creativity in Art, Religion, and Culture*, ed. Michael H. Mitias, (Amsterdam: Rodopi, 1985), 84. Jerome Berryman also refers to these two spiritualities. He says that one is based on the love of creating and the other on the fear of falling. See Jerome Berryman, *Godly Play: A Way of Religious Education* (San Francisco: Harper, 1991), 157.

26. Maria Harris, *Dance of the Spirit: The Seven Steps of Women's Spirituality* (New York: Bantam Books, 1989).

27. Ibid., 59.

28. Sylvano Arieti's *Creativity: the Magic Synthesis* (New York: Basic Books, 1976) is an excellent summary and discussion of all of these facets of creativity. For this book I have also relied on the theory and research about creative persons and process found in Jock Abra, *Assaulting Parnassus: Theoretical Views of Creativity* (Lanham, Md.: University Press of America, 1988).

29. Carl R. Hausman, "Originality as a Criterion for Creativity," in Mitias, 33. Also, Abra, 3–8.

30. In a similar way, our historical context shapes the moral and ethical criteria we use to distinguish good from evil uses of our human creativity. See above, p. 20.

31. Jock Abra and Suzanne Valentine-French, "Gender Differences in Creative Achievement: A Survey of Explanations," *Genetic, Social, and General Psychology Monographs* 117, no. 3 (1991): 235. Also, Rhona Ochse, *Before the Gates of Excellence: The Determinants of Creative Genius* (Cambridge: Cambridge University Press, 1990), 173; and Joelynn Snyder-Ott, *Women and Creativity* (Millbrae, Calif.: Les Femmes Publishing, 1978), 11.

32. In some research, confirmation is sought for hypotheses about the antecedent causation of creativity, such as Freud's sublimation of unconscious sexual conflicts, Jung's archetypes of the collective unconscious, or Winnicott's dynamics of the transitional space. In other research the data is distilled from factor analysis of questionnaires and then theoretical interpretation follows. Abra reports that, unfortunately, neither approach has resulted in conclusive data about creativity. Abra, xvi–xvii.

33. Ernest G. Schachtel, *Metamorphosis: On the Development of Affect, Perception, Attention, and Memory* (New York: Basic Books, 1984), 237–48. "Openness to the world" shares some similarities with spiritual openness, especially as it is exemplified in mystical illumination. Religious experience, like aesthetic experience, makes creative use of primary process thought to make abstract concepts meaningful (Arieti, 249). This is one possible explanation for Nancy Frankenberry's observation that aesthetic categories are useful for explaining religious experience (see above, p. 11). Jerome Berryman appropriates this insight in his theory of Christian nurture in *Godly Play*.

34. Arieti, 17.

35. Arieti, 346; Abra, 25.
36. Abra, 29–30; Arieti, 349.
37. Arthur Koestler, *The Act of Creation* (New York: Macmillan, 1964, 1969), 35, 59, 352; Arieti, 12–13; C. G. Jung, "The Transcendent Function," in *The Portable Jung*, ed., trans. R. F. C. Hull (New York: Viking Press, 1984, 1971), 273–300; Schachtel, 83.
38. Arieti, 15; Abra, 16. A thorough and entertaining description of the creative process can be found in Abra, 69–121. The important point about these stages or phases is not their smooth, linear progression. Actually, they probably originate, overlap, interact, and repeat more fluidly. The point of identifying stages is that they help to distinguish the different kinds of thought and experience that take place.
39. Abra, 76.
40. Ibid., 17.
41. Ibid., 87. Abra cites a couple of dissidents who insist that insight comes gradually, but these clearly represent a minority opinion.
42. Ibid., 17.
43. Arieti, 54–65.
44. Abra, 90.
45. Arieti, 312–25.
46. Virginia Woolf, *A Room of One's Own* (San Diego: Harcourt Brace Jovanovich, 1929). The broad range of sociocultural inhibitors of women's creativity is explored in *Remarkable Women: Perspectives on Female Talent Development*, ed. Karen Arnold, Kathleen D. Noble, and Rena F. Subotnik (Cresskill, N.J.: Hampton Press, Inc., 1996).
47. Rhona Ochse, "Why There Were Relatively Few Eminent Women Creators," *Journal of Creative Behavior* 25, no. 4 (1991): 341. See also Ochse, *Before the Gates of Excellence*, 172–75.
48. Paula Bennett, *My Life a Loaded Gun: Female Creativity and Feminist Poetics* (Boston: Beacon Press, 1986), 9.
49. Ibid., 222–23. Bonnie Miller-McLemore also ponders the pulls of creative work and family in *Also a Mother: Work and Family as Theological Dilemma* (Nashville: Abingdon Press, 1994). Instead of anger and separation, her resolution involves revisioning "generativity" in ways that value and enable creative work and relationships for both men and women.
50. Ibid., 266.
51. Ellen G. Levine, "Women and Creativity: Art-In-Relationship," *The Arts in Psychotherapy* 16 (1989): 309.
52. Abra, 442. Essays on creativity by these and other "third force" psychologists can be found conveniently collected in Harold H. Anderson, ed., *Creativity and Its Cultivation* (New York: Harper, 1959).
53. James E. Loder, *The Transforming Moment*, 2d ed. (Colorado Springs: Helmers & Howard, 1989; Harper & Row, 1981); "Creativity In and Beyond Human Development," in *Aesthetic Dimensions of Religious Education*, ed. Gloria Durka and Joanmarie Smith (New York: Paulist Press, 1979); "Transformation in Christian Education," *Religious Education* 76, no. 2 (1981): 204–21. Others using creativity in this way include Sharon Parks, *The Critical Years: The Young Adult Search for a Faith to Live By* (San Francisco: Harper and Row, 1986); Robert Kegan, *The Evolving Self: Problem and Process in Human Development* (Cambridge: Harvard University Press, 1982) and "There the Dance Is: Religious Dimensions of a

Developmental Framework," in *Toward Moral and Religious Maturity*, First International Conference on Moral and Religious Development (Morristown, N.J.: Silver Burdett Co., 1980); and Jerome Berryman, *Godly Play*.

54. Loder, *The Transforming Moment*, 153.

55. Ibid., 135ff. Loder compares his analysis with Carl Jung's description of transformation. The steps of the creative process have also been correlated with Jung's description of individuation by Anthony Storr, "Individuation and the Creative Process," *Journal of Analytical Psychology* 28 (October 1983): 329–43.

56. Loder, "Creativity," 230.

57. Process philosophy refers to those thinkers who hold that "process" or "event" best describes the fundamental nature of reality. Anything which is not processive is an abstraction from process. This assertion stands in contrast to substantialist philosophies that view reality as bits of matter or substance that exist through time and have attributes. There are several philosophers and theologians who have articulated their perspectives in terms of process, the most recent being Edward Farley, who also uses Creativity, empathy, and metaphor as fundamental aspects of his theology of God (*Divine Empathy*). I have chosen to focus on Alfred North Whitehead and his theological interpreters because of (1) Whitehead's comprehensive and consistent view of reality, (2) the centrality he gives to relationships, and (3) the compatibility I find between Whitehead's thought and certain Christian and feminist perspectives, as will be shown.

58. Charles Hartshorne, "The Idea of Creativity in American Philosophy," *Journal of Karnatak University—Social Sciences* 2 (1966): 8.

59. Alfred North Whitehead, *Religion in the Making* (New York: Meridian Books, 1960; Macmillan Company, 1926), 88.

60. Alfred North Whitehead, *Process and Reality*, corr. ed., ed. David Ray Griffin and Donald W. Sherburne (New York: Free Press, 1978; Macmillan Publishing, 1929), 21.

61. Ivor Leclerc, *Whitehead's Metaphysics* (London: George Allen and Unwin, 1965, 1958), 149. In a novel twist of his own, Whitehead makes beauty more fundamental than goodness, aesthetics prior to morality.

62. Sheila Greeve Davaney, introduction to *Feminism and Process Thought*, 5.

63. Whitehead, *Process and Reality*, 21.

64. Whitehead's "principle of relativity" is a rejection of the type of dualism feminists associate with the subject-object dichotomy that has rendered women the eternal object to the normative male subject. However, Whitehead persists in the use of this terminology, even though "subject" and "object" are merely temporal perspectives rather than concrete entities (David Ray Griffin, "Creativity in Postmodern Religion," 74). Davaney recognizes the need for caution in the use of these words and reframes the subject/object terminology in process philosophy as an assertion that we have intrinsic value in ourselves (subjects) as well as value for others also (objects). Davaney, *Feminism and Process Thought*, 5–6.

65. Alfred North Whitehead, *Adventures of Ideas* (New York: Mentor Books, 1955; Macmillan Company, 1933), 237.

66. Whitehead, *Process and Reality*, 21.

67. That is, generative novelty is made possible by God's primordial nature in the initial aim (or initial phase of the subjective aim) for the concrescing actual entity.

68. Whitehead, *Process and Reality*, 67, 247. Also, "reversion is a function of each actual entity's feeling of God's primordial nature, and conceptual reversion is the category by which novelty enters the world." Donald W. Sherburne, *A Key to Whitehead's Process and Reality* (Chicago: University of Chicago Press, 1966), 212.

69. Whitehead, *Process and Reality*, 232.

70. Charles Hartshorne, "Creativity as a Value and Creativity as a Transcendental Category," in *Creativity in Art, Religion, and Culture,* ed. Michael H. Mitias (Amsterdam: Rodopi, 1985), 9.

71. Whitehead, *Process and Reality*, 21. Charles Hartshorne highlights what I've called *constructive novelty* in his numerous discussions of experience as creative synthesis. See "The Idea of Creativity in American Philosophy," 8–9; also, *Creative Synthesis and Philosophic Method*.

72. These different nuances in Whitehead's thought recall Tillich's distinction between divine and human creativity, although an extensive comparison is beyond the scope of this work. God's creation *ex nihilo*, which is rejected by most process theologians, seems nevertheless quite parallel to generative novelty that is introduced only by God's initiative. "From nothing" and "wholly new" are not identical concepts, but there are some similarities in their explanation of the distinction between divine and worldly activity.

73. John B. Cobb, Jr., "Feminism and Process Thought: A Two-Way Relationship," in *Feminism and Process Thought*, ed. Sheila Greeve Davaney (New York: Edwin Mellen Press, 1981), 32.

74. Pete A. Y. Gunter, "Creativity and Ecology," in *Creativity in Art, Religion, and Culture,* ed. Michael H. Mitias (Amsterdam: Rodopi, 1985), 107–16.

75. Ibid., 109.

76. Bowers, 42.

77. Bowers, 66.

78. Whitehead, *Process and Reality*, 345, 88.

79. These are conceptual feelings cohering in the primordial nature.

80. For example, there are a mere 5 listings for "consequent nature" in the Index to *Process and Reality* compared to 15 places that the discussion includes God's "primordial nature." Similarly, Nancy Frankenberry writes that "the problem of how to talk meaningfully of the concrete actuality of God [the consequent nature] has gone largely unaddressed" (*Religion and Radical Empiricism*, 23).

81. Cobb, "Feminism and Process Thought," 33. Cobb says that, in contrast, "the primordial nature appears androgynous."

82. Cobb and Griffin observe that "the feminine and masculine images of God...tend to cluster around the Consequent and Primordial Natures, respectively." John B. Cobb, Jr. and David Ray Griffin, *Process Theology: An Introductory Exposition* (Philadelphia: Westminster Press, 1976), 135. However, these observations should be qualified by noting that God's consequent nature is also the source of judgment and consciousness, both stereotypically "masculine" attributes.

THREE

CREATIVITY AS COMPASSION

Empathic Attunement to the World

I should reiterate here that empathy, for the purposes of this discussion, is conceived as one person's actively and sensitively sharing in and understanding the momentary psychological experience of another.[1] As social beings, we humans find that empathy is an important tool with which we make connections with our world, learning what it means to be human and who we are as individuals. It is "the process through which one's experienced sense of basic connection and similarity to other humans is established."[2]

We have seen that openness is important to the creative process and fundamental in process philosophy. The dynamics of an empathic encounter involve two forms of openness. First, the one exercising empathy must be open to the perspective and experience of the other, in all of its dissemblance. His/her own perspective must be suspended as much as possible so that it does not filter or shut out the other's experience. Just as creativity is enhanced when we do not prematurely close off alternatives, empathic connection is promoted when we remain open to alternative perspectives and perceptions. In fact, one study has shown empathy to be positively related to creativity and inversely related to dogmatism, or closed-mindedness.[3] Empathy requires a *receptive* openness. Metaphorically, we might describe it as an attitude of "hospitality to the stranger."[4]

The second form of openness involved in an empathic encounter is the self-disclosure and vulnerability required of the one receiving empathy from another. Empathy presumes openness in the form of personal revelation, or *expressive/revelatory* openness. Someone may assume that they understand my experience and sympathize with me, but without my self-disclosure and confirming response to their perceptions, the empathic connection is not established. Openness is a fundamental requirement of both or all of those involved in an empathic encounter, but the experience of empathy is still very different depending on whether one is in the position of giving or receiving it. Our question is, how does empathic openness, in both its giving and receiving (receptive and revelatory) modes, nurture the creation of self?

Empathy's Role in Psychological Development

The importance of empathy has long been recognized by personality theories and therapeutic models that stress the significance of interpersonal relationships for self-development. Heinz Kohut's "self psychology," a branch of object relations theory, and Carl Rogers's "client-centered therapy" are the most well-known conceptualizations of the power of an empathic presence to foster selfhood and facilitate personal transformation.[5] These two theorists have argued that the intersubjectivity achieved by having one's experience "mirrored" by another's empathy confirms and clarifies one's identity as a person.

Empathy is important in these theories because they give precedence to the social character of personhood and the formative power of relationships. However, traditional approaches that emphasize interpersonal dynamics, including object relations theories, tend to be limited by a unidirectional focus that views "the relationship" and "the other" as contributions to understanding and maintaining the self rather than conceiving self and other as *co-constituted* within the relationship.[6] Hence, the powerful results of *receiving* empathy from another have been described, while little or no attention has been given to the effects on personal development of the extension of empathy to another. That is, empathy has been recognized as an important quality of the "holding environment" that is conducive to growth, but little attention has been given to how our human selfhood develops through the experience of "holding" otherness.[7]

An emphasis on the mutuality of growth in relationships is replacing the traditional unidirectional focus on development in a number of more relational models of selfhood that challenge the hegemony of western phallocentric models.[8] The images of self held by many other cultures and marginalized groups within western culture tend to portray identity within a web of relationships, rather than placing a separate individuality at the center of their images of health. These models stress a more mutual pattern of giving and receiving through relationships, expounding on what Beverly Harrison has called our "power...literally to create one another."[9] However, they are by no means all identical or even equivalent, reflecting as they do particular perspectives and contexts shaped by complex historical factors. Together they are creating new values, categories, and terms that are enhancing our understanding of human selfhood.

Among these relational perspectives, the feminist revision proposed by the Stone Center for Development has most explicitly dealt with empathy as the fundamental dynamic of human growth in relationship. The Stone Center model is distinctive in the importance it gives to empathy as a two-way, interactional process that serves the primary human need for connection and emotional joining with others.[10]

The Self-in-Relation as Women's Core Self-Structure

The model of selfhood being set forth by theorists associated with the Stone Center attempts to balance the overemphasis on separation and autonomy found in mainstream developmental theories extrapolated from male experience. By attending to women's experiences of self-development, they hope to increase our understanding of the dynamics of human connection.[11] Their alternative model uses the term "self-in-relation" to describe women's core self-structure that is organized and developed in the context of important relationships. The theory seeks to "account for the centrality and continuity of relationships throughout women's lives"[12] in ways that overturn psychology's customary pathologizing of women's investment in relationships. At the same time, the theory emerges from, and attempts to stay faithful to, some common problems that clinicians see in their women clients. Hence the theory emerges from a context that values women's experiences and is then tested by its applications within feminist revisionist approaches to therapeutic encounters.

Rather than being formed by a process of increasing separation and objectification of whatever is "not-self," the self-in-relation is articulated by differentiation within an increasing complexity of relationships, a process similar to the gradual differentiation observed in embryological development. Maturity is not achieved by disconnection and the sacrifice of relationships. Characteristics like competence, agency, and initiative are still important, but they evolve within a context of relationships and are viewed in light of their impact on those relationships. The goal of development is modified from autonomy to the deepening capacity for relationship and relational competency.[13]

There are many ways to express our relatedness. Dominance and submission are common ways of relating in our society. Even hatred creates a certain type of bond between persons. So what constitutes a healthy relationship? In the Stone Center model, healthy relationships are defined as those that lead to the psychological development or growth of the people in them, and the "essential feature is the interplay of mutual empathy created by both (or all) participants."[14] Each person's experience is recognized and granted full value. Each person has an impact on the other because both see that their actions, feelings, or thoughts affect the other, and they in turn open themselves to the influence of the other. In mutually empathic relationships, there is a sustained interest in, and responsiveness to, the inner world of the other.[15] Even the earliest relationship between child and mother (or primary caregiver) can be understood to be a reciprocal or mutual relationship in which both participants give and respond to cues from the other because of their investment in that relationship.

The self-in-relation model envisions mutual empathy as the fundamental developmental process, but that does not mean that every interaction is bilaterally empathic in growth-promoting relationships. Instead of an "equal time" or "tit-for-tat" connotation, mutuality is taken to mean "a kind of matching of intensity of involvement and interest."[16] Mutuality is an interactive process that fluctuates with persons' abilities to offer empathy in certain affective areas or at certain times. However, when empathy is consistently experienced unilaterally rather than mutually in a particular relationship, the relationship does not meet basic needs for recognition and affirmation and may degenerate into tyranny and abuse. Particularly if one person adjoins with an attitude of entitlement and the other "with mutuality or accommodation, imbalances and injustices abound."[17] In this case, one person is responsive to the needs and concerns of the other but is not heard, valued, or cared for themselves. Then the relationship is truly "self-sacrificing" in that one person's selfhood is not being nurtured by the relationship. These kinds of relationships form an inevitable part of our communal lives; however, persons extended in this way are dependent on the nurture they receive elsewhere to sustain their unreciprocated empathy. As Bonnie Miller-McLemore describes the parent-child relationship, "the necessity to give, in response to the needs of a child, depends upon a broader context of give-and-take....A parent cannot give to a child unless that giving is refreshed by the supportive attentions of another, whether spouse, neighbor, friend, or relative."[18]

In our society, destructive imbalances in empathic responsibilities are most often created by differences in power. Those with less power in a relationship are expected to empathically respond to those with greater power, the latter's resistance to the influence of the subordinate being equated with strength. Clearly, a new understanding of power is required if we hope to create contexts that nurture our human connections. Mutuality in relationship is based on shared power, "power with," or "power emerging from interaction."[19] This is contrasted with unhealthy relationships in which "power over" or "power for oneself only" diminishes or destroys people, especially when power differentials are unchangeable and go unrecognized. "Power with" is accompanied by humility because it takes seriously the shared responsibility for creative relationship. *Em*-powerment, like *em*-pathy (the prefix *em* meaning *with*), recognizes the value for selfhood of both giving and receiving. Relationships, when no longer viewed as a drain on personal resources and competency, can actually be a source of power and effectiveness.

Traditional definitions of power hold that having an influence or impact on another is an exercise of power. As a way of reframing this definition, we should recognize that being "held" within another's empathic response is affirming and empowering. If you empathize with me, I am exerting an influence on you at the same time that you are "holding" me. I am having an effect upon you; you are empowering me with your presence. Shared power recognizes both the power of influence and the power of response. For example, the power of response is manifested when women gain self-esteem from their capacity to perceive and respond to others and to "take care" of their relationships. Both receiving and giving empathy changes us, and this effect is amplified if the giving and receiving is mutual. Empathic connections leave persons "feeling more aware of self and other and, therefore, more energized to act."[20] The synergistic power or "zest" of mutually empathic relationships is characteristically generalized to action in other relational contexts, thereby increasing personal confidence and satisfaction.[21] The resulting sense of self forms concurrently with an evolving "response/ability" within an expanding web of mutually empathic relationships.

Self-in-relation theory has been criticized for its idealization of harmonious relationships and the resulting increased risk of self-denial. However, shared power does not mean an absence of conflict. On the contrary, the ability to engage in conflict—while maintaining the emotional connection—is an important part of healthy development.[22] Conflict creates an opportunity to elaborate the relational connection so that each person can change and grow. Mutuality is fundamental to "good conflict," in which the goal "is not to eradicate difference but to move beyond mere tolerance of existing difference to the creation of new opportunities."[23] In this new emergent synthesis we recognize the fingerprint of creativity as it is actualized by the self-in-relation. One metaphor that has been used to portray these dynamics of mutual empathic connection is that of an orchestra tuning to the same pitch so that different instruments can play together harmoniously. Connection requires continual emotional and cognitive "tuning" and adjustment so that each "instrument" is enhanced.[24]

The Co-Creative Dynamics of Mutual Empathy

Empathy is not some mysterious fusion of psychosystems involving a loss of identity. It is a complex, highly developed process that involves both cognition and affect, action and receptivity. "Developmentally, we believe that empathy evolves slowly over time as the individual engages in increasingly complex, shared, affective interactions which are mutually enhancing and out of which new, mutually informed understandings emerge."[25] One identifies with the feeling-state of the other person while cognitively structuring the experience in ways that articulate the differences and similarities between self and other. Empathy is bifocal in this attention toward self and other; it is mutually informing, with self and experience of both participants interpenetrating.[26]

Some understandings of empathy have posited a loss of identity inherent in the empathic connection with the affect of another person, but to suggest that we cannot empathically respond to someone without losing our self-awareness underestimates our ability to integrate multiple levels of experience. Empathy as it is described here actually sharpens the contrast of our similarities and differences. "The paradox of empathy is that in the joining process, one develops a more articulated and differentiated image of the other and hence responds in a more accurate way—quite the opposite of what regressive merging would lead to."[27]

The philosopher Edith Stein, in her classic phenomenological study of empathy, argues for the clear distinction between empathy and feelings of oneness with the other: "That the subject of the...empathized experience...is not properly an object is in agreement with our conception. But we do not agree that there is a complete coincidence with the...empathized 'I,' that they become one."[28] Stein insists that empathy is "differentiated from our own experience." What we empathically perceive (physical or emotional feelings) is "continually brought into relief as foreign in contrast with our own sensations....Now, however, it has a new dignity because what was presented as empty has found its fulfillment."[29]

Research on empathy supports an analysis of two distinct parts.[30] The affective part of the empathic process speaks to the interpenetration of feelings between two persons, creating a deep sense of connectedness. The cognitive part maintains "an integral sense of self," structures the experience, and acts on the basis of that selfhood.[31] The simultaneous experience of affective connection and cognitive differentiation seems contradictory, but we recall that this same juxtaposition of seemingly incompatible elements to create a novel entity is recognized by psychologists as creativity. Alexandra Kaplan even uses the metaphor of "empathy as creativity" to call attention to the sophisticated processes involved in our relational connections.[32]

Empathy and Boundary Disputes

Self-identity has often been articulated in terms of ego-boundaries so that "firm boundaries" describes adequate personal independence and initiative. The importance of empathy in self-development intimates a higher value for flexible boundaries that can extend to include the experience of another person. Judith Jordan calls attention to the stage in the empathic process in which one must "surrender" to affective arousal in oneself that is stimulated by temporary identification with the other's psychological state.[33] This surrender is receptive openness that involves a de-centering of one's own experience. But surrender also describes the willingness to reveal one's inner states, or revelatory openness, giving the other access to one's subjective world through self-disclosure. In either case, surrender is *not* passive. Empathy must be intentional, just as creativity has an important intentional element.[34] Shifting self-boundaries means openness and vulnerability to the pain of misunderstanding or rejection. Hence, courage and respect are also characteristic of relationships of mutual empathy in which selves are "transcended" in mutual surrender to a shared reality of their relational process.[35]

The accommodation of the self to receive the impression of the other is constantly balanced by the cognitive assimilation of the experience into the existing self-framework. Thus identity remains differentiated even though the so-called "boundaries" of selfhood are permeated by the feelings of the other person. The process of extension and withdrawal of self-boundaries that enables differentiation and connection to coexist has been described as the "oscillating self-structure."[36] This notion replaces the dichotomy between distinct/autonomous and merged/embedded that has perpetuated gender stereotypes and the pathologizing of women's experience. It also fits the post-modern view of a fluid, nonsubstantial selfhood.[37]

Valuing empathy as a central dynamic in growth-promoting relationship does not mean difference and distinctness are not important. On the contrary, it is the difference between persons that creates the gap which empathy traverses. It is our encounter with difference that creates the potential for integrative change like that associated with creativity. "We gain strength and harmony in similarity, but we learn and expand in difference."[38] If empathy involved simply "mirroring" the affect of the other, it would lead to stagnation. Marie McCarthy has punned that empathy is not "immaculate perception," but rather a "bridge between" differences.[39] Arguing for the possibility of empathy in intercultural classrooms, she explains:

> Empathic engagement is a dynamic process. It evolves over time, growing in increments as we engage one with another. There is a groping, unfolding quality to the empathic process, for it is the product of mutual vulnerability. As I am empathic with others and they are empathic with me, we become learners together, listening and responding to each other's points of view, seeing new possibilities, and expanding our range of awareness and appreciation. As we share story and presence, as we experience the invitation to share ourselves and our worlds, we come to understand and appreciate each other. And gradually the pool of empathy deepens and expands.[40]

Self-expression becomes increasingly full and clear as each person enlarges on his or her shared feeling-thoughts, thus creating movement and potential growth. "The combination of emotional responsivity and yet difference allows each of us to add something to the interplay."[41] As empathic abilities increase and mature through childhood and into adolescence and adulthood, we become more attuned to similarities and differences within and among various relationships. That is, we learn more about ourselves; we increase in self-awareness through comparison and contrast with those we encounter empathically. When we meet someone new and different, we must stretch to empathically connect with such diverse experience, and we are creatively "enlarged" as a result of this enrichment.[42]

Self-in-relation theory instructs us to value human diversity as a natural and perpetual stimulus for maturation, just as diversity was identified as a stimulus for creative activity in the previous chapter. "The more numerous and diverse the perspectives one has connected with, the broader the relational context, and the more enhanced will be the sense of being both connected to and empowered to respond to a larger 'human' reality."[43] That does not mean that embracing difference is easy. Audre Lorde says that our differences create sparks: "Difference must be not merely tolerated, but seen as a fund of necessary polarities between which our creativity can spark like a dialectic."[44] Empathic surrender necessarily involves some chaos and uncertainty. Empathy, like creativity, "is marked by restraint of the desire to master and control. It is rooted in the capacity to tolerate uncertainty, ambiguity, and doubt."[45] Empathic encounter with difference de-centers us for a time, but in our reintegration lies the opportunity for creative growth.

It is indicative of the limitations of language that "difference" places important limits on empathy at the same time that it is one of its fundamental ingredients. While difference stretches our abilities to connect with our world, there are also experiences so different from our own that we simply cannot comprehend them. We cannot transcend (literally, "cross over") the gap that distinguishes us. To insist that we can in such instances is presumptuous and discounts the other by denying the particularity of their experience. This "pretense to a homogeneity" is the dangerous seduction that Susan Thistlethwaite denounces as "the genius of patriarchy": to deal with difference by obliterating it through projection, obfuscation, and suppression. Thistlethwaite's insistence that "the boundaries of difference must be respected" is a reminder of the empathic disability of white feminists who have yet to come to terms with the conditions and pervasiveness of our race and class privilege.[46]

Ethical limits to empathy pertain to individuals as well as groups. Sharing someone's "feeling-thoughts" is a gift to be offered by invitation. The attempt to empathize without permission is impositional and may be an unethical invasion of the privacy and integrity of the self. It is especially important to honor the personal boundaries of those who are victims of violence, who have been abused by the intrusion and presumed entitlement of others and denied the dignity of self-definition and agency.[47] Placing value in relatedness does not undermine the importance of solitude. Solitude and relatedness need not be contradictions in terms, as even solitude can be reframed as a cultivation of relationships of different types—"to nature, books, animals, or one's internal images."[48] These relationships also enrich the quality of our other connections.

Some negative restrictions on our ability to empathize are socially systemic. The patriarchal structure of our society has made it difficult for persons to develop empathic skills in healthy ways. Hierarchy rather than mutuality has been the norm in most types of relationships, breeding anger that is not allowed expression except as it is displaced onto those lower and with less power than oneself.[49] Cultural stereotypes of male-female differences have channeled development into lopsided caricatures of relational skills. Self-in-relation theory "is not in any way an attempt to idealize women's altruism or relational capacities."[50] The point is not that women have some special standpoint that is more true and liberatory than others,[51] but that women in our culture are carriers of certain aspects of the human experience that must be included in a comprehensive understanding of human selfhood.

Some of these socially produced gender differences are apparent in attitudes toward emotional vulnerability in empathy. Jordan has found that males tend to have difficulty, symptomatic of overly rigid self-boundaries, with the necessary surrender of affect and momentary joining with another.[52] Discomfort with self-disclosure and difficulty allowing another to have emotional impact are major impediments to mutual relationality.[53] Men might feel threatened by the passivity and loss of control they associate with empathy. Because they deny themselves the direct access of empathic connection, their knowledge of the other may be a distant and intellectualized version that is highly contaminated by their own projections and/or narcissism. In more extreme cases, perceived vulnerability in others "evokes exploitation and violence in those socialized toward dominance."[54]

Whereas men seem to have more difficulty with the affective aspect of the empathic process, Jordan has found that women often have more difficulty cognitively structuring the experience so as to maintain self-differentiation. They also have more trouble developing what Jordan calls self-empathy, or "bringing an empathic attitude to bear on themselves."[55] Having been socially conditioned to attend to others' needs first, and feeling the empathic pull very strongly, women may be unable to identify their own desires and needs, much less trust and act on these perceptions. A further complication may be the inability to disengage from destructive relationships or to demonstrate self-determination outside of certain intense dyadic relationships.

By expanding our exploration from intra/interpersonal relationships to their social and systemic contexts, we discover impediments to mutually empathic relationships built into our cultural worldviews as well. Just as creativity is qualified by its contextual limitations, so is the development of empathy inhibited by gender stereotypes. Catherine Keller has written extensively about the tenacity of the patriarchal assumption that separation equals superiority, which undergirds sexism's claim "that men, by nature and by right, exercise the primary prerogatives of civilization."[56] Only when our worldviews shift to support our experiences of human connection—only when we have struggled with language and models to conceptualize those connections—only then will relational views of self have the power to change our cultural patterns of dualism and domination. A process perspective on empathy can help by providing conceptual support for (and a cosmological interpretation of) women's experiences of empathy in relationships. Process descriptions of creativity resonate with the characteristics of empathy that we have just identified, including openness, contrast, analysis or judgment, synthesis, and limitation.

A Process Perspective on Empathy

Whitehead's cosmology describes the nature of reality in ways that affirm empathy's central role in self-creation. The following four points guide our discussion of the intersection between process thought and the Stone Center analysis of empathy:

1. Reality is fundamentally relational.
2. Difference adds value to experience.
3. Mutuality characterizes growth-producing relationships.
4. There are important limits to empathy.

In what follows I employ Whitehead's methodology of drawing analogies between descriptions of the most fundamental levels of reality and human experience. Whitehead believed that the coherency of his theory was demonstrated by the continuity between the structure of human experience and the structure of physical nature.[57] By implication, we might inversely state that our presuppositions about reality at the microlevel inform our understanding and descriptions of human experience at the macrolevel.[58]

Reality as Fundamentally Relational

> *Relation...is more than a feminine or feminist preoccupation; it is the best metaphor for the nature of the universe.*
> —Catherine Keller[59]

In Whitehead's view, reality is composed of events rather than substances. The smallest unit, an actual occasion or actual entity,

Creativity as Compassion

consists of that occasion's synthesis of data from its past into a single unity of identity. All of space and time (or "space-time") is made up of actual entities becoming concrete ("concrescing") and perishing. In Whitehead's words, "An epochal occasion is a concretion. It is a mode in which diverse elements come together into a real unity....Thus an actual entity is the outcome of a creative synthesis, individual and passing."[60]

Each becoming receives the data from past actual entities as the "raw material" for its self-creation, and each completed entity then contributes the "emergent fact" of its feeling as data for future occasions. The actual entity is both the mode (concrescing) and outcome (transition) of the creative synthesis, or growing together, of its experience of the universe of past actual entities. In this way, all reality is interrelated because "an actual entity has a perfectly definite bond with each item in the universe."[61] In the creative activity of concrescence and transition, Whitehead explains, an actual entity

> ...is not self-sufficient. The aspects of all things enter into its very nature. It is only itself as drawing together into its own limitation the larger whole in which it finds itself. Conversely it is only itself by lending its aspects to this same environment in which it finds itself.[62]

Whitehead distinguishes the interconnections in the universe as internal rather than external relations. In other words, actual entities are *constituted* by their relationships rather than being impacted (like billiard balls) while not essentially changed by them. "For each relationship enters into the essence of the event; so that, apart from the relationship, the event would not be itself."[63] Keller draws out this point for us by describing the influence of one individual on another:

> If the other enters my experience, then it enters as an influence upon me: it makes a difference, and so I am no longer quite the same. But influence, to be more precise, is not working *upon* me so much as *into* me; in-fluence is that which flows in. If the other flows into the self, then the other is immanent to the self, to the inside being of that self. This is the philosophical meaning of internal rather than external relations: relations between different subjects that are internal to what those subjects *are*—part of their very essence, for good or for ill.[64]

Because relations are internal to existence, the Cartesian subject-object dualism between knower and known is dissolved. Attempting to convey this epistemological subversion, Whitehead says that the subject "has a 'concern' for the object" rather than an external knowledge of it.[65] The distinction is consistent with Judith Jordan's observation of an empathic/love mode of knowing as contrasted with an objectifying/power/control mode that fears openness. For Whitehead, objects exist only as immanent in experiencing subjects, that is, as components of the subject.

An entity's "concern" for its world is made up of positive prehensions, or feelings. These describe *how* past entities influence the present concrescing subject. Whitehead's choice of "feeling" emphasizes that emotion is the basis of all experience, although Whitehead does not mean the high-level affective states associated with human experience. Rather, "feeling" describes the intuitive bond between an entity and its universe.

> The primitive form of physical experience is emotional—blind emotion—received as felt elsewhere in another occasion and conformally appropriated as a subjective passion. In the language appropriate to the higher stages of experience, the primitive element is *sympathy*, that is, feeling the feeling *in* another and feeling conformally *with* another.[66]

In Whitehead's view, as in the Stone Center model, our most basic connection with the world, a connection that is part of our essence, is experienced as sympathy (or empathy).[67]

Valuing Difference

Whitehead stated that the most fundamental order is aesthetic order. Beauty is the aesthetic value that entities strive for in their becoming. Creativity is individualized in their subjective experience. Beauty is created by the maximum harmony and intensity that can be synthesized in a particular occasion of experience. Harmony as an aspect of beauty is experienced when things fit together or connect with each other. Harmony in relationships strengthens our identity and makes us feel secure. However, too much harmony becomes repetitious and boring, so it must be balanced by intensity. Intensity is created by contrast and tension between differing prehensions. Difference introduces novelty, and novelty, according to Whitehead, makes something alive.

If we draw an analogy with human empathy, we see that "fusion," that infamous threat to women who invest in their connections with others, translates into process terminology as mere repetition. It is too much harmony, the domination of conformal feelings, and lacks the novelty that difference provides. The important cognitive dimension of empathy that draws contrasts between the thought-feelings of self and other is analogous to the conceptual feelings (or the mental pole) in concrescence—they introduce the possibility of novelty.

Things in the universe strive for the greatest beauty both in their subjective experience of becoming and in their objective contribution to the future. That would involve achieving the greatest amount of contrast which can be creatively integrated into a final unity. Because of the important role of contrast and intensity, Whitehead's unity never connotes a simplistic harmony. It always includes the tension of contrast—as much contrast as can possibly be brought together in a particular moment of experience while still preserving "an aptitude for final synthesis."[68] Bernard Loomer's classic translation of this principle is "size." As the measure of a person, "size" is

> ...the stature of a person's soul, the range and depth of his [her] love, his [her] capacity for relationships. I mean the volume of life you can take into your being and still maintain your integrity and individuality, the intensity and variety of outlook you can entertain in the unity of your being without feeling defensive or insecure. I mean the strength of your spirit to encourage others to become freer in the development of their diversity and uniqueness. I mean the power to sustain more complex and enriching tensions.[69]

Loomer's definition of "size" correlates with the psychological claim that a person matures through an increasing complexity of relationships that embrace more and more diversity. Jean Baker Miller reminds us that "relationships have to encompass many disparate and conflicting thoughts and feelings. There has to be room for oppositional thoughts and feelings, negative and destructive thoughts and feelings, and many misperceptions and misunderstandings."[70] We are "enlarged" by our ability to empathically connect with (contain or "hold") more significant difference.

Mutuality in Relationship

In Whitehead's cosmology, mutual relatedness or mutual influence is the basis of order. Order is not understood to be a rigid structure that opposes all novelty, like that described in Chapter 2 as an oppressor's squelching of resistance. Order is simply Whitehead's way of talking about how groups of entities are interconnected to create more complex forms (societies). Aesthetic order expresses how entities are grouped by harmony and intensity. The "togetherness of things" involves mutual immanence.[71] Increasing complexity is the only distinction between the continuum of so-called "lower" and "higher" forms of existence. People are complex societies of actual occasions that are related to each other by their mutual prehensions because mutuality contributes to order, and order supports increasing complexity.

Whitehead's principle of mutual relatedness provides a way to re-envision power, which, as we have seen, is an important dimension of every relationship. For Whitehead, "the 'power' of one actual entity on the other is simply how the former is objectified in the constitution of the other."[72] Bernard Loomer demonstrated how this understanding expands the traditional conception of power as "the ability to produce an effect" to suggest that power is also "the capacity to absorb an influence."[73] Receiving the influence of other entities enriches the possibilities of the experiencing subject, which, in turn, empowers it by making its satisfaction more interesting and likely to influence future occasions. Relational power, as Loomer has called it, is expressed in both giving and receiving. Importantly, "receiving is not unresponsive passivity; it is an active openness. Our reception of another indicates that we are or may become large enough to make room for another within ourselves."[74]

We have observed that the richness of the otherness that we hold in empathy does not only empower our own becoming. When we demonstrate receptive openness to others, they are also empowered by our confirmation of their being (Whitehead's objective immortality). Power like this is released in the therapeutic relationship, for example. If power is redefined from "power-over" to include "power-with," we see that both giving and receiving empathy are channels for creative power. Empathy demonstrates the "active openness" that is relational power.

Jean Baker Miller often uses the concept of "enlarging" in her struggle to find language to describe psychological growth-in-connection, revealing remarkable parallels with process thought:

> For the moment, perhaps it will suffice to say that the important thing is that both people were connected through the interplay of their "feeling-thoughts." They both created something new together. Both are enlarged by this creation. Something new now exists, built by both of them. This is "the connection between," the relationship. It does not belong to one or the other. It belongs to both. Yet each feels it as "hers," as part of her. She contributed to its creation. And it contributed to her, to what she now "is," which is <u>more</u> than she was a few moments before.[75]

Mutuality and shared, relational power indicate the Stone Center's shift in focus from the psychological *structure* of a discrete, separate entity to the relational *processes* of a de-centered subject.[76]

The Limits of Empathy

A final important point of intersection between process and feminist thought on empathy concerns the limitations to connection that we experience. Although each entity is essentially connected to the universe of other things, it has the limitation that Whitehead calls a "perspective" of the universe. Perspective limits the infinitude of alternatives according to their relevance for this particular actual entity.[77] In the first phase of concrescence, an actual entity positively prehends or feels only a portion of the past universe. Some of the past is negatively prehended, which means it is still "involved in the production" of an entity but it is not included in the final concrete unity of feeling.[78] Some of the past is negatively prehended on the basis of its incompatibility with other feelings in that entity.

The concept of perspective is Whitehead's technical approach to something like our human experience of diversity. There are limits to our ability to empathize with experiences very different from our own. Some things are simply beyond our ability to comprehend due to the "subjective insistence on consistency."[79] This is the limitation of our given world. That an entity's "location" renders some data irrelevant for its concrescence explains the impact of social location and cultural context upon our ability to empathically connect in particular situations. It is not surprising that our ability to empathize is increased by our exposure, if we are receptive, to a wide variety of people, places, and situations.

As we have seen, under certain circumstances empathy can be invasive and connection can be camouflage that conceals privilege. Distinctiveness and privacy must also be accounted for in an ontology of relational selfhood. Whitehead's schema protects the individuality of each actual entity by the privacy and absolute self-constitution, or self-enjoyment, provided to it in its act of creative synthesis.

> The individual immediacy of an occasion is the final unity of subjective form, which is the occasion as an absolute reality. This immediacy is its moment of sheer individuality, bounded on either side by essential relativity. The occasion arises from relevant objects, and perishes into the status of an object for other occasions. But it enjoys its decisive moment of absolute self-attainment as emotional unity....[The word 'individual' properly applies] to an actual entity in its immediacy of self-attainment when it stands out as for itself alone, with its own effective self-enjoyment.[80]

Whitehead's understanding of individuality is circumscribed by the presupposition of "essential relativity," or that the nature of reality is that all things are interrelated with one another. Individuality describes the "I-ness" or uniqueness that is the entity at the moment of its completed becoming. It is individuality that is not apart from its internal relations with past and future worlds. Separateness of experience exists only for contemporaries, which Whitehead technically defined as those occasions that happen in causal independence of each other.

Whitehead's interpreters have had trouble with this point, and critics have argued that true intersubjectivity, which would seem to be central to a theory of relatedness, is made unfeasible because, in Whitehead's schema, no two subjects can share internal relationship. For example, Nancy Howell argues that this point reveals how Whitehead continues to be limited to subject-object relations while feminists should hold to the centrality of intersubjective relationships; intersubjectivity is foundational to relationality.[81] However, the boundaries of an actual entity are what guarantee true individuality that is characterized by its own unity of existence. Otherwise, there really would be no distinction between you, me, and that chair—only continuous process. Intersubjectivity as it is used in such critiques is

Creativity as Compassion

undesirable and cannot be equated with relationality. It would be fusion. I concur with Marjorie Suchocki that "each concrescence is like a breathing space in a sea of relationality, the aloneness through which one becomes a self in the integration of many relations."[82] I affirm Whitehead's insight that there is ultimately a difference between my self-constitution and another's perception of it, that there is space for solitude, and that my agency in the form of invitation or aim for the future is required for your empathic presence, and yours for mine.

Theological Interpretations of Empathy

Religion is about making connection with the divine, and when the divine is imaged as a personal God, that connection is viewed in terms of relationship. If empathy is the fundamental dynamic of healthy relationships, what could this imply about our relationship to God? How could the exploration of empathy's role in emerging selfhood illumine our theological reflection on the divine nature?

The importance of empathy in human relationships challenges traditional masculine images of God on issues of mutuality and power, notions that feminist and process theologians have been particularly interested in reworking. Receptivity and revelation, two types of openness found in mutually empathic relationships, are themes that might resonate with feminist process reformulations. At the same time, a process theological context for empathy lends itself to new understandings of love, justice, incarnation, and spirituality.

Mutual Empathy and the Receptivity of God

The insistence that growth-producing relationships are mutually empathic issues a direct challenge to conventional understandings of divine transcendence. Descriptions of God as transcendent Being emphasize the difference between the divine and human. Hence God is "wholly other," not subject to temporality, and self-sufficient in God's perfection. In this understanding, the divine-human relationship is anything but mutual because, while humans are totally dependent upon God for their existence, humans can contribute nothing to God's unchangeable perfection.[83] When influence is unilateral, dominance and submission are the means by which separate parts experience connection. Unity is experienced through assimilation of the weak into the strong, without influencing the latter. Feminist theologian Carter Heyward gives a scathing description of this "narcissistic God who demands her self-negation" as One who thrives on our alienation and weakness because it forms the basis of our dependent relationship with Him.[84] Rita Brock concurs that preoccupation with God's transcendent, external power discourages self-awareness and personal power.[85]

In a radically transcendent God there is no accommodation to the impact of human existence because God's relations do not affect God's existence. From God's impassible (impossible?) nature we are to draw the illogical conclusion that God is both loving and self-sufficient. Theologian Tom Driver claims that "the Church has fabricated a myth of a God who is self-sufficient yet loving. This myth makes the church schizophrenic" by breeding "either self-contempt or the arrogance of purity."[86] Beverly Harrison sees a connection between God's aseity and our western compulsion for independence. She writes that "by stressing that God is 'being itself' or is 'the wholly other,' the Christian tradition implies that a lack of relatedness in God is the source of divine strength. And this image of divine nonrelatedness surely feeds images of self that lead us to value isolation and monadic autonomy."[87] Catherine Keller concurs that this separatist view of God is intricately connected with our cultural model of independent and autonomous selfhood: "The absolute separateness of deity has symbolized the separative aspirations of a Mankind created in His image....Indeed this is the ultimate separate subject, eternally self-sufficient, immune to the influence of those others, whom he has created....In our culture this God could only take the pronoun *he*."[88]

Keller and other process theologians have argued that this is an inadequate view of God and God's love.[89] A process view flatly denies that God is the "unmoved mover" who remains unchanged by God's relations. As a special kind of actual entity, or what John Cobb calls an "energy-event," God is internally related to the world and therefore influenced or affected by that relationship.[90] Whereas traditional theism radically separates God from the world, Cobb explains how God is interconnected with the world in a way that protects the integrity of God. God is not identified with the world, but God and the world do not exist apart from each other. In other words, process theologians describe God in ways analogous to the self-in-relation, who is distinct but not separate, related without being "fused" to the world or "lost" in relationships.

God's immanence names how God's presence is felt as a part of every concrescing occasion. Whitehead associated God's immanence in the world with God's primordial nature as "being *with* all creation," luring it toward beauty by providing ordered potentials in the form of its initial aim.[91] God's immanence in every entity as its initial aim is a presence so definite that Marjorie Suchocki writes, "It is as if every becoming occasion in the world begins with the touch of God."[92]

Whitehead's notion of internal relations helps us reflect on the implications of immanence as a mutual occurrence. God is not only immanent in every occasion of experience, but the world is also immanent in God's experience. "The character of the world is influenced by God, but it is not determined by [God], and the world in its turn contributes novelty and richness to the divine experience."[93] The divine nature exhibits Whitehead's idea of mutual immanence in that we also enter into God's experience of becoming as an aspect of God's consequent nature. It is through this receptive pole of God's nature that God "feels" the world, consciously and everlastingly, in the immediacy of its becoming actuality.[94] Traditional theism has difficulty conveying this responsive aspect, which is part of our human experience of loving relationships, because traditional theism has a high investment in God's impassibility. In process theology, God and the world influence one another. God's influence is felt in the world as the activity of God's primordial nature, and the world's influence on God is accounted for in God's consequent nature. The consequent nature is how God feels what we feel with us. This is the aspect of God's nature that characterizes God as "the great companion—the fellow-sufferer who understands."[95]

Daniel Day Williams amplifies the meaning of mutuality in the God-human relationship in his discussion of love. "Love presupposes beings who can both give and receive in relation to one another, and therefore God must have ways of receiving and responding to what happens in the world."[96] Williams calls this capacity to be acted upon "suffering" and speaks of the suffering of God as an essential requirement of love; love cannot be impassible. Instead of a "God who condescends to humankind in the name of love without getting his essence dirty,"[97] process theology envisions God as receptive to our experience. God's consequent nature "takes account" of our feelings in order to respond to us with the best possibilities for our next moment. "God feels the world, and thus can fashion for the world lures deeply suited to its variant realities."[98] So God's love is manifested in God's responsive attunement to the moment-by-moment actuality of the world. This is very different from the usual connotation of agape as the love of God. Agape is characteristically interpreted as a unilateral love that expects nothing in return, a love that is disinterested and sacrificial in that it is given without regard for the characteristics of its recipient.[99] That is, agape is the love of an immutable God for His creatures.

While process theologians like Daniel Day Williams have made an issue of mutuality by reinterpreting agape, I described in Chapter 2 the efforts of several feminists to balance the unilateral emphasis of agape by reclaiming eros. Keller writes that a God who demonstrates a responsive and therefore credible love "is as much Eros—desire—as Agape, the unilaterally self-giving, sacrificial 'love' of the theological mainstream."[100] These reformulations recognize that love requires an ongoing knowledge of—a desire for—the other. Love requires seeing the other clearly so that our response will be informed and relevant to the other's particular need. Too often our human imitation of agapeic love is patronizing and paternalistic rather than truly responsive because we maintain our distance (our separateness) and resist knowing the other. In mutually empathic relationships, both persons surrender rigid boundaries in order to know the other. Both are transformed by the encounter. In empathic connection there is real risk of rejection, but there is also potential communion with shared pain and shared joy. Identity is not lost, but enriched.

It is obvious that our ability to influence God means compromising the omnipotent unilateral power of traditional theism. However, process and feminist theologians argue that mutual or relational power is superior to the power to compel or force, "in all the ways that matter."[101] Rita Brock calls relational or erotic power "the power that nurtures life" because it represents acts of giving and care as acts of strength.[102] We have seen that empowerment, not power over, characterizes empathic connection. When God's power is understood as relational power, then divine empathy does not contradict divine power. Relational power tends to generate power and freedom in others. When feminists refer to God's power as erotic power, they draw attention to the creative power that is released or becomes available when connections are made. Hence divine power results in creativity, communion, integration, and insight.

Mutual influence and relational power reconfigure our conception of the divine and blur traditional boundaries between God and humans (one can imagine traditional theists joining dubious therapists to cry, "Beware of fusion!"). One thing that does distinguish the divine nature from our human version is that God feels the world in the fullness of its actuality, discarding nothing as irrelevant. Our human knowledge is always partial, as it is filtered and conformed to our expectations and perspective on "what this is for me" or "what this is compared to that." God is different from all other actual entities in that God feels the world without limitation. Nothing is eliminated because of its incompatibility. This is the divine acceptance which is unconditionally receptive to the world, acting in "tender care that nothing be lost."[103]

Loomer applies his principle of stature to describe the size of God as involving "the transformation of incompatibilities and contradictions into compatible contrasts" within the interconnected web of the world.[104] That is, God perfectly holds the universe of past and present actualities in compatible contrasts, and God feels them as everlastingly present. Marjorie Suchocki brings this reality to life:

> The consequent nature of God is God's feeling of every occasion that ever existed....It rains in a city called Chicago on a certain day. Does God know it? How? In the process understanding, God knows it by feeling it, both through the reality of the drops of moisture as they fall and through the experience of wetness as the drops touch the earth, be it upon the pavement, or a leaf upon a tree, or the wet cheek of a secretary rushing to reach shelter from the unexpected noontide storm. Every actuality that comes into existence, human or otherwise, is felt by God in its entirety, just as it felt itself.[105]

This is the extent of God's empathy for us! No one and nothing is left out. "Holding" presents a powerful image for empathic attunement. As we [or God] hold others, our own personhood [God's Personhood] is enriched. "Welcoming" is another image that Keller has used to describe empathic openness, and McCarthy has depicted mutual empathy as being alternatively the host who makes room and the guest who resides there.[106] These images capture what Whitehead defined as "peace." Instead of construing peace as something gained by closing out the world and its chaos, Whitehead understood peace to be found in the removal of inhibition—in openness. Peace, according to Whitehead, is our dim intuition of our acceptance in God's consequent nature.[107] Peace is the fruit of maximized creativity!

Our concern to keep discussion rooted in women's experiences cautions us to qualify this appreciation for immanence and mutuality with another word about privacy and solitude. Because women are socialized to be receptive to others, feminists have rightly resisted anything that would compromise women's already fragile self-awareness. With regard to Whitehead's notion of absolute individuality as it was summarized above, theologians have found difficulty with what would seem to be God's sharing our subjective experience only "after the fact," that is, after the actual entity has perished in its subjective immediacy. As we have seen, this point arises because of the causal independence of contemporaries and issues forth in the complaint that "God cannot prehend [persons] in their hearts, in their processes of becoming."[108] That is, critics insist that process theology discredits God's compassion.

However, compassion is better portrayed by mutuality than by perpetual togetherness. Just as our human relatedness is limited in its intersubjectivity, so also the privacy of the individual entity is preserved from God's knowledge, which amounts to limiting God's omniscience. The tension between God's "feeling with us" and individual privacy becomes significant when we recognize how knowledge can be used to intimidate and control. In our society women experience the judgmental and all-seeing normative male gaze as conditioning and controlling in both public and private spheres.[109] The importance of this limitation to immanence is painfully illustrated by the experience of battered women who literally cannot escape their tormentor's possessive and jealous watchfulness and control. "Where can I go from your spirit? Or where can I flee from your presence?" (Psalm 139:7) The image of an all-seeing, all-knowing God leaves me nowhere to be alone with myself, when I so choose. Divine omniscience, like omnipotence, contains some implicit associations with unjust hierarchical social relations that must be exposed in theological reformulations of relational selfhood.

Mutual Empathy and the Revelation of God

Just as the receptive openness of empathic encounters has important parallels in our understanding of receptivity in the divine nature, so also the revelatory or expressive openness of such encounters resonates with certain conceptions of divine revelation. For example, the Christian community has understood Jesus to be the self-disclosure of God. In Jesus, one could say, the boundaries between God and humanity were "permeated" in a way analogous to our human experience of empathy.[110] Incarnation would then describe how God extended Godself into empathic relation with our humanness, a relation that process theology asserts transforms both. Jesus' life has been interpreted as revealing God's character and intention; in Jesus, God identified with our human joys and struggles. "The disclosure of who God is has come through Jesus not primarily in miraculous powers, but in [God's] self-identification with the suffering of the world for the sake of love."[111]

The hymn in Philippians 2 portrays God's kenotic activity to strengthen the divine-human relationship. Similarly, incarnation could describe the emptying of our assumptive world to be open and receptive to another's world. Incarnation expands us in "size." We are diminished by what Judith Jordan calls *"pathological certainty* about one's perception of reality," an anti-relational orientation of entitlement that shuts out others in our world.[112] At the same time that incarnation empties us to receive another perspective, it also exposes us through self-disclosure and vulnerability to the other's rejection. For Christians, Jesus' life was a testimony to the power of these dynamics to open up new and richer worlds of meaning.[113]

Carter Heyward writes insightfully about the power of disclosure in the lives of gay and lesbian persons. She views "coming out" as an issue of authentic connection. It is a way of moving into shared power for the struggle for justice. "As a profoundly relational movement, the coming-out process among gaymen and lesbians can be paradigmatic for all efforts toward right and honest relationships."[114] God's incarnation as the man Jesus could be viewed as God's "coming out," an act of love that risked everything in order to gain a more mutually empathic relationship with the world. At the same time, Heyward recognizes the "profound theological wisdom in the tension between revelation and concealment."[115] Sometimes the divine is characterized by hiddenness because humans are not regarded as able to comprehend or accept the divine truth. Similarly, Heyward observes that gaymen and lesbians have to be sensitive in their disclosure, weighing situations and times for personal safety and compassion for others' readiness to hear. There is risk involved in opening oneself emotionally to another, exposing vulnerability in order to create a close relationship. Such a risk requires great courage, but courage of a different sort from the worldview that pictures the brave as standing alone and free from relational encumbrances. It is a courage that acknowledges vulnerability while continuing to act faithfully to strengthen human connections, a courage which Rita Brock calls "heart."[116] For Christians, Jesus' death was evidence of the human rejection of relationship with the divine as well as rejection of life as Jesus lived it in mutual relation with others. "The rejection and crucifixion of Jesus signaled the extent to which human beings will go to avoid our own relational possibilities."[117] Risk of rejection is clearly part of mutual relationship, but the point of risk is not to invite physical or emotional martyrdom. The risk is a profound affirmation of the possibility of life beyond the poles of domination and oppression.[118]

Transformative power is grounded in loving openness. It is empathy that provides the fundamental data for creative, redemptive transformation. Marjorie Suchocki explains redemption in process terms:

> God's full openness to who we are involves God in the pain of who we are, symbolized most profoundly in the revelation of God in Jesus on a cross. But this unsurpassable truth of God's knowledge is the means whereby God knows precisely what possibilities will be redemptive for us in the next moment of our existence. Through God's crucifixion, God provides us with a resurrection fitted to us.[119]

Empathic acceptance links creative transformation with redemption. "What is typical of *soteriological* activity is typical of *creative* activity."[120]

Jesus' death and resurrection also has meaning for Christians as an expression of God's solidarity with those who suffer. In this view resurrection is both transformation and liberation, a particularly meaningful perspective for African-American and third-world women whose multivalent experiences of oppression make central Jesus' identity as liberator. Womanist theologian Jacquelyn Grant proclaims that the message of the resurrection is that liberation from oppression is immanent.[121] As co-sufferer, God empathically participates in human life at its deepest and most profound level, and that presence empowers persons to resist oppression.

Empathy and Human Response/Ability

Pastoral theologian Larry Graham has defined justice as "right relationships between persons and the various components of their worlds."[122] If "right" or healthy relationship is characterized by mutual empathic connections, then justice is, as Carter Heyward describes it, the "shape of mutuality in our life together, in our societies and relationships—friendships, families, local and larger communities, the world itself."[123] Sin names the self-in-relation's experience of disconnection from lack of relationship or in dysfunctional, abusive relationships. Sin can be described in terms of the failure of empathy; that is, sin is traceable to over-identification or under-identification of self with another. In either case, the relational bond is broken so that persons "are disempowered to grow, love, and/or live."[124] If justice-love is "right relation," sin is denial or violation of right relation—a rejection of mutuality in any relationship, including humans' relationship with nature. As an essential part of a feminist structure of meaning, empathy must empower us in the struggle for justice. How does it do so?

Empathic openness increases our response/ability. Our ability to "feel" the world, to literally "bring it in, to give it a home, to let its objective manyness turn into a new subjective oneness"[125] with our emerging selfhood, stirs in us grief for the pain. It motivates us to action to resist personal and systemic evil and to lessen suffering in our world. Megan Boler has critiqued the risks of a false or "passive empathy" that is not mutual but "allows the voyeuristic pleasure of listening and judging the other from a position of power/safe distance" that does not have to change.[126] Mutual empathy means mutual transformation, and that is the foundation of social change.

God's receptivity and revelation models for us the response/ability to enlarge ourselves and our worlds by expanding the web of authentic and loving connection. "Since the divine harmony is one of enormous inclusiveness, wherein all the world is integrated into God's own being, reflections of that harmony in history will also push the world toward societies with the widest possible forms of inclusive well-being."[127] God's creative power is the power of interconnection—not to bind or constrict, but to hold us accountable to one another in community to be co-creators of justice.

Daniel Day Williams locates sin in our attempts to make ourselves invulnerable, going against our inherently relational nature that seeks communion. "The forms of sin are ways of seizing substitutes for communion or of smothering anxiety about its loss."[128] Sin is closing ourselves off from others (including the "otherness" of our own past and future) because these are too threatening to our illusions of fortified selfhood. "Always, in sin, we build a prison for ourselves. The refusal to live toward others from the depths of who we are then acts as a way of filling those depths with stones, until finally they have been reduced to shallowness."[129] Sin diminishes our "size."

We have seen that Jordan perceives a male susceptibility to under-identification in relationship due to excessively rigid self-boundaries. Her observations correlate with Valerie Saiving's description of a particularly "male" experience of sin: "pride, will-to-power, exploitation, self-assertiveness, and the treatment of others as objects rather than persons."[130] By constructing rigid boundaries, this "fortified" self tries to allay anxiety about its own inadequacy and to avoid vulnerability that might lead to suffering (that is, "being acted upon"). Human freedom is experienced alongside fear for the self's survival, so "power-over" is the chosen mode because "power-with" is too risky. The self is absolutized as subject and others are objectified in an effort to clarify the self's protective boundaries; then the gaps in knowledge of the other are filled in with the self's own projections.

This view of self and power that is commonly encouraged in males in our society produces a "self-identity that is brittle and isolated, is afraid of relatedness, associating intimacy with violence, and is oriented toward the domination and control of others."[131] As the pattern by which males are socialized into a patriarchal culture, it also reflects the dominant values pervading our society. Hence Carter Heyward says that we actually learn sadism, to "enjoy the 'power' in separating and distancing ourselves from those who display their own, and represent our, vulnerability: children, women, differently abled men and women, gaymen and lesbians, animals, students, patients, prisoners, poor people, elderly people, members of racial ethnic, cultural, or religious minorities."[132] I would include nature in this list. Viewing nature as the expendable "other" has brought our world to the brink of self-destruction.

The tendency that Jordan observed in women toward over-identification in relationship is also sinful because it breaks the relational bond by default of one self from its mutual contribution. Persons who are empathic to the needs and feelings of others but are unable to admit or feel their own reveal a lack of respect for the integrity of both the other and themselves. They make themselves the object for all others and deny the fullness of their own subjectivity.[133] Rita Brock calls this a "loss of heart" or a "broken heart" because such a person has lost touch with the vital meaning and organizing core of his or her selfhood.[134] Softer, more tentative self-boundaries can lead to diffuseness, stagnation, and sacrifice of the self's creativity and initiative. Nevertheless, enmeshment in another's life can be appealing in that it provides a certain invulnerability to loneliness and meaninglessness. Fusion seems a safe, if inferior, alternative to communion. Passivity, devaluing oneself, and resentment of the other often combine as deadly ingredients in ennui and depression. While Thistlethwaite has identified passivity as a poisonous fruit of white women's socialization, sins of over-identification also resonate with Delores Williams's description of black women's temptation to self-destruction through "bearing a disproportionately large burden in the work of community [that is, relationship] building and maintenance."[135]

Sins of over- and under-identification make relationships essentially unilateral, whether power is exercised openly or covertly, thereby denying the transformative power of mutual co-creation and mutual relational responsibility. These distorted ways of relating have coexisted symbiotically in patriarchal societies for thousands of years. Their representations in social and systemic evil compel us to pursue socio-ethical dimensions of empathy that cross over from personal to political realms of life.

If sin is the denial of right relation, then righteousness is the desire to live "in harmony with the fully real."[136] Spirituality would then be our intentional attempts to integrate our total living with the purposes and meanings we perceive in our wider reality.[137] Spirituality is a way of life that continuously creates our relationship with "the fully real." It is an attitude or a way of orienting one's life. Empathy can also be an attitude, "a disposition, a way-of-being-in-the-world, which is characterized by a sense of openness, wonder, flexibility, and play."[138] A spirituality based on empathic connection with God and the world would involve empathy that is acted out or "put to use." Our common word for this is compassion. Matthew Fox defines compassion as "feeling with" another that results in action to promote healing and celebrating.[139] Compassion is empathy seeking to change the world rather than merely understand it. Spirituality as compassion acts in justice-love to restore right relations within the cosmos. A spirituality of compassion involves cultivating an empathic disposition in order to strengthen our sensitivity to injustice and our capacity to creatively work for change.

Fox links creativity and compassion as ways of living that recognize and pursue the intrinsic interconnections among people and things.[140] Creativity, which is the reason for the origin of an actual occasion, is manifested in our moment by moment response to the influence of God and the world. Our spirituality and our self-fulfillment is to participate in God's own care for the world through acts for the world's well-being. That we do so is the fruit of God's influence upon us (in the initial aim), but our doing so also enriches the life of God (via the consequent nature). "We have become a worker with God, helping to shape the good of the world."[141]

To summarize, we have seen how empathy functions as a fundamental ingredient in the development of women's sense of self. Receptive and revelatory openness, mutuality, relational power, and flexible self-boundaries are all necessary accouterments of the type of empathic attunement that nurtures healthy relationships. Creativity requires such openness in order to avail itself of the richest possible combinations of elements and, as a conceptual framework, presents a picture of self-emergence as reliant upon inclusion. Whitehead's explanation of each entity's creative self-construction confirms the centrality of empathy, as feeling-the-world, at the most basic level of reality. At the same time, important limitations to empathic presence are maintained. Theological reflection upon these reformulations of the self-in-relation highlights the receptive openness of immanence and the revelatory openness of incarnation. New understandings of love, power, sin, and justice emerge when we consider the importance of mutuality and co-creation. Creativity weaves through the discussion as the recognizable refrain that openness is a precursor to transformative power. We continue in the next chapter with a similar excursion into the creative dimensions of a second aspect of the self-in-relation as set forth by theorists with the Stone Center.

NOTES

1. R. Schafer, "Generative Empathy in the Treatment Situation," *Psychoanalytic Quarterly* 28, no. 3 (1959): 342–73. Quoted in Ellen S. More, "Empathy as a Hermeneutic Practice," *Theoretical Medicine* 17 (1996): 244. Also, Judith V. Jordan, Janet L. Surrey, and Alexandra G. Kaplan, *Women and Empathy—Implications for Psychological Development and Psychotherapy*, Work in Progress, no. 2 (Wellesley, Mass.: Stone Center, 1983), 2. Some of the most recent research of empathy is reported in *Empathic Accuracy*, edited by William Ickes (New York: The Guilford Press, 1997).

2. Judith V. Jordan, *Empathy and Self Boundaries*, Work in Progress, no. 16 (Wellesley, Mass.: Stone Center, 1984), 2.

3. Alfred F. Carlozzi, Kay S. Bull, Gregory T. Eells, and John D. Hurlburt, "Empathy as Related to Creativity, Dogmatism, and Expressiveness," *Journal of Psychology* 129, no. 4 (1995): 365–73.

4. Hospitality to the stranger is a biblical theme that has been explored by Stanley Hauerwas, *The Peaceable Kingdom* (Notre Dame: University of Notre Dame Press, 1983), and Thomas W. Ogletree, *Hospitality to the Stranger* (Philadelphia: Fortress Press, 1985), among others. I will discuss this metaphor further in Chapter 5 in connection with "dwelling."

5. Heinz Kohut, *Analysis of the Self* (New York: International Universities Press, 1971); Carl Rogers, "Empathic: An Unappreciated Way of Being." *Counseling Psychologist* 5, no. 2 (1974): 2–10. Empathy as it is associated with heightened pro-social behavior has been another area of research, but "no 'grand' theory of structure and development exists." Nancy Eisenberg and Janet Strayer, eds., *Empathy and Its Development* (Cambridge: Cambridge University Press, 1987), 186. I have chosen not to deal here with the research on sex differences in empathic abilities as it remains inconclusive at this time and is not germane to this argument; however, an excellent summary can be found in Marie-Lise Brunel, "Empathie, Femmes, Fèminisme et Prèfèrence de Genre en Psychothèrapie, *Revue Quèbècoise de Psychologie* 8, no. 3 (1987): 89–118.

6. Feminist critics argue that treating mothers (and therapists) as objects to be evaluated in terms of the child's (or client's) needs ignores the participating subjectivity of the former. It does not consider what the self contributes to the other, perpetuating a psychology of ownership and possession. In this way, models for relating degenerate into overt or covert manipulation in order to obtain what one needs. See Nancy J. Chodorow, *Feminism and Psychoanalytic Theory* (New Haven: Yale University Press, 1989), 185; Judith V. Jordan, *The Meaning of Mutuality*, Work in Progress, no. 23 (Wellesley, Mass.: Stone Center, 1986), 3–5; Janet L. Surrey, Alexandra G. Kaplan, and Judith V. Jordan, *Empathy Revisited*, Work in Progress, no. 40 (Wellesley, Mass.: Stone Center, 1990), 11.

7. For example, Ross A. Thompson, writing on the early development of empathy, cites research that gives "account of the emergence of [infantile precursors to] empathy in the context of the mother-infant bond....Although heuristically interesting, this formulation has failed to generate a substantial body of research concerning early empathy." Ross A. Thompson, "Empathy and Emotional Understanding," in Eisenberg and Strayer, 145.

8. Examples include the "self-with-other," Rebecca C. Curtis, ed., *The Relational Self: Theoretical Convergences in Psychoanalysis and Social Psychology* (New York: Guilford Press, 1991); the "extended self," Wade W. Nobles, "Extended Self: Rethinking the So-Called Negro Self-Concept," in *Black Psychology*, 3d ed., ed. Reginald L. Jones (Berkeley: Cobb & Henry, 1991), 295–304; Ruthellen Josselson, "The Embedded Self"; the "familial self," Alan Roland, *In Search of Self in India and Japan: Toward a Cross-Cultural Psychology* (Princeton: Princeton University Press, 1988); the "ecological self," Joanna Macy, "The Ecological Self: Postmodern Ground for Right Action," in *Sacred Interconnections*, ed. David Ray Griffin (Albany: State University of New York Press, 1990), 35–48; and the "relational self," Archie Smith, Jr., *The Relational Self: Ethics & Therapy from a Black Church Perspective* (Nashville: Abingdon, 1982).

9. Beverly Harrison, "The Power of Anger in the Work of Love," in *Weaving the Visions: New Patterns in Feminist Spirituality*, ed. Judith Plaskow and Carol P. Christ (San Francisco: Harper & Row, 1989), 217.

10. Janet L. Surrey, *Empathy Revisited*, 2–3. Another important distinction of the Stone Center model may be its embodiment of theory-building as a cooperative venture, wherein the epistemological process consists of regular, ongoing discussion within a group of women educators, therapists, doctors, and theologians. See Arnold, *et al.*, 44.

11. A weakness of the Stone Center model is that it relies heavily on the experience of white middle-class women for its theorizing. This is a sociocultural limitation that will necessarily qualify any broad conclusions, but it fits our postmodern guidelines that render such conclusions important but partial. See Laura S. Brown, "Cultural Diversity in Feminist Therapy: Theory and Practice," in *Bringing Cultural Diversity to Feminist Psychology*, ed. Hope Landrine (Washington: American Psychological Association, 1995), 143–61. It is a weakness that Stone Center theorists begin to address in *Women's Growth in Diversity: More Writings from the Stone Center*, ed. Judith V. Jordan.

12. Janet L. Surrey, *The Self-In-Relation: A Theory of Women's Development*, Work in Progress, no. 13 (Wellesley, Mass.: Stone Center, 1985), Abstract.

13. Surrey, *Self-In-Relation*, 2.

14. Jean Baker Miller, *What Do We Mean by Relationships?*, Work in Progress, no. 22 (Wellesley, Mass.: Stone Center, 1986), Abstract.

15. Jordan, *The Meaning of Mutuality*, 6.

16. Ibid., 3.

17. Judith V. Jordan, *Courage in Connection: Conflict, Compassion, Creativity*, Work in Progress, no. 45 (Wellesley, Mass.: Stone Center, 1990), 6.

18. Miller-McLemore, 166–67.

19. Janet L. Surrey, *Relationship and Empowerment*, Work in Progress, no. 30 (Wellesley, Mass.: Stone Center, 1987), 4.

20. Ibid., 6.

21. "Zest" is Jean Baker Miller's term for the "increase…in a feeling of vitality, aliveness, energy" produced by empathic connections. Miller, *What Do We Mean by Relationships?*, 7.

22. Alexandra Kaplan and Nancy Gleason, *Women's Self Development in Late Adolescence*, Work in Progress, no. 17 (Wellesley, Mass.: Stone Center, 1985), 5.

23. Jordan, *Courage in Connection*, 4, 9. See Harriet Goldhor Lerner, *Women in Therapy* (Northvale, N.J.: Jason Aronson Inc., 1988), 271–83, for a feminist

critique of self-in-relation theory on this point. For Jordan's response, see *Courage in Connection*, 3.

24. In a talk given at the Society for Pastoral Theology (Atlanta, 1992), Marie McCarthy attributed this metaphor to Chris Schlauch, Professor of Psychology and Religion, Boston University.

25. Alexandra G. Kaplan, "Empathy and Its Vicissitudes," in Surrey, *et al.*, *Empathy Revisited*, 7.

26. Chris R. Schlauch, *Faithful Companioning: How Pastoral Counseling Heals* (Minneapolis: Fortress Press, 1995), 90, 96.

27. Judith V. Jordan and Janet L. Surrey, "The Self-in-Relation: Empathy and the Mother-Daughter Relationship," in *The Psychology of Today's Woman: New Psychoanalytic Visions*, ed. Toni Bernay and Dorothy W. Cantor (Hillsdale, N.J.: The Analytic Press/Earlbaum Associates, 1986), 85.

28. Edith Stein, *On the Problem of Empathy*, trans. Waltraut Stein (Washington, D.C.: ICS Publications, 1989), 12–13.

29. Ibid., 58, 60.

30. Janet Strayer, "Affective and Cognitive Perspectives on Empathy," in Eisenberg and Strayer, 218–44; Changming Duan and Clara E. Hill, "The Current State of Empathy Research," *Journal of Counseling Psychology* 43, no. 3 (1996): 261–74.

31. Jordan, *et al.*, *Women and Empathy*, 14.

32. Ibid.

33. Jordan, *Empathy and Self-Boundaries*, 3.

34. Sandra Lee Bartky associates intention with imagination and believes that imagination is the intentional element that makes empathy transformative. Sandra Lee Bartky, "Sympathy and Solidarity," in *Feminists Rethink the Self*, ed. Diana Tietjens Meyers (Boulder, Colo.: Westview Press, 1997), 177–96.

35. Jordan, *The Meaning of Mutuality*, 8.

36. Jean Baker Miller, *The Development of Women's Sense of Self*, Work in Progress, no. 12 (Wellesley, Mass.: Stone Center, 1984), 5, and Ellen S. More, "Empathy as a Hermeneutic Practice," 244. A similar dynamic is accorded the "extended self" in African psychology (Nobles, "The Extended Self").

37. Carrie Doehring describes the poles of self-boundaries as disengagement and fusion, with empathy as a midpoint between these two extremes. I prefer the less static image of an oscillation in either direction. See Carrie Doehring, *Taking Care: Monitoring Power Dynamics and Relational Boundaries in Pastoral Care & Counseling* (Nashville: Abingdon Press, 1995).

38. Jordan, *Courage In Connection*, 4, 9.

39. Marie McCarthy, "Empathy: A Bridge Between," *Journal of Pastoral Care* 46, no. 2 (Summer 1992): 119–28.

40. Ibid., 122–23. We will return to the topic of empathy and interculturalism in Chapter 5.

41. Miller, *What Do We Mean by Relationships?*, 18.

42. Ibid., 8.

43. Surrey, *Relationship and Empowerment*, 11.

44. Lorde, 111.

45. McCarthy, 125.

46. Thistlethwaite, *Sex, Race, and God*, 2, 8. Regarding the limits of an oppressor's empathy, see also Una Narayan, "Working Together Across Difference," *Hypatia* 3, no. 2 (1988): 31–48.

47. The role of boundaries in interpersonal relationships and their ability to hurt and protect is the subject of complex and powerful debates in therapeutic communities. See Katherine Hancock Ragsdale, ed., *Boundary Wars: Intimacy and Distance in Healing Relationships* (Cleveland, Ohio: Pilgrim Press, 1996).

48. Judith V. Jordan, *Relational Development: Therapeutic Implications of Empathy and Shame*, Work in Progress, no. 39 (Wellesley, Mass.: Stone Center, 1989), 4.

49. Jean Baker Miller, *The Construction of Anger in Women and Men*, Work in Progress, no. 4 (Wellesley, Mass.: Stone Center, 1983), 5.

50. Jordan and Surrey, "Self-In-Relation," 94.

51. Feminist standpoint theory is still hotly disputed among feminist theoreticians. See Susan Hekman, "Truth and Method: Feminist Standpoint Theory Revisited," and other feminists' responses in the same issue, *Signs* (Winter 1997): 341–402.

52. Jordan, et al., *Women and Empathy*, 3.

53. Jordan, *The Meaning of Mutuality*, 8.

54. Jordan, *Courage in Connection*, 2.

55. Jordan, et al., *Women and Empathy*, 3.

56. Keller, *From a Broken Web*, 2.

57. Whitehead, *Adventures of Ideas*, 190–91.

58. My use of analogy follows Whitehead's example and bottom line prerequisite that there is consistency between my experience of the world and my experience of God, so that God's love is recognizable to me and God's justice is understandable. William Placher has argued against this basic process presupposition in *The Domestication of Transcendence*: "Something we can understand and adequately account for in terms of our human categories is not God. And therefore, the deity of process thought who in Whitehead's words, 'is not to be treated as an exception to all metaphysical principles' but as 'their chief exemplification' is not the God of Christian faith. Transcendence that fits our categories has been domesticated" (10). I disagree with Placher's insistence that faith must remain blind to have the proper attitude toward God.

59. Catherine Keller, "Toward a Postpatriarchal Postmodernity," in *Spirituality and Society: Postmodern Visions*, ed. David Ray Griffin (Albany: State University of New York Press, 1988), 75, italics hers.

60. Whitehead, *Religion in the Making*, 90.

61. Whitehead, *Process and Reality*, 41; *Religion in the Making*, 89.

62. Alfred North Whitehead, *Science and the Modern World* (New York: Macmillan Company, 1925), 96.

63. Ibid., 125.

64. Keller, *From a Broken Web*, 27.

65. Whitehead, *Adventure of Ideas*, 178.

66. Whitehead, *Process and Reality*, 162.

67. Whitehead uses "sympathy" in the same way that I have defined "empathy," i.e., "feeling in and with." The prefixes *sym* and *em/en* both mean *into*. "Sympathy" was more commonly used in Whitehead's day because "empathy" was just beginning to be used with regard to interpersonal relationships, having been introduced in the field of German aesthetics in the late 1800's. Today researchers distinguish sympathy as feelings of concern that are focused on one's own experience of another's pain. In contrast, empathy connotes a more active, deliberate intellectual effort to identify with the full range of another's affective state or situation. See Eisenberg and Strayer, 5–8, and Davis, 5.

68. Whitehead, *Process and Reality*, 249.
69. Bernard M. Loomer, "S-I-Z-E Is the Measure," in *Religious Experience and Process Theology: The Pastoral Implications of a Major Modern Movement*, ed. Harry James Cargas and Bernard Lee (New York: Paulist Press, 1976), 70. Edward Farley also writes about empathy as enlargement (282–311), but he emphasizes the influential power or efficacy of empathy that works to promote "attractions between what is self-isolating and competitive" (296). Farley's treatment of empathy does not take into account women's experience of the receptive power of empathy and its concomitant risks of hiding and enmeshment.
70. Miller, *What Do We Mean by Relationships?*, 15.
71. Whitehead, *Modes of Thought* (New York: Macmillan Publishing, 1938; Free Press, 1968), 164.
72. Whitehead, *Process and Reality*, 58.
73. Bernard Loomer, "Two Conceptions of Power," *Process Studies* 6, no. 1 (Spring 1976): 5–32.
74. Ibid., 18.
75. Miller, *What Do We Mean by Relationships?*, 15.
76. Judith V. Jordan, "Relational Development Through Empathy: Therapeutic Applications," in Surrey, et al., *Empathy Revisited*, 11.
77. Whitehead, *Modes of Thought*, 67.
78. Whitehead, *Process and Reality*, 236–37.
79. Ibid., 227.
80. Whitehead, *Adventure of Ideas*, 179.
81. Howell, *A Feminist Theory of Relations*, 3.
82. Marjorie Hewitt Suchocki, *God, Christ, Church* (New York: Crossroad, 1982), 52.
83. It is interesting that this image of God is quite similar to traditional models of the therapist's role as impassive, "neutral," and non-self-disclosing. Feminist therapy and feminist theology replace this model, which they view as essentially disempowering and abusive, with one that advocates increased mutuality in the relationship.
84. Isabel Carter Heyward, *The Redemption of God: A Theology of Mutual Relation* (Washington, D.C.: University Press of America, 1982), xv.
85. Brock, *Journeys by Heart*, 54.
86. Tom F. Driver, *Patterns of Grace: Human Experience as Word of God* (San Francisco: Harper & Row, 1977), 165.
87. Harrison, "The Power of Anger," 221.
88. Keller, *From a Broken Web*, 37, 35.
89. Process theologians are not the only ones to have emphasized God's vulnerability. Consider reform theologian William C. Placher's *Narratives of a Vulnerable God: Christ, Theology, and Scripture* (Louisville: Westminster John Knox Press, 1994).
90. John B. Cobb, Jr., *God and the World* (Philadelphia: Westminster Press, 1969), 75, 80.
91. Whitehead, *Process and Reality*, 344.
92. Suchocki, *God, Christ, Church*, 39.
93. Cobb, *God and the World*, 80.
94. Whitehead, *Process and Reality*, 345.
95. Ibid., 351.
96. Williams, *The Spirit and the Forms of Love*, 10.

97. Driver, 165.
98. Marjorie Hewitt Suchocki, "Earthsong, Godsong: Women's Spirituality," *Theology Today* 45, no. 4 (January 1989): 398.
99. As the supreme Christian virtue, agapeic love has been increasingly criticized for "its complicity in reinforcing social inequality. By making self-sacrifice the primary criterion of the virtuous life, Christianity has given powerful religious validation to the situation of oppression." Linell E. Cady, "Relational Love: A Feminist Christian Vision," in *Embodied Love: Sensuality and Relationship as Feminist Values*, ed. Paula M. Cooey, Sharon A. Farmer, and Mary Ellen Ross (San Francisco: Harper & Row, 1987), 140.
100. Keller, *From a Broken Web*, 214.
101. Cobb, *God and the World*, 89.
102. Rita Brock, "Power, Peace, and the Possibility of Survival," in *God and Global Justice: Religion and Poverty in an Unequal World*, ed. Frederick Ferre and Rita H. Mataragnon (New York: Paragon House, 1985), 26.
103. Whitehead, *Process and Reality*, 346. However, there is still divine judgment, as we shall see in Chapter 4.
104. Loomer, "The Size of God," 51.
105. Suchocki, *God, Christ, Church*, 67. In another place Suchocki states that God's love is "the fullest possible form" of empathy. See *The Fall to Violence: Original Sin in Relational Theology* (New York: Continuum, 1995), 158.
106. Keller, *From a Broken Web*, 92; McCarthy, "Empathy: A Bridge Between." These are the images of hospitality to which we will return in Chapter 5.
107. Whitehead, *Adventures of Ideas*, 283–85. God's primordial nature, on the other hand, is depicted as luring us to adventure.
108. Robert C. Neville, *Creativity and God: A Challenge to Process Theology* (New York: Seabury Press, 1980), 15.
109. Anne Marie Hunter, "Numbering the Hairs on Our Heads: Male Social Control and the All-Seeing Male God," *Journal of Feminist Studies in Religion* 8:2 (1992): 7–26.
110. Edward Farley also links the Incarnation with divine empathy, but he does not link it with God's self-disclosure (278–283). Instead it is more of a capacity for suffering, which, I believe, resurfaces the problems of overemphasizing suffering love that were discussed earlier. Marie McCarthy uses the mystery of Incarnation as a metaphor for our empathic possibilities and limits in "Empathy: A Bridge Between." J. E. Barnhart explores a metaphysical comparison of empathy and incarnation in "Incarnation and Process Philosophy," *Religious Studies* 2 (1967): 225–32.
111. Williams, *The Spirit and the Forms of Love*, 167.
112. Jordan, *Courage in Connection*, 7.
113. McCarthy, 128.
114. Heyward, *Touching Our Strength*, 21.
115. Carter Heyward, *Coming Out and Relational Empowerment: A Lesbian Feminist Theological Perspective*, Work in Progress, no. 38 (Wellesley, Mass.: Stone Center, 1989), 8.
116. Brock, *Journeys by Heart*, xiv. "Courage" derives from the Latin word for "heart" (*cor*).
117. Heyward, *The Redemption of God*, 48.
118. Brock, *Journeys by Heart*, 94.
119. Suchocki, *God, Christ, Church*, 110.

120. Grey, 384. Regarding the connection of creativity and redemption, see also Don S. Browning, *The Atonement and Psychotherapy* (Philadelphia: Westminster Press, 1966).

121. Jacquelyn Grant, *White Women's Christ and Black Women's Jesus: Feminist Christology and Womanist Response* (Atlanta: Scholars Press, 1989), 216.

122. Graham, 44.

123. Heyward, *Touching Our Strength*, 190.

124. Heyward, *Redemption of God*, 18. Marjorie Suchocki provides a helpful and extensive examination of sin as a failure of empathy in *The Fall to Violence*, especially pages 36–41.

125. Keller, *From a Broken Web*, 183.

126. Megan Boler, "The Risks of Empathy: Interrogating Multiculturalism's Gaze," *Cultural Studies* 11, no. 2 (1997): 260.

127. Suchocki, *God, Christ, Church*, 70.

128. Williams, *The Spirit and the Forms of Love*, 145.

129. Marjorie Suchocki, *God, Christ, Church*, 23.

130. Valerie Saiving, "The Human Situation: A Feminine View," in *Womanspirit Rising*, ed. Carol P. Christ and Judith Plaskow (San Francisco: Harper & Row, 1979), 35.

131. Brock, "Power, Peace," p. 26.

132. Heyward, *Touching Our Strength*, 107.

133. Suchocki, *God, Christ, Church*, 26.

134. Brock, *Journeys by Heart*, xiv, 10.

135. Delores Williams, "Womanist Theology," in *Weaving the Visions: New Patterns in Feminist Spirituality*, ed. Judith Plaskow and Carol P. Christ (San Francisco: Harper & Row, 1989), 182.

136. Cobb and Griffin, 14.

137. This definition is informed by Suchocki, *God, Christ, Church*, 20, and Mary Grey, *Towards a Christian Feminist Spirituality*.

138. McCarthy, 124.

139. Matthew Fox, *A Spirituality Named Compassion* (San Francisco: Harper & Row, 1979), viii. Mary Grey has also written about spirituality as compassionate empathy in *Towards a Christian Feminist Spirituality*, 468.

140. Fox, *A Spirituality Named Compassion*, 127.

141. Suchocki, "Earthsong, Godsong," 401.

FOUR

CREATIVITY AS COMPOSITION
Clarity Through Complexity and Contrast

In the previous chapter, we examined the central role that empathic attunement to one's world plays in emerging selfhood. However, when we extol our connections, the question arises as to how to account for difference. Given the importance of mutual empathic connections with a diverse group of persons, how is it that one achieves and maintains a distinct identity amid the multiplicity and complexity of this web of relationships? If we are indeed constituted by our internal relationships with the various components of our world, how then do we understand individuality and personal agency?

As we have seen with other aspects of human selfhood, these questions about identity intimate issues both deeper and broader than a model of psychological development. For example, the conundrum of how to affirm difference while prioritizing relationship continues to plague feminism as a political movement. As feminists become more aware of the subtleties and compounded effects of racism, classism, and heterosexism, it is imperative that we find ways of enhancing individuality that do not obscure our connections, and vice versa.

If one's standpoint recedes to an even more generalized perspective, one finds the postmodern stance defending itself against accusations of total relativism and nihilism because of its adherence to the perspectival and localized nature of truth. In this context our question is formulated as: How can we affirm the interconnections of a global existence and still be clear about our values, commitments, and moral judgments when we are confronted with our own embedded provincialism? On what basis can we act with passion when that act violates what others claim to be a different truth? Perhaps our contemporary obsession with unity and wholeness is a utopian fantasy that violates what post-colonial critics are helping us recognize as the different spaces and values of particular civilizations.[1] It is dangerous to use holism like a plaster to smooth over ruptures or deny the plurality of our inner and outer worlds. In his book *Remembering Esperanza*,[2] Mark Taylor gives voice to questions like these as he ponders how to celebrate plurality in a way that stimulates us to discern and resist domination.

If it seems a bit grandiose to approach an answer to these vast questions through issues that have arisen in the psychology of women, at least it is a beginning from which to explore new ground about the nature of connection and difference, of unity and diversity, the one and the many. This is the issue of selfhood I have defined as achieving clarity amid the complexity of relational living. It is creativity at work in composing a complex beauty from radically disparate elements.

Clarity and Selfhood

I have chosen the word "clarity" to refer to how we know ourselves as something unique within, and distinct from, the components of our worlds.[3] It means that, while I may share your feeling-thoughts in empathic connection, I am able to distinguish my own and integrate them into a focused, though fluid, image of who I am as a person. Achieving clarity about oneself is energizing, gratifying, and produces a sense of well-being. It is something like the "aha" experience of illumination in the creative process. It is the sigh of relief we feel when the unknown is named.

"Clarity" shares some similarities with "identity," but the former is intended to highlight the perpetual process involved in creating identity as opposed to fixing it to a substantial self. "Clarity" is also similar to "differentiation" when the latter indicates distinctiveness but not necessarily separation. Personal clarity is important as a basis for personal agency, or acting with conscious intention toward a goal. It connotes a focus of experience that is imperiled by diffuseness and fragmentation. Clarity is about self-knowledge; it is a specific and articulated awareness that evolves in and through contrasts with other components of one's world.

Traditional Paths to Clarity

The Western psychological tradition has viewed selfhood almost without exception as an individual identity that achieves clarity through increasing separation, objectification, and abstraction.[4] Its Freudian roots depict the trajectory of personality development as the fragile self gradually emerging from an undifferentiated amalgam of infant-mother-world. The goal of adulthood lies at the opposite extreme: a self-contained, autonomous, and independent individual. The developmental pathway to clear adult identity lies through a series of separations from the mother and the family unit as identity is increasingly crystallized. These separations are engendered by conflict, which is understood to be the central dynamic of our formative relationships.[5] Catherine Keller, describing this dominant view of personality as it is shaped by patriarchal culture, has written, "Motives of defense direct the process of differentiation from the start."[6] Close relationships, according to this view, can endanger the self, at least until it is strong and well developed, because the individual's desires, fears, and perceptions might be contaminated by something like the empathic resonance that the Stone Center describes. Only after a clear identity is established, advocates insist, are we considered able to enter healthy relationships with other autonomous selves, relationships which then reestablish the important dimension of connection with fellow humans.[7]

In response to this generally accepted scenario, it can be argued that these relationships tend to be systematized in terms of power, rights, and entitlement to ensure that the needs of the self are met. A sense of uniqueness, which I am calling "clarity," must then be maintained by comparative, hierarchical measuring wherein "your gain is my loss" and vice versa.[8] Restated more existentially, the dominant western model of selfhood teaches us to fear opening ourselves to others because we risk losing ourselves in the encounter. Relationships are secondary to our establishment of a core self as "the real me." Sharing of self with another somehow threatens to reduce my own personhood, as though I am giving self away, or expending a nonreplenishable treasure.[9]

Dangers of the Separation Model

Separation as a Goal of Therapy

A chorus of voices has declared that this traditional model of self-development through separation is fraught with problems at many levels. The most direct challenge arises from women in psychology who say that the version not only does not reflect women's experience, but that the separation model has also contributed to the pathologizing of what may be many women's preferred interpersonal style. Diagnostic categories like "enmeshment," "merged," "fusion," and "codependency"[10] reflect our cultural biases about how self-clarity must be preserved by separation from the corrupting influence of others. The over-representation of these diagnoses in populations of women suggests that the bias goes much deeper, into the Catch-22 of prescriptive roles for women that are contrary to models of healthy functioning. Hence, at the same time that they are designated as society's caretakers, women are often pronounced to be overly dependent or inadequately differentiated. Traditional therapy with women usually encourages them to become increasingly autonomous and assertive in order to become more self-defined and clear about their identity.[11]

The problem escalates when the gender bias of the traditional model is compounded by heterosexism in therapeutic interventions with lesbian women. Intimacy between women that is intensified by the interplay of their *mutual* relational skills and dependency is often labeled as fusion and has been marked as a "prominent problem in lesbian relationships."[12] Measured by male heterosexual norms, intimacy patterns among lesbians that might shed light on many women's relational preferences are considered dysfunctional.[13] Advances in our understanding of lesbian psychology are hindered by our entrenchment in the separation model, which is so paranoid in its fear of fusion that alternative relational models not based on male dominance cannot be appreciated.

Even in family systems theory, which purportedly embraces a contextual view of personhood as it is embedded within a system of relationships, there is a tendency to judge as undesirable or pathogenic female behavior that attempts to maintain or increase interpersonal connection. A "primary archetype" that is regularly diagnosed is "the triad of enmeshed mother, disengaged father, and symptomatic child."[14] Feminist critics of family systems theory insist that the common focal point of "over-involved mother-child" reveals a dangerous bias against women that implicates them as the cause of most family dysfunction. These critics say that the male-based norms of the clarity-through-separation model have infected systems theory so that the emotionally invested mother is villainized while the "so-called 'peripheral fathers' [are let] off the hook."[15] Women end up being punished for making affiliations central in their lives when treatment dictates that they should "back off" as a way of "courting" the distant men toward greater relational involvement.

If development could be redeemed from its defensive portrayal as escape from an absorptive relationship with the mother, then the phenomenon of fusion might be more accurately discerned and, in some instances, productively reframed. Relational dynamics might be improved without "mother-blaming." Therapists who challenge the fusion fallacy call for more adequate relational language that constructively defines women's strengths and offers richer descriptions for failure of attachment. They point to the need for a more balanced focus that reworks the stereotype of the "detached" father to explore new male roles.[16]

In a similar way, reframing "enmeshment" might mean reinterpreting lesbian relationship as a creative, women-centered model of living that transcends isolating ego boundaries, or even "a healthy development of boundaries that serve to protect the couple from a homophobic culture."[17] Taking into account our embeddedness in broader cultural systems contributes to a more accurate evaluation of our interpersonal functioning. It helps to "render visible and to legitimate what is currently camouflaged or invalidated" by socially constructed norms.[18]

Separation in Modern Epistemology

Reexamining labels like "fusion" and "enmeshment" to ferret out their covert gender bias is part of the larger task of analyzing and acting against the pervasive and tenacious power of the clarity-through-separation model in western culture. The belief that clarity or knowledge—of ourselves, of others, and of our world—is gained by means of separating the self from the object to be known has not only dominated western psychology. It pervades western culture as the definitive epistemological paradigm. It is modernity's assertion that detachment is the key to reason.

The radical separation of self and other leads to knowledge through possession and control. The focus of progress becomes mastery, which is then measured by the degree of one's autonomy and independence. Aggression toward an objectified "other" becomes the common way to obtain that to which one is entitled. "Since objectivity demands separation from and control over...the objective knower is driven to dominate."[19] The pursuit of objectivity is an outgrowth of modernity's assertion of a foundation or core of truth. The latter has spilled over into a concomitant search for a "core" of personhood that is uncorrupted by its contextual embeddedness.

As we have seen, a postmodern perspective opposes this conception of encapsulated selfhood. Alan Fogel argues that a postmodern perspective views the self as a dynamic relational system: "From a postmodern perspective, therefore, the self is defined in social *relational* terms and is never fully individuated. The self has *multiple* voices and themes, and is always part of *cultural dialogues* with people and objects."[20] Catherine Keller and Mark Taylor have specifically connected the emphasis on separation in personality development with some of the fundamental errors of modernity as well as with prevalent structures of pain in our society. Keller has argued that the self that can only emerge by means of separation from the mother is the self that perpetually fears and hates women as the primordial enemy. Keller unveils the roots of misogyny in myth and history, both individual and cultural, as they give definition to the male separative self, ever bound to its quest for power over its sticky connections with the engulfing, devouring female.[21]

Taylor extends Keller's connections and makes them more explicit by indicting the developmental model of "matriphobic separation" as the operating dynamic of domination in western culture.[22] According to Taylor, sexism, "hetero-realism," classism, and racism are all traceable to the matricidal psychological myth of the infant's extremes of longing and rage toward an all-encompassing mother.

The abstracting from the mother, from the infant-mother symbiosis that is a matrix from which we never really become totally free, not only involves the continual subordinating of women to men celebrated in various mythologies of the dismembering of Tiamut (sexism); it also involves the alienation of women and men from intimate friendship with their own gender and from being at home with their own bodies (hetero-realism), the alienation of women and men from just distribution of the earth's goods (classism), and, further, the systemic dismemberment of black men and women's bodies and lives (racism).[23]

Taylor recognizes the ubiquitous influence of "culturally disseminated beliefs about human development and maturity"[24] and exposes them as part of systemic exploitation and oppression. The clarity-through-separation model is the psychological window into selfhood that is imported by other disciplines to inform their theories of economics, politics, education, medical ethics, and religion.[25] Any effective transformation of our images of self must deal with "this matriphobic dynamic of separation from the woman and from the maternal...which powers and reinforces structures that reinforce recurring pain."[26] As long as mothers are viewed as the fundamental threat to our autonomy, our culture will support matriphobia and misogyny. As long as relationship is viewed as a threat to our distinctive selfhood, women with their relational affinities will be perceived as the primordial enemy.

An Alternative View of Development

Efforts to recast human development in ways that do not place maturity in opposition to our relational ties have found support in recent advances in infant research. Daniel Stern, whose research has played a central role in feminist revisioning of psychological development, argues that infants "never experience a period of total self/other undifferentiation. There is no confusion between self and other in the beginning or at any point during infancy."[27] Instead, Stern's observations of developmental changes in infants' level of organization have led him to infer "the sense of self as a developmental organizing principle" *from birth*.[28] More recently, Alan Fogel is able to point to "a growing consensus that a sense of self exists long before infants recognize their own image in a mirror, before the acquisition of language or symbolic abilities."[29] It appears that infants interact with their primary caregivers as distinct beings from the beginning, and that the traditional model of clarity of selfhood through separation is rooted in a "male-made-up notion about the life of mothers and babies that never existed."[30] According to Stern, the sense of self-and-other is central to the way we pattern our awareness, and the emerging self does not lose early interpersonal patterns, but elaborates these as new forms of "being with another" throughout the life span. Fogel adds that the infant self is "able to construct nonverbal narrative frames across repeated encounters."[31] These personal narratives provide internal coherence as the self continuously evolves in multiple relationships. Note how Stern reconstructs a twelve-month-old baby's subjective experience of looking for his favorite toy with his mother:

> I found it! Here!
> A wave of delight rises high in me. It swells to a crest. It leans forward, curls, and breaks into musical foam. The foam slips back as the wave passes, and disappears into the quieter water behind.
> Does she feel the wave too?
> Yes!
> She calls back the rising and falling echo of my wave. I ride her echo up and down. It passes through me, and I sense my delight in her.
> It now belongs to both of us.[32]

Stern's imagination captures the sheer joy of being with another that we continue to experience throughout life. His and Fogel's analyses of infant research help us see that distinctive personhood is the result of organization and reorganization of experience, or the restructuring of relationships rather than separation.

Recent interpretations of infant research suggest that development is more about integration than separation. Rather than separation from Mom, the developmental task is the creation of relationships. Clarity of selfhood has less to do with remaining pure and uncontaminated by other selves and more to do with integrity and authenticity as it is reflected in one's particular relation with, or appropriation of, otherness. Instead of fusion, the very real danger becomes fragmentation or *dif*fusion because of the multiplicity that tugs at our "organizing principle" of selfhood.

An image that may be useful for conceptualizing this alternative approach to clarity of self is the kaleidoscope. Its pieces of colored glass suggest the diversity of relationships that connect each person with his/her animate and inanimate worlds. As humans, we find these connections—these pieces of glass—shifting, changing, realigning until a pattern or gestalt emerges from the incoherence; there is meaning.[33] But the pattern never freezes. Our relationships are constantly changing, and with every shift we are aware of the risk of fragmentation. The kaleidoscope turns, releasing the bits of glass from their pose, and new patterns appear, beautiful and intricate in the contrast of their interconnections. Theorists working with the Stone Center model of women's development have given attention to how a clear "pattern" of selfhood coalesces within our relational embeddedness.

Clarity in Women's Psychological Development

Clarity That Results From Connection

The careful attention that Judith Jordan gives to the role of empathy in the development of the self-in-relation naturally led her to question how we become clear about who we are in the midst of all of these empathic connections. She explains that the basis for clarity lies in the mutuality of empathic relationship. Experiencing an empathic response to our own self-disclosure sharpens our awareness of the subtleties of our experience. So, Jordan reminds us, the listener powerfully influences the quality of the emerging voice. "The expectation that someone will listen and make an effort to understand greatly enhances the clarity and sureness of the message presented."[34] Being empathically "heard" helps us become more clear about what we are trying to express. This resonates with Nelle Morton's powerful message about women "hearing each other into speech"[35]—until we speak our truth and know it is heard, we do not know it wholly ourselves.

An empathic response from another is not necessarily identical with our own experience but expresses the other's interest in understanding us. It enables us to trust our experience as real and valid so that it becomes available for examination and articulation. "The validation of our responses by others helps form and crystallize this self knowledge."[36] Actually, the imperfections in our empathic attunement to one another help each of us articulate our own affect, differentiate it from the other's, and extend it into the thoughts and feelings of the next moment. In other words, I welcome and enjoy the other's different feeling-thoughts as necessary new factors that clarify who I am and make me more than I was a moment ago.

The importance of mutuality is once again highlighted by the role of the "interplay of increasingly full and clear expression of each person's thoughts and feelings."[37] Ideally, mutual self-expression enables each person to move toward a fuller and more accurate picture of herself and of the other person. Self-perceptions grow increasingly delineated and better articulated. Hence, clarity of self is a process. Stressing this point, McCarthy writes, "Paradoxically, we come to self-knowledge only through the encounter with the other. In the surprise of genuine difference, we begin to mark out the boundaries of our own selves and our own worlds. And we experience ourselves and our worlds changing in the process."[38]

When empathy is absent from a relationship, clarity of self decreases as the feedback loop of information and acceptance is cut. Jordan has noted, "If the other person does not really wish to know my experience, or does not wish her/his experience known, I may become confused about my desires....If the other is not empathically attuned, disappointment and a sense of being unheard or invalidated results; one's sense of clarity diminishes."[39] For example, when anger or sadness is not acknowledged, or it is invalidated by a nonempathic reception, the result is often confusion and depression.

Another common situation is illustrated by relationships in which one person denies the empathic connection being made by another: "No, I am not upset." The denial may be a defense against one's need for others or simply an unwillingness to become vulnerably exposed. In either case, the result is that the other person feels confused about his or her perceptions and intentions: "I must be mistaken. Perhaps this is my issue rather than yours." Consequently, there is confusion and isolation rather than clarity and increased connection. Jordan identifies the accompanying sense of being locked out of connection as shame, a particularly potent emotion that prevents one from reaching out for the very connections that could assuage it. Shame immobilizes one with a sense of unworthiness that coexists with one's longing for relational connection.[40] In contrast, an empathic connection might increase clarity so that a person could move from a vague depression into a sharper, more accurate identification and experience of sadness or anger. Or, if we know more about how we feel and why, the paralysis of a diffuse anxiety might be overcome by revealing specific, and therefore potentially manageable, fears.

A dramatic illustration of self-confusion is provided by Susan Brison from her work with trauma victims.[41] She observes that trauma inflicted intentionally by other humans convinces victims that they cannot be themselves in relation to others. Because they are treated as objects and worthless, the self is lost and must reconstitute itself after this obliteration at the hands of another. "Vulnerable enough to be undone by violence," the self is nonetheless "resilient enough to be reconstructed with the help of empathic others."[42] Trauma victims need empathic listeners who help them frame an autobiographical narrative by listening to their stories and "hearing" them into recovery.

This is not to say that clarity about self is always enhanced through empathy with others (unless we choose to define "true empathy" by those parameters). Fusion and enmeshment are still dangerous potentialities of our contextual embeddedness. The self can indeed drown in vulnerability and openness. What distinguishes relationships that nurture selfhood is their mutuality of empathy and therefore their mutual or shared power to influence. Loss of self through fusion or diffusion reveals a lack of mutuality. Mutual recognition maintains the balance between our assertion of "I am, I do," and our recognition of the other who completes us by her confirmation mingled with her own self-assertion.[43] We discover our unfolding selves in the other's response. As one of Jordan's clients put it, "I connect with myself through connecting with you. I know myself partly through your knowing me."[44]

Critics of relational theory see a danger in emphasizing this mutuality in psychological development, especially in the inherent inequality of parent-child interactions. Alice Miller's work on "toxic parenting" provides poignant examples of what happens when a child must "take care of" a needy parent in a reversal of the parental nurturing role.[45] The child's emerging selfhood is coopted by a narcissistic parent whose needs dictate how the child will be recognized. Marcia Westkott, seeing a propensity in the Stone Center's relational model to contribute to this dynamic, writes, "A mother who turns to her daughter in order to meet her own needs does not create the conditions for the blossoming of the self but instead confounds her own needs for care and recognition with her responsibilities as a caretaker. By turning to her daughter to provide *adult mutuality,* a mother can, in effect, create a nurturing reversal, seeking care from one who is too young to give it" (italics mine).[46]

By identifying mutuality as a characteristic reserved for adult relationships, Westkott demonstrates how deeply entrenched is the traditional developmental representation of the child as a passive, undifferentiated, and enmeshed self. According to Stern's research, even infants demonstrate a *mutuality* of engagement with their environment. It is a misrepresentation of the Stone Center model to equate mutuality with caretaking, in the therapeutic sense of the word. The dangerous dynamics that result in one person's using another for their own narcissistic purposes, as Miller and Westkott describe, do not represent a mutual empathic connection. Instead, the motivation for mutual connection is the challenge of what Janet Surrey has called "relationship authenticity."[47] Authenticity rather than equality describes the condition we seek in all of our relationships, and it grows out of our human need for mutual recognition. There is mutuality in student-teacher, parent-child, doctor-patient, and other relationships of temporary inequality[48] when each person is striving to remain purposeful, attentive, and honest. The pleasure and fulfillment—as well as challenge—of authentic relationship is what motivates us to seek self-clarity through connection rather than to seek clarity by means of separation. Your validating acceptance and responsiveness, in tandem with your own self-disclosure, help me articulate my unique personhood.

Clarity Obtained Through Coordinating Multiplicity

We have seen that clarity of selfhood is aided by the connections with others that provide us with information about ourselves in relation to our world. Clarity accompanies our awareness of our own boundaries and how those interact or ebb and flow with the boundaries of others. At the same time, a second dimension of clarity requires organizing the incoming data into a synthesis that we recognize as meaningful. We must bring our complexity of experiences into focus as a coherent unity that makes sense of our past and orients and empowers us for our future. Just as a kaleidoscope uses a prism to relate shards of colored glass to each other in a beautiful pattern, so we must coordinate the complex data flowing in from our relationships. If we do not, our "conception of self is a scatter plot, a labyrinth with someone always around the corner, a diagram of competing vectors."[49] Then we feel scattered and in pieces.

The delicate and essential key point, however, is that the emerging synthesis must not be accomplished by merely censuring certain divergent influences or relationships. It must do more than acknowledge difference, yet it must not be paralyzed by it; it must obtain coherence, but through engagement rather than dissociation or relativity. Gathering the relational self into focus counters the traditional approach to clarity, which has been to consolidate "the many" into one through domination. Domination denies or overrules the diversity of our inner and outer worlds. Differences are muted or squelched by a dominant part or point of view, which can then profess a false unity.

This is not only true in interpersonal and international relations in which people use their power to impose singularity, but it is also the case intrapsychically where defensive denial keeps certain "shadow" portions of our internal images, memories, and feelings "cut off" in silence. Modernity's association of clarity with separateness, exemplified in traditional models of personality development, has contributed to the illusion that a person is a monolithic, unified whole. Nevertheless, the fact remains that our lives are full of multiplicity, and personality is not homogeneous. We experience many feelings, thoughts, desires, and memories all at once. Archie Smith, Jr., writes that "the self cannot be grasped or known in its totality, but only in its fragments. The self is always fragmented in its roles, functions, and appearances. All such roles, and appearances express the relational character of the self."[50] Hence, every person is presented with the task of blending a kaleidoscope of social experiences in "that act of creation that engages us all—the composition of our lives."[51]

Mary Catherine Bateson is among those who believe that women have developed particular skills for actualizing this type of creativity, which she calls "improvisation." Improvisation involves combining familiar and unfamiliar components to respond to new situations in ways "especially sensitive to context, interaction, and response."[52] Bateson writes about life as an improvisatory art in which we strive for balance and diversity, coherence and fit—not through the simplification of singleminded purposes, but through the creative blending of simultaneous commitments to many different people and projects. Historically, the circumstances of women's lives have given them a particular proficiency at improvisation because their lives have typically been a collage of tasks, interruptions, shifting commitments, and marginality. As a result, women learn to cope with ambiguity and discontinuity. The interpersonal and cognitive skills that enable women to practice "multiple attention"[53] without fragmentation are aptly depicted by Michele Bograd as "including the exquisite sensitivity to the often unspoken, subtle, emotional, and physical needs of others; the ability to note, retain, and organize the voluminous and diverse details of the daily lives of the family members; and the capacity to simultaneously attend to a variety of distinctly separate activities."[54] Underneath, Bateson claims, there persists an underlying unitary quality, an integrity of structural soundness, which is born out of women's perpetual creative life-task of discovering what the different parts—of self, life, or world—have in common.

Women's improvisational skills enable them to fill multiple roles in their mosaic of relationships (daughter, mother, wife, worker, volunteer, student, and so forth), and they develop coping techniques and personality styles that enable them to move comfortably among various roles. One woman calls her negotiation of career, motherhood, community involvement, and personal spirituality "speaking in tongues" to convey the plurality of discourses that intersect in her life.[55] Another woman's work with women from several ethnic groups and social classes has convinced her that, from girlhood, women learn strategies with which to manage complexity, including decision-making, flexibility, cooperation and teamwork, delegating tasks, and stress management.[56] Contrary to the literature that predicts lowered self-esteem, confusion, and burnout from role overload, recent research has found that women involved in multiple roles often report better overall physical and emotional health.[57] In addition, they demonstrate more sophisticated role articulation at an earlier age and advanced relativistic and dialectical thinking because of their handling of more complex social relations.[58] Role theorists recognize that the ability to articulate and synchronize one's relations within the "plurality of life worlds" is vital to a coherent and meaningful existence.[59] Thus women may be better equipped with a key feature of adult thinking, the "ability to make choices and commitments in the context of uncertainty, contradiction, and plurality."[60]

Along these lines, Sara Ruddick has identified what she calls "maternal thinking," a distinctive mode of cognition that arises from the social practices of protecting, nurturing, and training children to take their place in society, activities which are still largely carried out by women.[61] Ruddick argues that, because these activities are frequently in competition, people who "mother" learn creative ways to resolve what seem like irreconcilable conflicts. She confirms Carol Gilligan's observation over a decade ago that women seek ways of "solving conflicts so that no one will be hurt."[62] They practice a special kind of attentiveness that Ruddick connects with the capacity for empathy, and which conveys a simultaneous commitment to both preservation and change—the overall preservation of a child that is tempered by a welcoming response toward growthful change. Maternal thinking, as Ruddick explains it, enables women to merge diverse and often discordant concerns and responsibilities.

Living with ambiguity and being receptive to differences and alternatives makes obvious the ultimate necessity to make choices. Multiple commitments must finally be prioritized and fulfilled according to values that protect and nurture what we love. Developing a many-sided, multiple-role sense of self is a characteristic that cuts across racial and class lines among women. Making decisions that adjudicate conflicting demands is a skill that lower and working-class women have developed in the context of their struggle for survival.[63] Their skills in using money, power, and organization have contributed to strong self-concepts, group identity, stress management, and leadership qualities in ways that white upper-class feminists have not experienced. For women who suffer race and class oppression, making difficult choices is a product of reality orientation and adaptability. Bell hooks encourages white bourgeois women who are seeking to build confidence and self-esteem to use as models these decisive women who have developed this strength of character in the face of injustice.[64]

Just as it was necessary to qualify the contribution of openness to clarity in the last chapter by reemphasizing the importance of mutuality, so it is also necessary to acknowledge the very real confusion and fragmentation that sometimes plague women as they try to hold together multiplicity. Women do not have some inherent female quality that enables them to perfectly integrate their plural lives, just as men are not lacking in some essential propensity for nurturing connections that safeguard diversity. What we can learn from women's psychological development is that multiple commitments need not be automatically viewed as a liability.[65] Studies show that fragmentation and "role strain" in women should be associated with the quality of environmental support that is available to them.[66] Rigid gender expectations and "the intrinsic conflict between success, as defined in our culture, and the qualities that women value for themselves" continue to pose very real barriers to women's happiness.[67] What is required is that the complexity be somehow, even momentarily, resolved through choices that emerge from a synthesis of personal and contextual values.[68] The kaleidoscope pauses and the shards of glass settle into a patterned whole.

In summary, when we reframe our understanding of selfhood to make relationships central rather than peripheral, we must also reframe our understanding of the integrity and particularity of the self. It is in Whitehead's process-relational philosophy that we find help to conceptualize inherent relatedness that can still produce difference and distinctiveness.

Clarity in Process Thought

Marjorie Suchocki has written, "When an occasion is open to a wide range of influences...then the manyness of influences itself presents a ground for contrast, plus a problem for integration."[69] The "ground for contrast" and the "problem for integration" are precisely the two perspectives on clarity that we have identified in the literature on women's relational selfhood. There is a clarity that grows out of or is due to increasing complexity. This clarity is achieved when vague or fuzzy ideas and feelings become more distinct. This we see in a mutual empathic connection where the contrast from juxtaposing one's own feeling-thoughts with those of other persons produces greater clarity of self. That is, clarity is aided by an increase in complexity because complexity enhances the "ground for contrast." As we have seen, this offers an important alternative to the traditional idea of clarity through separation and decontamination.

At the same time, in the midst of our contextual embeddedness, there also exists a need to create the sort of clarity that emerges from the coordination of a multiplicity of influences into a unity of experience or identity. This type of clarity is required if we are to speak of the self as a moral agent, making choices and acting in ways that impact one's environment. From this perspective, complexity presents a challenge to clarity, or a "problem for integration." Multiple influences and possibilities must be combined in a way that empowers self and resists diffuseness and fragmentation.

Whiteheadian process thought preserves an ontology of relatedness while articulating these two types of clarity. The questions about identity that arise at the interpersonal level when we consider psychological development from a relational perspective are quite similar to questions Whitehead dealt with in his systematic approach to a relational cosmology. His analysis helps us conceptualize difference without discounting connection.

Clarity Through Contrast

A central assertion of process thought is that all existence is interrelated at the most basic level of reality. From this premise issues a concern for how distinctiveness can be explained, just as a self that emerges from relationships requires a fresh interpretation of how individual identity coalesces. Whitehead proposed a profound alternative to obtaining difference by separation from contaminating influences. In what may prove to be the single most significant contribution to the feminist dilemma of selfhood, Whitehead conceptualized clarity as conceived in the midst of multifarious connections by means of *contrast* rather than separation.

Whitehead introduces the notion of contrast for the very purpose of describing how the many components of a complex datum are felt as a unity by an actual entity. For Whitehead, contrast is the opposite of incompatibility rather than being the opposite of fusion.[70] Contrast is the basis for including rather than dismissing others in one's self-constitution.

According to Whitehead, in the initial phase of every concrescing occasion, feelings of the world are vague or diffuse. This is the most elemental form of experience or "causal efficacy," the indiscriminate feeling that characterizes inert matter and "lower" forms of life, as well as unconscious experience in "higher" forms like humans. Contrast becomes important because it is a condition for intensity, and the aim of every becoming entity is to increase the intensity of this initial vague experience, both for itself and for others, including God. The end result is the maximum satisfaction for that entity.

Intensity is achieved by maximizing the amount of compatible contrasts that an entity can synthesize as its objective identity. The aim at intensity reflects God's aim for each entity's depth of satisfaction through vivid experience. "Thus God's purpose in the creative advance is the evocation of intensities."[71] While the intensity of experience, the "size," beauty, and satisfaction of an entity, is increased by contrast, it is reduced by excessive similarity, which Whitehead identified with "vagueness."[72]

We begin to see the significance of this argument for our discussion when we relate clarity to the key role that contrast plays in increasing consciousness. Whitehead differentiated consciousness from the dim apprehension of raw experience. Consciousness is a result of succeeding phases of concrescence in which increasing contrasts are held together. "Consciousness originates in the higher phases of integration and illuminates those phases with greater clarity and distinctness."[73] Consciousness is a function of contrast; it is the felt contrast between present actuality and future possibilities, or between the "in fact" and the "might be."[74] Marjorie Suchocki explains, "Always, in the creation of consciousness, there is a contrast between the data at hand and possible ways in which the data might be ordered. There is a contrast between what is and what might be, between past and future."[75]

The confirmation we glean from Whitehead's explanation of consciousness is that complexity that is patterned into contrasts actually contributes to clarity because it increases consciousness of portions of our experience. "Consciousness arises by reason of intellectual feelings, and *in proportion to the variety and intensity* of such feelings" (italics mine).[76] When complexity is dismissed as incompatible, contrast is reduced and consciousness never emerges from vagueness. In process thought, this type of separation results in less clarity, not more!

Judith Jordan's description of the dynamic process by which women achieve clarity of selfhood through empathic relationships parallels the process understanding of clarity enhanced by contrast. At both the interpersonal and metaphysical level we find that relationships provide rich contrasts that contribute to the clarity of one's immediate experience and coalescing identity. Whitehead's use of contrast affirms that vague, diffuse experience can be transformed into clarity of identity and purpose without requiring detachment from that experience. To the contrary, separation that results from valuing relations negatively promotes vagueness, confusion, and loneliness.[77]

Clarity and Composure

While the clarity that accompanies increasing consciousness demonstrates the value of complexity for contrast, consciousness is limited to a very small domain of experience. The second type of clarity, which has been related to the coordination of complexity, is necessarily obtained by every actual entity as it terminates in a completed unity of feeling. This is the clarity of unique identity which, in relational selfhood, must be composed or "improvised" from multiple relationships (or roles). Whitehead summarizes this clarity of distinctiveness when he writes, "The problem which the concrescence solves is, how the many components of the objective content are to be unified in one felt content with its complex subjective form. This one felt content is appropriately called the 'satisfaction,' whereby the actual entity is its particular individual self."[78]

"Constructive novelty" is the term I have used to designate the creative activity by which an actual entity integrates "the many" feelings that flow in as its datum into "the one" complex unity of feeling that is its satisfaction. For Whitehead, this self-creating activity defines the parameters of individual freedom, for although every other past actual entity is prehended or felt by the concrescing entity, *how* those entities are felt and integrated by its subjective aim is a function of its own constructive novelty.[79] Our interrelatedness with our world is a given, but our unique personhood is the expression of our creative improvisation with the materials at hand. "The actual entity, in a state of process during which it is not fully definite, determines its own ultimate definiteness. This is the whole point of moral responsibility."[80] Thus the self is a manifestation of limited freedom or contextual creativity; things like role expectations and material resources place contextual limitations on our creative possibilities in that place and time, or space-time. However, the blending of multiple influences into a particular identity is always a creative expression of individual personhood.

Whitehead refers to this activity of individual freedom technically as "decision" (not necessarily involving consciousness), which causes a limitation of possibilities in order to bring about the unique satisfaction of this concrescing subject. Past actualities must be included as objects in the concrescing actualities, but "'how' they are included does not depend on the past actualities, but on the 'decision' of the concrescing actual entities."[81] Definiteness, which I am linking with clarity of identity, is dependent upon decision.

Decision enters concrescence in the form of the mental pole or conceptual prehensions, which are acts of evaluation. When we must limit possibilities, we decide what to eliminate on the basis of relative value. We also give varying weights to certain possibilities as we decide how to combine them. For Whitehead, the act of valuation explains the decisions that give definiteness to actuality. In women's complex and conflictual lives, the act of valuation explains how decisions are made that weave multiple commitments together in mutually enhancing ways. Hence, decision-making is more in accord with synergy than hierarchy; it is more about integration than competition.[82]

The determination of exactly *how* feelings are integrated is a function of the value placed on given feelings in concordance with the lure of the subjective aim.[83] The subjective aim is the purpose that guides the creative synthesis of an entity. It is the final cause that lures feelings into unity, or the focus around which the entity coalesces. It is represented in women's lives by what Bateson calls an "internal gyroscope" that helps one stay effectively centered in self-definition while remaining sensitive to one's surroundings.[84] The subjective aim at self-constitution is a "double aim," taking into account its potential contribution to both the immediate present and the relevant future.[85] That is, the subjective aim considers not only what the occasion can be for itself, but also what it can be for others. Judith Jordan provides an example when she reframes behaviors ordinarily assessed as infantile (seeking acceptance or approval, trying to please others) as expressions of responsiveness aimed at strengthening an interpersonal connection. "An empathic awareness of you will alter the experience of how and what I want."[86]

The process description of decision, valuation, and aim clarifies the ongoing creative improvisation of self from a multiplicity of relationships. Whitehead affirms that "self-knowledge...is the knowledge of [self] as a complex unity, whose ingredients involve all reality beyond [self], restricted under the limitation of its pattern of aspects. Thus we know ourselves as a function of unification of a plurality of things which are other than ourselves."[87] The struggle for focused individuality is the locus of creativity in every moment of becoming. Instead of viewing clarity of self as being endangered by our relational commitments, it is more accurate to simply recognize that clarity requires evaluation and action regarding how those commitments come together in our lives. The end result is what Whitehead identified as the satisfaction of closure[88] and what Judith Jordan discerns as the joy that accompanies self-clarity.

Whitehead's conceptualization of the most elemental level of reality provides one potential resolution of the problem of dealing with multiplicity without negating particularity. Just as it encourages and undergirds explorations of our relational web at the intrapsychic and interpersonal level in psychology, it also may contribute to other conversations whose similarities we have noted. Mark Taylor writes that dealing with "the sheer multiplicity of factors that need attention" is the "key mark of our time, a central element of our postmodernism."[89] Taylor insists that a central task of postmodern stances must be to develop ways to cope with this pluralism and fluidity. We must move beyond the mere "celebration of the flux" that allows us to avoid really dealing with authentic differences, especially those which pertain to the distribution of power. Taylor and others like Nancy Frankenberry argue that pragmatic, empirical criteria can adequately inform our decisions and actions and critique the status quo of injustice.[90] Valuation and decision in the concrescence of a single actual entity, in the self-composure of a woman's relational life, and in the construction of a postmodern worldview, hold diversity together in a tentative, temporary, but authentic harmony.

Theological Implications

Clarity Through Judgment and Transformation

In Chapter 3, we explored God's radical receptive and revelatory openness to the world as an extension of recognizing the value of empathic openness for our human selfhood. Process theology associates these aspects with God's consequent nature. In this chapter, we have considered how such radical openness is then brought into focus as a unity of feeling and purpose. For process theologians, the corollary is to ponder how the profusion of uncensored feelings flowing in from the world are dealt with in the divine nature. This activity is most often explained in terms of God's primordial nature, which is how God's compassion for the world converges into the lure toward truth, beauty, and goodness.

According to Whitehead's schema, it is necessary to have an ordering or limiting principle that conditions the relevant possibilities for each actual occasion. Otherwise there could be no synthesis into a particular actual entity, but only chaos. Whitehead conceptualized the primordial nature of God as "the principle whereby there is initiated a definite outcome from a situation otherwise riddled with ambiguity."[91] God orders the possibilities, relevant according to the entity's past actual world and directed toward depth of satisfaction or beauty, and presents them as the initial aim for that entity. The primordial nature describes how God is involved with the becoming of each actual entity. Nevertheless, how that initial aim, in addition to the rest of the world, is felt and appropriated by the entity still reflects its individuality and freedom—as expressed in its subjective aim for its own becoming. "It derives from God its basic conceptual aim, relevant to its actual world, yet with indeterminations awaiting its own decisions."[92]

God's primordial nature not only initiates the personal process that draws our experience together; it also interweaves with God's consequent nature as God's own unison of becoming.[93] God's primordial nature describes the possibilities for the future. When these possibilities are woven with God's physical feelings of the world, it creates the contrast that is God's valuation or judgment. It is judgment in that it is the contrast of "what is" with "what might be," but it is not only the evaluation of the past. We tend to think of judgment as condemnation since our human past always falls short of perfection, and then judgment becomes a critical expression of God's "power-over" us. Here judgment as an act of integrative weaving is also a valuation or ordering of possibilities for the future. Based on the feelings of the past, the possibilities for the next moment are ordered according to their relevance and intensity and presented as God's presence in the initial aim. This is the form of a truly loving response (underplayed as it is in traditional theology) that begins in radical openness and is then adaptive to the needs of particular entities. While one aspect of God's response is inevitably judgment, it is inseparable from compassion and transformation. They are a unity

Creativity as Composition   105

in God's experience of the world. God feels with us, values that experience according to what was possible, and then offers us a lure toward the best possible future, given the past we have jointly experienced.

God's contribution of this lure, or the initial aim, introduces novel possibilities for the becoming entity. This is "generative novelty" (see Chapter 2), by which God enables us to break free from bondage to the past. Creativity manifested in this way is the foundation of hope in and for the world. It is "love's transformative energy, in which love seeks to promote 'new beings' in a 'new creation' whose fecundity is novel and unprescribable."[94] Each act of self-creation possesses the potential for generative and constructive novelty as it fulfills its own unique becoming. Subtle but irrepressible, creativity keeps its stand against the loss of hope.[95]

For Whitehead, this is the meaning of transcendence. "It is to be noted that every actual entity, including God, is something individual for its own sake; and thereby transcends the rest of actuality."[96] And again, "Every actual entity, in virtue of its novelty, transcends its universe, God included."[97] In process thought, transcendence is the act of creating clarity of self, a new thing, from the multiplicity of the "in-fluencing" world.

Hence, transcendence need not be displaced by immanence in feminist theological reframing of the divine as relational and dynamic.[98] Instead, transcendence can be rendered as the freedom to bring new possibilities into existence. Divine transcendence then describes how complexity is integrated into an interconnected universe. That is, all actuality as preserved in God's consequent nature is woven into the harmony of possibility within the primordial vision. Whitehead explains, "The wisdom of subjective aim [from the primordial nature] prehends every actuality for what it can be in such a perfected system...woven by rightness of feeling into the harmony of the universal feeling....The image...is that of a tender care that nothing be lost."[99]

This view of transcendence resembles the word's root meaning of "crossing over" or "linking" more than does its long tradition of interpretation as a spatial separation from or opposition to another. Transcendence is the space-time event of concrescing being that bridges the past with the next moment of becoming. We transcend our past (self), but not by separating from it. As clinical studies of childhood trauma and delayed stress reactions have demonstrated, such dissociation from the past leads only to greater fragmentation. We transcend what was—what we were—by creating of it something new, something for ourselves as well as something for others in our common future. Similarly, God's transcendence is perhaps best expressed in the transformation that Christians affirm as the Resurrection—not a separation from the life and death of Jesus, for the risen Christ bore the scars of that past experience, but a transformation of that past into promise for the immediate and future moments.

For humans, transcendence is nothing less than our authoring of self in response to the inflowing world and God's lure in the initial aim. Every moment of self-composition is "an act of transcendence, for it expresses a fundamental freedom to create [one]self out of the components of [one's] world—not merely to rearrange the parts."[100] We have seen that decision according to graded valuation is the means by which multiplicity becomes the singular fulfilled entity. Hence transcendence involves freedom, intentionality or aim, and choice. Tom Driver, who explores the nuances of transcendence as "choosing," argues that the opposite of transcendence is not immanence, for immanence is a necessary precursor to transcendence. That is, openness or immersion in the world is what sets up the situation of possibilities that requires us to choose.[101] Instead, the opposite of transcendence is best thought of as not-choosing, or inertia. Being stuck or "simply removed from the scene"[102] prevents our own actualization as well as any potential contribution to God's vision of beauty for the world.

There is no doubt that indecision and inaction can contribute to evil in the world. "Sins of omission" are particularly potent in their complicity with injustice. Whenever diversity is celebrated and openness and tolerance encouraged without the accompaniment of decision and accountability, we become vulnerable to paralysis and apathy. Remaining open and plural can be a way of avoiding a true encounter with otherness. "Discovering our differences" can become a scam for wallowing in them with no intention of allowing those differences to critique my particular selfhood and its culture of embeddedness. True encounter involves just this type of radical impact followed by a decision that initiates transformation.

We have described decision as judgment based on valuation. Just as God's judgment is coterminous with God's compassion and transformation, so are we required to judge with our compassion and to be compassionate in our judgment. Carter Heyward notes insightfully that those of us who value inclusivity and diversity, "taking seriously the relative and open-ended possibilities of all that is true or good,...are reluctant to pass judgment on anything or anyone."[103] It is appropriate that we should abhor judgment that, handed down from on high as a reflection of power-over, points a finger and makes demands without compassion—without first truly encountering the other. Judgment with compassion turns the critical gaze upon the self at the same time that it accuses others, recognizing that we are interconnected in destructive as well as growth-producing relationships. Heyward insists that, just as there is no judgment without compassion, neither can there be compassion without judgment, and so she exhorts us to use our prophetic voice of "judgment with compassion" to work for justice in our own and others' lives.[104]

Inaction not only permits injustice to continue. Inaction also means allowing multiplicity to degenerate into confusion. Instead of increased clarity and value, experience is then characterized by diffuseness and fragmentation. In process thought evil enters our experience through lost intensity, triviality, and discord. As God's aim for the world is for greater intensity and satisfaction, triviality and vagueness are deficiencies resulting from lack of contrasts.[105] Vagueness is the result of over-identification or too much similarity; vagueness is the sin of conformity to others' expectations and dull habit. On the other hand, triviality, according to Whitehead, results from a lack of coordination. Data is treated as incompatible rather than being worked into patterned contrasts. Triviality is the lack of focus or fragmentation that threatens to pull us apart because of conflicting concerns.

Feminist theologians have noted that traditional notions of sin need to be broadened to include aspects like fragmentation that better characterize the difficulties that many women experience. Valerie Saiving's well-known list of feminine temptations includes "triviality, distractibility, and diffuseness; lack of an organizing center or focus; dependence on others for one's own self-definition; [and] tolerance at the expense of standards of excellence...."[106] Rather than replacing the familiar conceptions of sin as pride, the abuse of power to control, and the attitude of superiority and entitlement, these additional examples, which reflect our struggle against inaction and inertia, fill out our understanding of sin as the diminishment of relational selfhood.

While decision is an essential part of composing one's self and life with courageous creativity, process thought also makes apparent that every decision involves loss. The choice between competing possibilities inevitably means that some will not be realized. Some possibilities are preserved and encouraged only at a cost. Jean Lambert, writing from a process perspective about decisions women must make regarding pregnancy and abortion, reminds us that every choice means lost possibilities. "Any creation involves losing some good; thus no choice is free of evil."[107] Lambert concludes with the sobering assertion that each decision "bears moral components calling for grief, celebration, and humility."[108] Of course, our multitudinous decisions vary in the moral weight that each carries. Nevertheless, the creative act that is the ever-emerging self cannot escape the loss that is inherent in process. For Whitehead, this is the ultimate evil, or "perpetual perishing," that "selection is elimination."[109]

Whitehead goes on to say that this is not the whole story, for God everlastingly retains as immediate what is lost in the temporal process. We have seen that God's consequent nature describes how God feels with us and preserves the fullness of those past experiences, without limitation, in the divine nature. Our lives are made meaningful by the unfading importance of our experience and actions. Our intuition of this "everlastingness" is what Whitehead means by "peace." Peace is "the intuition of permanence," "a grasp of infinitude," "a trust in the efficacy of Beauty."[110] Peace is our dim perception of God's consequent nature, in which our lives are valued and perfected in harmony with God's primordial vision of beauty. We are accepted and loved. God's presence sustains us as we live the decisions of the present moment. In spite of our mistakes, there is hope for the future. Peace is our intuition that, for this moment, all is well.

Finding the Center

Our longings for peace testify to the turbulence and uncertainty that are the real threats inherent in the plural self. My insistence that clarity actually coalesces within our connections (rather than requiring separation) is not a "naive glorification of connection."[111] As we have seen, connections can indeed be entangling, stifling, and fragmenting. We can be imprisoned or splintered by others' demands and expectations, and we often manipulate others in our efforts to secure our connections. Nevertheless, the defense against such temptations is to nurture clarity, not to withdraw from relationship.

The subjective aim of an actual occasion is its unifying goal, the intention that coordinates the complexity of feelings. We might think of it as its internal focusing mechanism or "center." One way that women describe their attempts to nurture clarity in selfhood is through activities that help them become more "centered." Strengthening their inner focus helps to establish something like an "internal gyroscope" that balances the complex interplay of external forces with personal integrity.[112]

Centering has a rich history in Christian spirituality as an act of disciplined attunement with God. As a response to the complexities (and distractions) of daily life in the world, centering prayer is intended to take one "beyond thought and image, beyond the senses and the rational mind, to that center of our being...where we are our truest selves...."[113] This true self, often described as the heart of a person, is the convergence experienced when we bring our "scattered thoughts and feelings together to allow for a certain deepening."[114] However, it is a sense of coherence, not a static identity—as psychologist Alan Fogel describes it, "a flexible and dynamically stable coalition of many voices playing many parts in the self-drama. From the perspective of relational narratives, therefore, the self is an open system of emerging possibilities and creative processes."[115] Our heart or center is the place of the loving creative action that births us anew in every moment.

We recognize in this ancient image of our "center" many of the qualities that characterize clarity in selfhood. It is indeed appropriate that aligning with the dynamic center of our being is envisioned as drawing closer to God. However, this "work of the heart," as a monastic view depicts it, has also suffered from the traditional paradigm that associates (spiritual) clarity with separation. Monks have traditionally withdrawn from the "webs woven by society" to a place where they could create a new and more spiritual center within which to meet God.[116] Moving away from family and outside of culture, the monk's worldly passions would lose their power to entrap him as he drew near to God at the holy center.

The picture of monastic withdrawal recalls the significant distinction between sacred and profane activities and space, and feminists remind us that women and the body have historically carried the burden of the natural and profane as a foil for masculinized spirit. Ever so subtly, woman once again represents the enemy, from which men must pull away in order to be saved. And once again, we must delicately discern what nourishes clarity without vilifying the connections that create us.

Some feminist reworkings of centering carefully attend to the multiplicity that characterizes many women's experience. Consequently, the center depicts an orientation in the middle of life's complexities rather than a place apart and unpolluted by them. Instead of spirituality as moving us up, out, and away from our bodily and emotional immanence in the natural world, it moves us into physical reality in "life-affirming rather than life-separating or life-distancing" ways.[117] Delese Wear demonstrates the difference in a reflection on the commonly used metaphor of the web: "I, the spinner of my web, was at the center, but it was a center that existed within the architecture of the rest of the web. The threads leading outward and around were essential, reassuring, and secure."[118]

Solitude is still important because webs can entangle and connections can be knotted, and solitude provides the space-time for reflection, integration, and orientation. But aloneness, which need not always entail physical distance, means remaining intensely aware of the integral value of one's relationships. Marjorie Suchocki contrasts aloneness with loneliness, where the latter involves the devaluation or negative valuation of relationships.[119] Solitude is necessary for us to bring our interpersonal relationships into synchrony with our intrapsychic plurality. One woman writes of solitude that it is "the place where I can temporarily and contingently unfix and allow my many selves to float. A place where I can luxuriously and deliciously trace through my words, feelings, heart, and spirit the effects that various responses, selves, and meanings might have for me."[120] For women, centering our multiplicity must incorporate this dialectic of a solitude that strengthens connection.

The activity of centering nurtures clarity because it generates power, creativity, satisfaction, and peace. With the monks who practice centering prayer, one can affirm that one sinks "down into the quiet depths, where there is only a simple, peaceful flow from our Source into the Ocean of Infinite Love. What serenity, what tranquillity, what peace; what vitality, what power, what refreshment!"[121] Finding our center is empowering and energizing because one is laying claim to who one is, becoming attuned to "who I am as I act out of my most authentic self."[122] Being centered releases the creativity of self-expression. As one artist writes, "My creativity is the truest aspect of my self, the essential source of my being, the whole and holy nature of my human experience."[123] And, finally, the convergence of our centering yields the satisfaction of closure, the integration of our multiplicity. The fruit of being centered is peace; it is our feeling of God's "yes" sustaining this momentary clarity of selfhood. It is to images that can convey the creativity of such peace that we now turn.

NOTES

1. Naomi Southard and Richard Payne, "Teaching the Introduction to Religions: Religious Pluralism in a Post-Colonial World," *Teaching Theology and Religion* 1, no. 1 (February 1998): 51-7.

2. Mark Kline Taylor, *Remembering Esperanza: A Cultural-Political Theology for North American Praxis* (Maryknoll, N.Y.: Orbis Books, 1990). See especially Ch. 1. See also William Dean, *History Making History*.

3. My understanding of "clarity" relies heavily on Judith Jordan's work on clarity and desire in adolescent sexuality. See Jordan, *Clarity in Connection*.

4. In the discussion that follows, I am referring most directly to psychology descending from Freud, the father of personality theory and easily the most influential theorist for interdisciplinary applications. At the same time, neither behavioral, cognitive, nor humanistic schools have questioned basic assumptions of psychoanalytic psychology about selfhood emerging from union with the mother. For example, behaviorism concurs with drive theory, posing attainment of personal gratification in opposition to relationships with significant others. The point is that a truly alternative version of the development of self-clarity has never found acceptance in the dominant Western cultures.

5. Fred Pine, *Drive, Ego, Object, and Self: A Synthesis for Clinical Work* (New York: Basic Books, 1990), 2.

6. Keller, *From a Broken Web*, 98.

7. Erik H. Erikson, *Identity and the Life Cycle* (New York: W. W. Norton & Company, 1980; International Universities Press, 1959), 101, 134.

8. Jordan, *Clarity in Connection*, 2.

9. Note how the language of "self-giving" and "self-sacrifice," prevalent in many strands of Christianity and differentially applied to women, carries this connotation of self as diminished by its connections. Religious sacrificial language, which has shown itself to be evocative and powerful, could be reclaimed in ways that are not destructive to women by opting for an alternative to the substantialist self. See Stephen G. Post, "The Inadequacy of Selflessness: God's Suffering and the Theory of Love," *Journal of the American Academy of Religion* 56 (1988): 213–28.

10. I am not making careful distinctions among these terms but referring more generally to all of them when they are used to describe one person's being overshadowed or subsumed by another's identity. Carrie Doehring makes a more technical distinction based on the dynamics of power imbalances in *Taking Care*, 91ff.

11. Michele Bograd, "Enmeshment, Fusion or Relatedness? A Conceptual Analysis," *Journal of Psychotherapy and the Family* 3 (Winter 1987): 65–80. Katherine van Wormer argues that the co-dependency label has been used in a discriminatory way against women in "Co-dependency: Implications for Women and Therapy," *Women & Therapy* 8, no. 4 (1989): 51–63. Natalie Porter adds that enmeshment is often a misdiagnosis that pathologizes familial patterns of people of color. See "Supervision of Psychotherapists: Integrating Anti-Racist, Feminist, and Multicultural Perspectives," in *Bringing Cultural Diversity to Feminist Psychology*, ed. Hope Landrine (Washington: American Psychological Association, 1995), 163–75.

12. Julie Mencher, *Intimacy in Lesbian Relationships: A Critical Re-Examination of Fusion*, Work in Progress, no. 42 (Wellesley, Mass.: Stone Center, 1990), 2.

13. Offering a traditional psychoanalytic interpretation of lesbian relationships, Beverly Burch writes that fear of engulfment by the mother and a generalized fear of the power of women are particularized in the woman who is the lesbian's lover. This leads to characteristic conflicts over power and nurturance within the relationship. Beverly Burch, "Barriers to Intimacy: Conflicts over Power, Dependency, and Nurturing in Lesbian Relationships," in *Lesbian Psychologies: Explorations and Challenges*, ed. Boston Lesbian Psychologies Collective (Urbana, Ill.: University of Illinois Press, 1987), 126–41. A more balanced view is presented in Joretta Marshall, *Counseling Lesbian Partners* (Louisville: Westminster John Knox Press, 1997).

14. Bograd, 65.

15. Betty Carter, "Fathers and Daughters," in *The Invisible Web: Gender Patterns in Family Relationships*, ed. Marianne Walters, Betty Carter, Peggy Papp, and Olga Silverstein (New York: Guilford Press, 1988), 112.

16. Lerner, *Women in Therapy*, 270. Paula Caplan proposed that DSM-IV include a personality disorder called Delusional Dominating Personality Disorder, or "Macho Personality." This category would represent stereotypical male feelings and behavior, like "inability to respond empathically to the feelings of intimates" and "having an excessive need to inflate the importance and achievements of himself and other males." Paula J. Caplan, "Driving Us Crazy: How Oppression Damages Women's Mental Health and What We Can Do About It," *Women & Therapy* 12, no. 3 (1992): 5–28.

17. Boston Lesbian Psychologies Collective, "Introduction," in *Lesbian Psychologies: Explorations and Challenges* (Urbana, Ill.: University of Illinois Press, 1987), 15.

18. Bograd, 78. Larry Kent Graham's psychosystemic analysis, which draws on family systems theory, makes an important advance in this area (*Care of Persons, Care of Worlds*).

19. Sara Ruddick, "Remarks on the Sexual Politics of Reason," in *Women and Moral Theory*, ed. Eva Feder Kittay and Diana T. Meyers (Totowa, N.J.: Rowman & Littlefield, 1987), 239. Judith Jordan contends that "aggression, domination, and entitlement" characterize how males are socialized in western culture (Judith Jordan, *Clarity in Connection*, 5). See also Jessica Benjamin, *The Bonds of Love: Psychoanalysis, Feminism, and the Problem of Domination* (New York: Pantheon Books, 1988).

20. Alan Fogel, "Relational Narratives of the Prelinguistic Self," in *The Self in Infancy: Theory and Research*, ed. Phillipe Rochat (New York: Elsevier Science, 1995), 118.
21. Keller, *From a Broken Web*, 137–38.
22. Taylor, 115, 117.
23. Ibid., 147.
24. Ibid., 114.
25. For example, see Pamela D. Couture, *Blessed Are the Poor? Women's Poverty, Family Policy, and Practical Theology* (Nashville: Abingdon Press, 1991), for a demonstration of how cultural models of separate, self-sufficient persons undergird public policies.
26. Taylor, 115.
27. Daniel N. Stern, *The Interpersonal World of the Infant: A View from Psychoanalysis and Developmental Psychology* (New York: Basic Books, 1985), 10.
28. Ibid., 26.
29. Fogel, 117.
30. This is Jean Baker Miller's addendum to Mencher's paper *(Intimacy in Lesbian Relationships*, 10). The high stakes bearing on such a radical departure from traditional developmental theory are recognized by Fred Pine, associate of Margaret Mahler of attachment theory fame. Pine devotes a chapter in his book, *Drive, Ego, Object, and Self*, to rescuing the symbiotic phase of attachment theory from its denouement by research on the cognitive and relational capacities of infants. In order "to preserve some of the explanatory potential [of the symbiotic phase] for clinical work" (234), Pine argues that "moments" of such sophisticated ego functioning when an infant is rested and alert are more than countered by "moments" of merger experience. In fact, Pine insists that the "moments" of symbiosis are much more emotionally charged and, therefore, more significant for psychological development.
31. Fogel, 129.
32. Daniel N. Stern, *Diary of a Baby* (New York: Basic Books, 1990), 101–2. Stern wrote this book as a diary "invented to answer questions we all pose about a baby's inner life," based on current research with infants (1).
33. Theologian Tom Driver finds the German notion of *gestalt* extremely helpful in describing the nature of human experience. "We actively structure and unify the overwhelming sensations that flood upon us from our environment. The patterns we make are our experiences." Driver, *Patterns of Grace*, xviii.
34. Jordan, *Clarity in Connection*, 2.
35. Nelle Morton, *The Journey Is Home* (Boston: Beacon Press, 1985).
36. Jordan, *Clarity in Connection*, 17. See also Mary Belenky, Blythe Clynchy, Nancy Goldberger, and Jill Tarule, *Women's Ways of Knowing: The Development of Self, Voice, and Mind* (New York: Basic Books, 1986), for more on the relationship between validation of a woman's experience and her self-knowledge.
37. Miller, *What Do We Mean By Relationship?*, 6.
38. McCarthy, 123. This resembles the creative person's ability to juxtapose seemingly disparate elements in order to bring about a new pattern of meaning. See Ch. 2, p. 32 above.
39. Jordan, *Clarity in Connection*, 3.
40. Jordan, *Relational Development*, 6.

41. Susan J. Brison, "Outliving Oneself: Trauma, Memory, and Personal Identity," in *Feminists Rethink the Self*, ed. Diana Tietjens Meyers (Boulder, Colo.: Westview Press, 1997), 12–39.
42. Ibid., 12.
43. Benjamin, *The Bonds of Love*, 12, 21. Benjamin considers the need to recognize the other, which balances the need for self-assertion emphasized in traditional theories, to be the single concept that unifies the various relational, or intersubjective, personality theories.
44. Jordan, *Clarity in Connection*, 4.
45. Alice Miller, *The Drama of the Gifted Child* (New York: Basic Books, 1981), *For Your Own Good: Hidden Cruelty in Child-Rearing and the Roots of Violence* (New York: Farrar, Strauss, and Giroux, 1983), and *Thou Shalt Not Be Aware* (New York: Farrar, Strauss, and Giroux, 1984).
46. Marcia C. Westkott, "On the New Psychology of Women: A Cautionary View," *Feminist Issues* 10, no. 2 (Fall 1990): 12.
47. Surrey, *Relationship and Empowerment*, 9.
48. Relationships of "temporary inequality" and "permanent inequality" are distinguished by Jean Baker Miller in *Toward a New Psychology of Women*, 4.
49. Delese Wear, "A Reconnection to Self: Women and Solitude," in *The Center of the Web: Women and Solitude*, ed. Delese Wear (Albany: State University of New York Press, 1993), 8.
50. Archie Smith, Jr., *The Relational Self*, 55. Others who write of the multiplicity of self include Roberto Assagioli (as "sub-personalities" in *Psychosynthesis*, New York: Penguin Books, 1976; Hobbs, Dorman & Co., 1965), James Hillman (as "multiple persons" in *Re-Visioning Psychology*, New York: Harper & Row, 1977, 1975), and William James (as the "various selves" and the "empirical selves" in "The Consciousness of Self," in *The Principles of Psychology*, vol. 1 (New York: Dover Publications, Inc., 1950; Henry Holt & Co., 1890), 291–401.
51. Mary Catherine Bateson, *Composing a Life* (New York: Atlantic Monthly Press, 1989), 1.
52. Ibid., 2.
53. Diana Somerville, "Mary Catherine Bateson: Men Disadvantaged by Single Focus When Multiple Attention Is Needed," *Boulder Daily Camera* (Boulder, Colo.), 14 September 1993, 1(B).
54. Bograd, 75.
55. Beverly M. Gordon, "Speaking in Tongues: An African-American Woman in the World and the Academy," in *The Center of the Web: Women and Solitude*, ed. Delese Wear (Albany: State University of New York Press, 1993), 153.
56. Brunetta R. Wolfman, *Women and Their Many Roles*, Work in Progress, no. 7 (Wellesley, Mass.: Stone Center, 1984).
57. Lynn M. Martire, Mary Ann Parris Stephens, and Melissa M. Franks, "Multiple Roles of Women Caregivers: Feelings of Mastery and Self-Esteem as Predictors of Psychosocial Well-Being, *Journal of Women & Aging* 9, no. 1/2 (1997): 117–31; Ravenna Helson, Teresa Elliott, and Janet Leigh, "Number and Quality of Roles: A Longitudinal Personality View," *Psychology of Women Quarterly* 14, no. 1 (1990): 83–101; Ingrid Waldron and Jerry A. Jacobs, "Effects of Multiple Roles on Women's Health—Evidence from a National Longitudinal Study," *Women and Health* 15, no. 1 (1989): 3–19; Faye J. Crosby, ed., *Spouse, Parent, Worker: On Gender and Multiple Roles* (New Haven: Yale University Press, 1987).

58. Deirdre A. Kramer and Jacqueline Melchior, "Gender, Role Conflict, and the Development of Relativistic and Dialectical Thinking," *Sex Roles* 23, nos. 9/10 (1990): 553–75. Also, Rose Laub Coser, *In Defense of Modernity: Role Complexity and Individual Autonomy* (Stanford, Calif.: Stanford University Press, 1991), 7.

59. Coser, 18; Robin W. Simon, "Gender, Multiple Roles, Role Meaning, and Mental Health," *Journal of Health and Social Behavior* 36 (June 1995): 182–94. Nevertheless, the lack of social and cultural support for women to integrate a career into the plurality of home life continues to be confirmed in research. See Holly Tingey, Gary Kiger, and Pamela J. Riley, "Juggling Multiple Roles: Perceptions of Working Mothers," *Social Science Journal* 33, no. 2 (1996): 183–91; Ellen Piel Cook, "Role Salience and Multiple Roles: A Gender Perspective," *Career Development Quarterly* 43 (Sep 1994): 85–95; and Mireille Cyr and Helene David, "L'Adaptation de Femmes Professionnelles à la Carrière, à la Maternitè et aux Responsabilitès Familiales," *Canadian Journal of Counselling* 25, no. 4 (1991): 520–30.

60. Kramer and Melchior, 554.

61. Sara Ruddick, *Maternal Thinking: Toward a Politics of Peace* (Boston: Beacon Press, 1989), 24.

62. Carol Gilligan, *In a Different Voice: Psychological Theory and Women's Development* (Cambridge: Harvard University Press, 1982), 65.

63. Karen Kollias, "Class Realities: Create a New Power Base," *Quest, a Feminist Quarterly* 1, no. 3 (Winter 1975): 28–43.

64. bell hooks, *Feminist Theory: From Margin to Center* (Boston: South End Press, 1984), 86–87.

65. Lois H. Grace Stoval writes about a job interview in which her commitment to the job was questioned because "women like you have so many distractions, children and all." See "A Woman's Path to Power as a Sacred Process," in *Sacred Dimensions of Women's Experience*, ed. Elizabeth Dodson Gray (Wellesley, Mass.: Roundtable Press, 1988), 23.

66. Cynthia Fuchs Epstein, "Multiple Demands and Multiple Roles: The Conditions of Successful Management," in *Spouse, Parent, Worker: On Gender and Multiple Roles*, ed. Fay J. Crosby, 29. Also, Coser, 113–35, and Arlie Russell Hochschild, *The Second Shift: Working Parents and the Revolution at Home* (New York: Viking, 1989).

67. Irene P. Stiver, *Work Inhibitions in Women*, Work in Progress, no. 3 (Wellesley, Mass.: Stone Center, 1983), 8.

68. For more on the person as a synthesis of values, see Graham, 84–88.

69. Suchocki, *God, Christ, Church*, 53.

70. Whitehead, *Process and Reality*, 83, 95.

71. Ibid., 105.

72. Ibid., 111. Here one sees the prevalence of aesthetic criteria in process thought. Whitehead asserts that "…contrasts [are] required for the fulfillment of the aesthetic ideal" (255). Intensity and harmony are complementary factors that create beauty. "A mere harmony of pattern, devoid of contrasts, is dull." Ivor LeClerc, *Whitehead's Metaphysics: An Introductory Exposition* (London: George Allen and Unwin, 1958), 214.

73. *Process and Reality*, 236. This is fundamental to Whitehead's argument that experience precedes consciousness rather than vice versa, refuting Hume and Kant. Bernard Loomer says that concrete existence, which is prior to ab-

straction, is irreducibly ambiguous. He cites the Whiteheadian axiom, "When you're clear, you know you're superficial." Loomer, "S-I-Z-E," 5.
  74. Whitehead calls this the "affirmation-negation contrast." *Process and Reality*, 267.
  75. Suchocki, *God, Christ, Church*, 45.
  76. Whitehead, *Process and Reality*, 267.
  77. Suchocki, *God, Christ, Church*, 53. At a more existential level, writing a book is definitely an exercise in increasing clarity. One's thoughts and communication are intensified, enriched, and slowly differentiated as one explores the literature on the subject. The thesis becomes clearer and more developed due to the increasing contrasts that are made with the work of others. Contrasts made in the mutual exchange of discussion rather than solitary library research seem to be even more effective.
  78. Whitehead, *Process and Reality*, 154.
  79. Ibid., 232.
  80. Ibid., 255.
  81. LeClerc, 190.
  82. This appropriation of process thought differs somewhat from Whitehead's conception of gradations of value, which has been attacked by feminists who take exception to its hierarchical applications. Nancy Howell discusses a similar modification that draws on the tenets of ecofeminism and the metaphor of motherly love ("A Feminist Theory of Relations," 135–53). Another potential alternative to valuation according to hierarchical thinking and the "economies of scale" is the "imaginal network" proposed by Andrew Samuels to account for the coherence of our pluralistic psyches (Andrew Samuels, *The Plural Psyche*, London: Routledge, 1989, 14, 40–41). All of these alternatives address what Bateson sees as an urgent need to develop "economies of combination" that yield decisions that are more responsible to ecological complexity and our ultimate survival than hierarchical decisions have been (179).
  83. Whitehead, *Process and Reality*, 240–41.
  84. Bateson, 41.
  85. Whitehead, *Process and Reality*, 27.
  86. Jordan, *Clarity in Connection*, 10. Jordan identifies "anticipatory empathy" or "empathic concern" as this "effort to take into account and care about the way another is going to be affected by what one says or does" ("Relational Development Through Mutual Empathy," in *Empathy Reconsidered: New Directions in Psychotherapy*, ed. Arthur C. Bohart and Leslie S. Greenberg, Washington, D.C.: American Psychological Association, 1997, 344).
  87. Whitehead, *Science and the Modern World*, 151.
  88. Ibid., 7.
  89. Taylor, *Remembering Esperanza*, 29.
  90. Ibid., 40. William Dean and Nancy Frankenberry argue that pragmatism, radical empiricism, and a sociohistorical method provide ways to value some things more than others, while still honoring the "insistence on the particulars in all their incorrigible plurality." Dean, *History Making History*, 33. See also Frankenberry, *Religion and Radical Empiricism*, 75, 84, 87; and "Pragmatism, Truth, and Objectivity," 512.
  91. Whitehead, *Process and Reality*, 345.
  92. Whitehead, *Process and Reality*, 224.

93. However, the poles are reversed in God so that God's "process of completion" is motivated by the consequent nature. Whitehead, *Process and Reality*, 345. Suchocki draws out the implications of this pole reversal in *God, Christ, Church*, 248–52.

94. Graham, 44. See also p. 180.

95. Judith Stone, "Creating the Possible," in *Sacred Dimensions of Women's Experience*, ed. Elizabeth Dodson Gray (Wellesley, Mass.: Roundtable Press, 1988), 43.

96. Whitehead, *Process and Reality*, 88.

97. Ibid., 94.

98. "The complaint voiced frequently against feminist theology is that we have no place in our theology for 'the transcendent.'" Carter Heyward, *Our Passion for Justice: Images of Power, Sexuality, and Liberation* (New York: Pilgrim Press, 1984), 244.

99. Whitehead, *Process and Reality*, 346.

100. Keller, *From a Broken Web*, 91.

101. Driver, 162. Hence, God's immanence as pictured in the consequent nature provides the physical feelings that are ordered by the primordial nature, expressing God's transcendence. Likewise, empathy (immanence) initiates self-emergence (transcendence) in women's development.

102. Ibid., 163.

103. Heyward, *Our Passion for Justice*, 208.

104. Ibid., 209–10.

105. Whitehead, *Process and Reality*, 111.

106. Saiving, 37.

107. Jean Lambert, "Becoming Human: A Contextual Approach to Decisions About Pregnancy and Abortion," in *Feminism and Process Thought*, ed. Sheila Greeve Davaney (New York: Edwin Mellen Press, 1981), 125.

108. Ibid., 131.

109. Whitehead, *Process and Reality*, 340.

110. Whitehead, *Adventures of Ideas*, 283–85.

111. Keller, *From a Broken Web*, 223.

112. Bateson, 41.

113. M. Basil Pennington, O.C.S.O., *Centering Prayer: Renewing an Ancient Christian Prayer Form* (Garden City, N.Y.: Image Books, 1982), 18.

114. Ibid., 61.

115. Fogel, 134.

116. John Eudes Bamberger, O.C.S.O., "Defining the Center: A Monastic Point of View," *Criterion* 20, no. 2 (Spring 1981): 9.

117. Elizabeth Dodson Gray, "Introduction," in *Sacred Dimensions of Women's Experience*, ed. Elizabeth Dodson Gray (Wellesley, Mass.: Roundtable Press, 1988), 2.

118. Delese Wear, "Introduction," in *The Center of the Web: Women and Solitude*, ed. Delese Wear (Albany: State University of New York Press, 1993), xi.

119. Suchocki, *God, Christ, Church*, 52.

120. Elizabeth Ellsworth, "Claiming the Tenured Body," in *The Center of the Web: Women and Solitude*, ed. Delese Wear (Albany: State University of New York Press, 1993), 74.

121. Pennington, 75.

122. Stovall, 24.

123. Stone, 40.

FIVE

DWELLING

An Experiment with Metaphor

> A creative paradigm of dwelling is taking hold in various fields of thought and action.
> —Gibson Winter, *Liberating Creation*[1]

> The assumption here is that belief and behavior are more influenced by images than by concepts, or to phrase it in a less disjunctive way, that concepts without images are sterile.
> —Sallie McFague, *Models of God*[2]

In *Models of God*, Sallie McFague offers a helpful admonition to refrain from relying too much on abstract theory to change the world, or even, perhaps, to make a point. While exploring the concept of women's selfhood and how it emerges, I have appealed to certain images, for example, a quilt, web, and kaleidoscope. Nevertheless, the main project has been to experiment with a *conceptual* framework for women's experiences of self in hopes of expanding our understanding of the human person. If practical impact and change is truly sought, then McFague's words remind us to examine the underlying images that fund and perpetuate traditional concepts and to explore new images that will depict and extend the concepts being advanced.

The Power of Metaphor

Part of the new consciousness that has been designated "postmodern" is associated with an appreciation of the power of language to shape as well as express human experience and thought. One offshoot of this realization has been a renewed interest in metaphoric language as a fundamental example of our use of imagery to help organize and mediate our knowledge of the unknown. Metaphor makes use of familiar images as tools with which to think and talk about things that we do not yet understand.[3] When we describe something by comparing it with something else, there will be ways in which the two are alike and ways in which they differ. This is the tension that is inherent in metaphor, the "is" and "is-not" whose conjunction sparks in us an experiential knowledge which then pursues refinement through conceptualization.[4] Some have argued, therefore, that metaphor is actually the foundation of thought and language. It is the way we know.[5]

Because it is an intermediate, less specific form of language that relies on images, metaphor is extremely important in our communication about areas of experience that are difficult to capture in words or are on the fringes of our awareness. We are dependent on metaphor when we try to communicate about the great unknowns, like religious ultimacy, or the qualities that make us human. We feel and know more than we can say.[6] The full range of human experience requires metaphor to mediate its reduction to conceptual clarity. Conversely, concepts removed from the images of concrete experience that engendered them can become stale and irrelevant. "The relationship...is symbiotic. Images 'feed' concepts; concepts 'discipline' images. Images without concepts are blind; concepts without images are sterile."[7] Our fullest understanding comes from the dynamic interplay of metaphors and concepts in "modes of mutual transfiguration."[8]

Nevertheless, it is metaphor that moves us. Nelle Morton insisted that images are "infinitely more powerful than concepts" because they function, with our emotions, even outside our awareness and, especially, beyond our willful control.[9] It is this power of metaphors to affect us at subconscious levels that makes them much more than literary devices for getting a point across. Metaphors actually organize our thinking about new information. They shape the questions we ask and the answers we find so that "different metaphors present different worlds."[10] Some "root metaphors" are so fundamental and comprehensive that we rely on them to provide coherence and understanding of broad areas of human experience.[11] These "root metaphors" embody basic assumptions by which we organize and then interpret our existence. For example, in *Pedagogy of the Oppressed*,[12] Paulo Freire shows how the "banking" metaphor of education has shaped methods of institutional control by portraying students as passive depositories for course content. Because scientific disciplines rely on metaphor to communicate and guide their theorizing, the chosen metaphor becomes a potent factor in the construction of social understanding and may be difficult to dislodge. Don Browning has written:

> We can see how potent our cultural disciplines are or can be in guiding our perceptions of reality. We both make discoveries through the lens of our metaphorical models and learn to see and perceive the world through these models. If this is the case, then the models that a particular discipline chooses to order its observations will limit its vision to what those models are able to account for and comprehend. Hence, one possible definition of reductionism can be stated in terms of a discipline's tendency to reduce the phenomenon it is studying to the metaphorical models it prefers to use. Human beings are complex phenomena and can be understood adequately only if a variety of metaphorical models are used to account for their action. Human action is thick enough and multifaceted enough so that many different kinds of models need to be used to account for its various aspects.[13]

Browning's insistence that we should use several metaphors in our descriptive efforts is echoed by others like McFague, who warn against our tendency to absolutize a metaphor so that it loses its open-endedness and is soon regarded as literal truth. A metaphor that has lost the tension of contrast, is overgeneralized, and cannot be surrendered becomes destructive and controlling. The nature and function of metaphor is pluralistic: "Many metaphors are necessary, metaphors which will support, balance, and illuminate each other."[14] The dialogue of image and concept is further enriched by the interplay of a variety of metaphors to extend our understanding.

New metaphors that counter old and absolutized ones become agents of social change. Just as an established metaphor can legitimate certain social patterns, a fresh metaphor can introduce new categories and ways of organizing, exploring, and describing our constructed worlds.[15] New metaphors become iconoclastic when they expose traditional or root metaphors that have imprisoned theory, research, and policy. They are then visionary as they guide our expanded explorations. Nelle Morton saw in this two-part process of iconoclasm and vision a powerful resource for women's liberation.

By understanding how patriarchal metaphors create us and how we create liberating alternatives, we begin to understand our own bondage and how to break that which binds us.[16]

Human becoming has been overly dependent on a single family of metaphors to guide our theorizing, just as it has been overly focused on male experience. As women's experiences challenge and expand traditional developmental models, iconoclastic and visionary metaphors that arise from women's experiences are needed to balance those that have portrayed life and guided theorizing from traditional male agendas. A new metaphor potentially illustrates and extends our approximations of a more inclusive picture of human becoming.

The Developmental Journey

It is this search for a more adequate and inclusive description of human becoming that led Sharon Daloz Parks to question our overdependence on the metaphor of journey as an image of human transformation. In a groundbreaking article,[17] Parks argues for the "companion metaphors" of home and pilgrimage to serve our personal and collective imaginings of human wholeness. Emphasizing the need for "multiple metaphors to correct the inevitable distortions of any single image"[18] for our psychological, social, or spiritual life, Parks suggests that the dominance of the journey metaphor has skewed our understanding of development. Images like journey, pilgrimage, and adventure suggest a process that is "more individual, more linear, and more preoccupied with discontinuity than is actually the case in human experience."[19] Yet journey is a very appealing image that resonates with our yearnings for improvement and excellence. Leaving our old selves behind and traveling toward something new and better is suggestive of the promise of emancipation and the path of progress. Heroes, pilgrims, and pioneers have been our models in myth and media. They (we) seek fulfillment, completion, or clarity of purpose and identity as the endpoint, recognizing ultimately that it is the process or journey itself that transforms us.[20]

However, the notion of a developmental journey has become increasingly problematic in a postmodern world that strives to recognize multiple perspectives and normative claims, the limitations of human mastery, and the abuse of power. In economics, psychology, and contemporary spirituality, development implies certain goals of maturity and excellence that, defined by those with more power, stigmatize as inferior those who are different and "don't measure up." At the same time, the developmental journey that the Enlightenment portrayed as unlimited progress now reveals itself to be ecologically disastrous. Our "passion for mastery" is rampant in patterns of domination and injustice that demonstrate disregard for nature and our own human finitude.[21] Alas, even the images of postmodern perspectives themselves portray the exhaustion of an ongoing search, "the infinite quest for more adequate approximations of reality"![22] Parks rightly concludes that development depicted as journey is, at best, a partial or incomplete image that desperately needs "the liberation, reappropriation, and renewed companionship" of the metaphors of home, homesteading, and dwelling.[23]

Parks hypothesizes that these missing metaphors are ones that express the experience of connection and relation that has been emphasized in women's explorations of selfhood. Alternately, Parks perceives that journey metaphors, especially as depicted in hero journeys of struggle and triumph, "may be particularly salient in male experience" because separation, mastery, and domination have played a central role in our culture's socialization of males.[24] Monica Furlong has observed that "literature abounds in spiritual combats and spiritual journeys, but it is striking that the voyager or combatant is rarely a woman. Woman is, again and again, the inspirer of the journey or the task (as she is also often the danger that lurks in the hero's path), but she is not the explorer."[25] This polarization of images by gender preference (rather than asserting anything about gender capacity) has meant that metaphors of homemaking and dwelling, as part of women's devalued and subjugated wisdom, have been displaced. Hence, attending to these exiled images from women's experiences may bring balance and greater comprehensiveness to our understanding of development.

When Parks explores home as a metaphor for development, she arrives at a more adequate definition of development as "the increasing embodiment of truth, compassion, and justice in our midst."[26] Rather than autonomy or self-sufficiency or detachment, increasing maturity correlates with "the capacity of justice...[where] justice is a matter of our ability to include more; justice is a matter of what we will tolerate in terms of who is included and who is neglected."[27] Parks' revisioning of development recalls our discussion of size and stature as markers for emerging selfhood. In similar attempts to rechannel what seems to be an encroaching "developmentalism," others have suggested alternative notions like "formation" or "completion" to convey a less linear and more inclusive image of human growth.[28] Fundamental to Parks' argument, however, is her insistence that metaphors of home and journey must be companions balancing each other as images of our coexistent yearnings for autonomy and communion. Parks affirms both of these human impulses and urges us to overcome "the split we have allowed between the values of body, connection, stability, belonging, familiarity, and hospitality as represented by the image of 'home' and the values of separation, cutting clean, openness to that which is strange, and search for the yet unknown as represented by the image of journey."[29]

However, Parks not only uses home to dislodge the dominance of journey metaphors; she also reminds us of the underside of home, using the metaphoric tension of "is" and "is-not" to advance our understanding of both home and development. My exploration of dwelling as a metaphor for women's experience of self is funded by Parks's initial consideration of home as a metaphor for development that emerges from women's experiences. This chapter "weaves the web further" by focusing more specifically on dwelling and by stressing its potential for reordering or incorporating elements of the developmental journey—not to replace it necessarily, but to help break its hegemonic power to organize social scientific theory and observations and legitimate traditional social patterns. Because dwelling is used as both a noun and a verb, a place and a practice, it is a particularly rich and apt image for emerging selfhood. Its notable religious heritage, along with the resistance it engenders by its negative connotations, will also be important signifiers of its iconoclastic and visionary qualities as a new metaphor.

Dwelling as a Place

Deep in the experiencing itself is the source of the new imaging.
—Nelle Morton, *The Journey Is Home*[30]

As child-bearer, nurturer, and keeper of the hearth, woman has long been associated with human dwellings. She has created these special spaces for others and herself for safety, nourishment, rest, and celebration. It has been woman's role from womb to tomb to embellish the human environment in ways that maximize the quality of human interaction in relationships. Deep in women's experiences of birthing, cooking, cleaning, decorating, clothing, nursing, and all of the other activities of caretaking lie the images that evoke the sense impressions of our "attachment to place," that "pervasive yet determinate feeling that is a ground tenor accompanying all the music of our activities."[31] This "ground tenor" of human dwelling emerges as a melody in itself when women begin to describe their particular reality by asserting the value of their daily activities.[32] They are activities that give continuity to the events of life, the repetition and predictability that root and identify us by their rhythmic connections.

Traditional western stereotypes presume men to be responsible for providing shelter for the family, that is, for providing the structures that are our dwelling places. Women, on the other hand, have most often been accountable for the quality of that space, along with the quality of the relationships within it.[33] It is through this responsibility that women have expressed their creativity, constrained as they have been to the limits of domesticity. Dwelling places are women's sacred spaces that are invested with time and care because these surroundings have a significant impact upon the relational persons that emerge within them. At the same time, because it has been woman's "place," women's creativity has been woven into their activities of making things special there.[34] Hence Alice Walker writes that her mother's flower garden was a creative "work her soul must have. Ordering the universe in the image of her personal conception of Beauty."[35] Actualizing one's creativity within the limits of one's context becomes an important "act of self-definition and spiritual confirmation."[36] The contextual creativity illustrated by Alice Walker's mother was a legacy of surviving, a way of holding on in small ways, even amid the most oppressive of circumstances.

Dwelling is a form of speaking, of self-presentation.[37] One of novelist Nora Ephron's female characters comments on squeezing creativity through the crevices of life's responsibilities: "It's hard to work in recipes when you're moving plot forward."[38]

The dwelling places that women create are designed to contain and preserve life. They are shared spaces. A dwelling provides a boundary or boundedness that enables us to make the interpersonal and existential connections that make sense of experiences from our broader life contexts. A household is "a place which can hold and contain the diversity of daily life."[39] Within its boundaries, the diversity is given coherence and meaning—just as creative "illumination" emerges from "incubation." Continuity is fostered within the walls that accommodate the metamorphosis like that "from baby to young woman, when every molecule in her body has been replaced and her mind has filled up with the world."[40] In Jungian psychology it is *temenos*, the sacred circle that protects us so that integration and transformation is possible. For object relations theorists it is the transitional space that allows us to creatively integrate our external and internal worlds. Our dwellings are places of transformation. A mother's womb is a container for perhaps the most miraculous transformation of all, the evolution of a single cell into a human baby. Dwellings house the passages of children to adults, of new marriages into established partnerships, or sometimes divorce. Most of life's major transitions are in some way played out within the boundedness of the dwelling place where, if we are fortunate, we feel most safe. A place of acceptance where we can rest and recharge can give us the courage we need in order to risk change. As containers of life, our dwellings provide "boundedness and bondedness" —protection and connection.[41]

However, a dwelling is not only a place of protection from the outside world. It is also a place of welcome and refreshment for the outsider. In their historical role as hostesses, women have created open and inviting atmospheres that convey an appreciation of others and an interest in their differences. Offering hospitality to the stranger is an important biblical theme that has been newly appreciated by those who write about creating coalitions and communities that can still affirm diversity. Biblical sources, while recognizing the risks inherent in hospitality, assure us that "strangers received will enlarge our total well-being rather than diminish it."[42] Biblical hospitality promises a mutual exchange of gifts between host and guest, including the gift of God's welcome to those who create a space for others.

It is hospitality's respect for otherness while linked in a host/guest partnership that Letty Russell finds to be a promising image of community in the church. Russell is especially sensitive to the very real differences of race and culture that are often distorted in order to dominate, so she proposes a "community of hospitality" as an image that expresses unity without uniformity.[43] Likewise, Judith Berling describes an orientation of "interfaith hospitality" that enables us to express the humility we need in order to learn from other faiths.[44] Hospitality expresses an attitude of openness and a measure of acceptance that de-center us from our self-centered lives. It contrasts sharply with an idolatry of development that suffers from "an inhospitable reduction of our perception of others to the shape of our own [self-image]."[45]

The gift of hospitality confirms that a dwelling is enriched by the diversity that is welcomed there. Conversely, the tragedy of homelessness that assaults us from our neighborhood streetcorners overwhelms us with the pain of those who have no place to dwell. Refugees displaced by natural or political disasters suffer the loss of dwelling in very visible ways. These examples indict homelessness as a symptom of impoverished relationships on a global scale.

Native Americans have articulated the dialectics of displacement and belonging with special skill because they value dwelling very differently from the European-American culture with which they struggle. For the former, space is primary and land is sacred; dwelling in a particular space is a religious act. For the latter, time receives more emphasis than space.[46] Hence, Native Americans concur with those who find roots to our contemporary ecological crisis in the casual treatment of earth as a temporary dwelling. Postmodern theological anthropology states that we belong to the earth; we are not tourists here.[47] We are not sightseers. We need to be at home on the earth—to be "centered" here. And from this realization flows a renewed commitment to care for the earth and its creatures in an attitude of partnership rather than seeking to gain whatever comfort we can from them in this "veil of tears" while we wait for some greater good in the life to come.

Similarly, feminists assert that we dwell as embodied selves, and that our particular bodily dwellings must also be embraced as where we fit, our situated perspective, our place in the whole.[48] We recall that creativity is embodied, erotic power. In *The Body of God*, Sallie McFague advocates an ecological theology that takes seriously our embodiment as a corrective to our preoccupation with time and progress, otherwise recognizable as that old orthodoxy that "movement is inherently good, staying put is bad."[49] The spaces in which we dwell root us momentarily in time and in the matrix of all our worldly relations.

Self as a Dwelling

Certainly psychologists have alerted us to the importance of the "holding environment" for the emergence of healthy selfhood.[50] However, when we metaphorically consider the self as a dwelling, we apprehend a fundamental reversal. Instead of a self that is unilaterally formed within a holding environment, we behold the self that is also constituted through holding otherness. Hospitality becomes a metaphor for empathic attunement. Creating a receptive and hospitable space welcomes others with an expectation of mutual sharing and transformation.[51] Mutually empathic relationships describe the interactions that nurture selfhood as alternating between the host who receives and responds to the self-disclosure of the other and the guest who is in turn then welcomed. Empathy is like the attitude of "holy regard" that Paul exhorts believers in the church at Philippi to convey toward one another.[52] Mutual empathy is hospitality in the multicultural classroom or workplace.

Developing one's gifts of hospitality is another way of talking about maturity as increasing in stature or "size," as Loomer describes it. Hospitality to the stranger expresses the extent to which we can welcome or integrate into our experience significant contrast or difference. With this image we are also able to differentiate between offering hospitality and actually making a home within the self indiscriminately for all strangers. We have seen that creativity requires assessment and decision. The metaphor allows us to distinguish between the growth-producing orientation of receiving the other's experience as a thing of value, and the destructive orientation of unquestioning affirmation of whatever is expressed. The welcome that is qualified by assessment and decision is analagous to the total acceptance we have in God's consequent nature that is always coupled with God's evaluative judgment. God's judgment is not condemnation, but assessment and decision that makes transformation possible.

Process theology affirms that, while God is transformed by God's welcoming of us, this acceptance also initiates the possibility of transformation in our lives. Our welcoming of God as indwelling spirit opens the door for our own transformation just as opening ourselves to empathic connection with another person will contribute to who we are becoming. Welcoming and/or being welcomed changes one in significant ways. The sacred dwelling is *temenos*, a place or container of transformation. The biblical testimony to this is consistent. Its images of dwelling resonate with our human associations of dwelling with presence, provision, acceptance, comfort, safety, and renewal. "Lord, you have been our dwelling place in all generations," the psalmist prayed (Psalm 90:1), and Isaac Watts penned in the beloved hymn, "My Shepherd Will Supply My Need":

> The sure provisions of my God attend me all my days;
> O may Your House be my abode, and all my works be praise.
> There would I find a settled rest, while others go and come;
> No more a stranger, or a guest, but like a child at home.

The tabernacle was the physical and symbolic presence of God in the midst of the community. The apostle Paul taught that God dwells *in* us through God's spirit.[53] When we welcome God in centering prayer, we create a space for God to dwell, allowing God's presence there to transform us. Because we know of the transformative power of God's indwelling Spirit, it is surprising that we do not recognize the invitation to transformation that every empathic encounter offers to us.

Reflecting on the self as a dwelling and attributing similar qualities to God as a dwelling highlights the power and creativity of transformative space. The image anchors the receptive nature of relationships while illuminating the unrecognized strength required to "hold" otherness. However, as we have seen, the plurality that welcoming receptivity engenders in us demands some synthesis or "locus of convergence."[54] The culture that requires of women "a competent sensitivity that holds multiple perspectives, histories, and possibilities simultaneously" also depends on them "to create, to invent, to find a way to hold things together."[55] Historically, in a dwelling the hearth was the center that gathered the diversity of daily life into coherence, creating a world around itself.[56] As the focus of the home, the hearth fire created bonds of community and acted as a stable integrative force. Our modern-day hearths, be they dinner table, television, car, or computer, continue to bring more (or less) cohesion to a complex web of interconnected lives. The dwelling that is the self relies on its hearth-center to coordinate multiplicity into clarity. Repeatedly, women speak of the importance of being centered in order to accomplish this integration or "knitting of self and world"[57] that I have identified with creativity.

An essential characteristic of metaphor that gives it dynamic power is that the two things being compared are both like and unlike each other. Hence it is not necessary to argue that a dwelling is a perfect image of the self and thereby ignore the aspects of dwelling that suggest unhealthy aspects of selfhood. The intent is not to romanticize the image. Associations that make us recoil from it are extremely important signposts for the contrasts that help clarify the conceptual inquiry. For example, a dwelling has often been used as an image of retreat and withdrawal. In this sense, it is a place where one is renewed and empowered so that he/she can then go out again to work in the world.[58] The Jewish philosopher Levinas used dwelling to refer to the intrapsychic welcome or "interiority" to which he thought an individual needed to retreat in order to be separate from the demands of others and recollect his/her own subjective identity.[59]

The image of retreat certainly has positive value, just as boundaries can be considered essential for self-definition, but these aspects of a dwelling can also connote escapism or entrapment. For women who have not had a choice about their location, their dwelling can seem like their prison. Locked into their nurturing roles by the expectations of others or by their own fear and uncertainty, they experience dwelling as separation. Indeed, dwellings have meant terrible forms of separation for the victims of residential apartheid and domestic violence.[60] Boundaries meant to form our connections with the world can become walls that lock others out. Some take refuge in their houses as a secure haven that enables them to stay closed off from reality, which is uncertain and changing.[61]

In conclusion, we can say that the self is a dwelling that welcomes the world and creatively uses that encounter to expand its empathic boundaries. Its hearth-center creates a plural or communal identity from many relationships. The dwelling-self undergoes continuous construction through remodeling or "adding-on," but not as a fortification from the world. Nor is it simply a quiet respite from the toil of the more serious and esteemed journey. Instead, viewing the dwelling-self through women's experiences discloses the risk and adventure of creating and maintaining a hospitable space for transformative encounters.

Dwelling as a Practice

One of the benefits of introducing dwelling as a new metaphor for selfhood lies in the dual function of dwelling as both a verb and a noun.[62] This gives it a special proclivity for representing the process understanding of reality as events or actual occasions, an understanding that Catherine Keller captures in her coining of "to selve" as the activity of identity.[63] Just as an exploration of dwelling as a noun encourages us to reevaluate our perceptions of space, reflection on dwelling as a practice engages us with a new approach to time. Whereas the metaphor of the journey tends to focus on a future goal or end and to emphasize the urgency of progress toward that goal, dwelling invites us to attend to the present. Nelle Morton's delightful twist of phrase, "the journey is home," captures the underside of the more commonly used metaphor. "Maybe 'journey,'" she explains, "is not so much a journey ahead, or a journey into space, but a journey into presence. The farthest place on earth is the journey into the presence of the nearest person to you."[64] Presence and the present come together in dwelling as a place and a practice.

Maria Harris contemplates the practice of dwelling in her depiction of women's spirituality:

> Dwelling.
> The sound of the word attracts. The meaning of the word comforts.
> Dwelling.
> To pause, to rest, to linger.
> To abide. To stay for a while. To inhabit.
> Dwelling.
> To let things remain as they are for a time, to let be, to let go.
> To stop, and to let ourselves be surrounded by the joys—
>   the healing joys—of rest, of contentment, of doing nothing.
> Dwelling.
> To give ourselves permission simply to *be*..[65]

These words present a different perspective on time from that of the dominant western attitude, which has viewed time as linear, historic, and moving. The pattern of questing presses the hero onward toward the goal and ever-greater achievement. As this has been played out in western culture, creativity is directed toward permanent, solid monuments to man's enduring greatness, like books, architecture, sculpture, and music. Some feminist thinkers have found this contrasted with "a traditional female mode [where] time is circular, boring, and repetitive."[66] While Odysseus wanders, Penelope waits, meanwhile investing her creative impulses "in what is perishable, transitory, fleeting, ephemeral...perishable foods, fleeting flower arrangements, sensitive relationships with people who grow old and die, in rearing children who grow up and go away."[67] Without reducing this observation to essentialism, we can note that, in a world preoccupied with progress and permanence, women's life experiences—even our bodies—reveal much that is repetitious and momentary. Self as the activity of dwelling invites us to consider "waiting...as a legitimate time pattern in its own right."[68]

Here we can learn from the connotations of dwelling and journey within monastic theology. The monastic vow of stability takes the form of a bond to a piece of land and a community of persons as the way to God. In her book, *Seeking God: The Way of St. Benedict,*[69] Esther de Waal asserts that the vow of stability is still relevant and valuable today because it is a recognition of our human need to be rooted and "at home" in order to establish a center from which we know ourselves and God. Sometimes we need to learn that "contentment and fulfillment do not consist in constant change, that true happiness cannot necessarily be found anywhere other than in this place and this time."[70] The repetition and monotony of monastic life is embraced by its adherents with the expectation that God is revealed in the ordinary, simple, and mundane. God is here; God is now. Instead of going or being sent to experience God, monastic dwellers seek the experience of God's spirit working in and among their present community. De Waal reminds us that attempts to find God by running away to a more appropriate and holy place may be in vain if we, in fact, are running from ourselves. We might extrapolate that achieving fame through some dramatic accomplishment is not necessary to establish our unique value. Dwelling can instruct us about self-acceptance.

Richard R. Neibuhr praises the journey metaphor for taking us away in order to find "fresh perceptions" and "radical experience" that awaken us from our stupor of day-to-day life, that "continuum of moments scarcely distinct from one another."[71] Such an emphasis can devalue the ordinary world, where most of us must remain, while promising salvation to a few elite who have the resources (whether material, psychological, or spiritual) to undertake the journey. In contrast, dwelling recognizes that "one of the marks of maturity...is to be able to see, and indeed to create, a sense of excitement and meaning in the prosaic and pedestrian dimensions of life with their responsibilities."[72] Instead of demeaning the ordinary, dwelling engages us in the artist's task of creative expression through the constraints of the materials at hand.

The appreciation that personhood is "a way of dwelling in the world"[73] has numerous biblical confirmations. One of the most important pictures of dwelling that is found in the Jewish and Christian scriptures is that of Sabbath, which in Hebrew means to rest or to cease. Finding its precedence in God's resting from the work of creation, Sabbath teaches us about the value of restful dwelling, an emphasis that counters our contemporary absorption with activity and productivity. "Sabbath asserts that humans become complete, not only by doing, but by not-doing, by *rest*."[74]

In addition to rest and completion, Sabbath dwelling teaches us to value an attitude of receptivity and responsiveness rather than always grabbing for more. The Sabbath day was to be kept as a day to enjoy and be grateful for God's provision. Its observance is a celebrative act of self-restraint, of letting go, that requires confidence that the world continues, even without our perpetual striving. Hence, Sabbath dwelling also helps us come to terms with our human finitude. Rather than encouraging our self- and world-destructive grandiosity, it reminds us that "life is more than human effort."[75] Indeed, our lives are only possible as we are the recipients of divine hospitality. Dwelling in God through rest allows God to provision us with what we need for ministry in the world. The dwelling that characterizes Sabbath frees us to live more fully in the present and empowers us to provide this sacred rest for others. Instead of the dominant theme of movement as inherently good ("Stand still, we are warned, and you die."[76]), we learn that "there are some things that can be accomplished, even by God, only in a state of rest....The precedent to quit doing and simply *be* is divine."[77]

At first glance, the instruction to rest might seem to be in conflict with a Whiteheadian emphasis on process. After all, Whitehead's central argument was that becoming is more fundamental than being. This particular manifestation of process thought, while valid, needs to be balanced by an appreciation of continuity and stability. John Cobb, writing to express agreement with Bernard Loomer's insistence on the value of the concrete, warns that "the one-sided emphasis on creative novelty and transformation, on imagination and prophesy, on purpose and goals, needs to be checked by a deep appreciation of the interconnected matrix of worldly relations."[78] While the process quality of reality has been presented as a series of events always becoming, the process of all existence can be just as truly described as a series of satisfactions. Resting or dwelling is not the same as stasis. Resting is simply a different type of process that values that which continues or repeats itself through time. By placing the accent on the satisfaction of an actual entity, we can more easily see that the perpetual becoming-ness of all things should not be equated with heroic striving.

The qualities of dwelling are further exemplified by biblical references to abiding. Especially in several Johannine passages, we discover that dwelling as abiding, remaining, or staying requires commitment. The Greek word (*menein*) is used to express a permanent relationship, for example, between a group of individuals, individuals and God, or God's Spirit and the believer.[79] The decision to dwell is a decision to "stick it out" or to make it work, an attitude that seems uncommon in our age of instant fixes and escalating divorce rates. Abiding means that we nurture the connections that characterize healthy relationships rather than immediately seeking a means of escape. Abiding or dwelling should not lock us into unjust and/or dangerous situations that require transformation, nor should it sentence us to tedious or trivial existence. These images simply point in a compensatory way to "the virtue and discipline of staying put."[80] The creative process often includes false starts and dead ends that test our persistence. The intention to abide or dwell is consistent with the attitude of resting in the present with one's full attention or presence.

Dwelling as a practice carries connotations of attending to the present place and moment, commitment to the quality of our relational connections, and an assessment of our human finitude. Because dwelling counterbalances an orientation toward perpetual striving, it affirms self-acceptance and encourages satisfaction and contentment. "Acceptance of one's finitude means ability to be grateful for life on whatever terms it has been given. In other words, it requires a certain maturity that can be contrasted with the spoiled child who cannot be happy with anything because he does not have everything."[81] Dwelling as a place and dwelling as a practice come together in self-acceptance, without which our own fears of inadequacy and potential rejection make us unable to offer hospitality, receiving others as the image of God.

Self-Emergence Through Dwelling

It seems somewhat paradoxical to use the practice of dwelling as a metaphor for the activity that is self-emergence. How can stillness portray process? The paradox is partially resolved when we realize that dwelling connotes stillness only in comparison with a certain type of vigorous activity like that imaged by "journey." Similarly, we have seen that in process thought synthesis, which produces continuity (or constructive creativity), is evaluated as boredom only when generative creativity is held as normative. The point is that the metaphor of dwelling reveals new understandings of creativity as our self-constituting endeavor when we begin by assuming the inherent value of women's experiences of dwelling. Just as women's experience of self is no longer assumed to be a simple derivative of some normative male representation, so the metaphor for relational selfhood cannot be simply derivative from the dominant one for separation. When we consider the ways that women dwell and how that experience contributes to their sense of self, we discover a metaphor that highlights the continuity in our lives as well as the disruptions and altered courses. As our contemporary world bombards us with the undeniable reality of continual change at an increasing pace, we must learn to spot the continuity and cultivate it rather than give in to the hopelessness of felt chaos. "We must come to a profound understanding of what constitutes radical continuity—the passion that guides us—not merely the circumstances which surround us....Ours must be not only a continuity of accomplishments, but a continuity of creativity."[82]

Dwelling as a practice describes one's intentional focus on maintaining connections in the midst of multiple intra- and interpersonal changes. Dwelling together as families or communities requires continual adaptation to the evolving needs and personalities of individuals. Continuity in relationships and individual and group identities is the fruit of an ongoing creation of relational connections through mutual empathy. The relationships that create us must be cultivated. "To cultivate, in its root form, means to inhabit, to dwell within."[83] If we can agree that nurturing others through empathic relationship does not deplete our own selfhood but truly enhances it, then cultivating, or dwelling, describes the experience of fashioning selfhood from internal relationships with our world.

Dwelling is an activity that requires endurance and persevering with patience, virtues that we do not hear much about today.[84] Instead, our western culture afflicts us with "overchoice" by offering us more alternatives to select from than we can often manage.[85] One common result is that we simply leave or switch when life becomes a little uncomfortable instead of persevering and tending to the present. Rather than suggesting evasive maneuvers, dwelling describes the life of faith that enables us to invest fully in the here and now because of our hope and participation in ongoing creative transformation. The commitment to remain when confronted with strangeness in people and circumstances is an important prerequisite for empathic connection. The threat of being abandoned inhibits the possibility of self-disclosure and mutual understanding. Today, when plurality tests our commitments by presenting a bewildering assortment of alternatives, the metaphor of dwelling encourages us to discern carefully the creative possibilities in our immediate "culture of embeddedness."[86]

This emphasis on nurturing and enriching what is already present conveys a more ecological view of growth as a process of deepening rather than expansion. Continuity in selfhood regains the stage when dwelling portrays maturity as establishing a center or unfolding (like a flower) rather than leave-taking. The practice of dwelling offers an apt representation of the stillness or sacred pause women speak of when describing their experience of clarity in connection. Dwelling brings integration, "a condition of clarity and focus...akin to what the Buddhists call mindfulness, what Christian contemplatives refer to as recollection, what Quakers call centering down."[87] In such a metaphoric context, serenity and peace become attributes of emerging selfhood without negating the potential for risk and adventure. Indeed, from serenity and continuity we draw the strength that makes possible our struggles for justice.[88]

There is a metaphoric tension inherent in dwelling as an activity that depicts self-emergence. For many women, dwelling is associated with stagnation rather than serenity, feeling stuck rather than being centered, and fear of risk instead of enduring commitment. For immobilized homemakers, life may not be an experience of contentment and dwelling deeply but of finding themselves locked into a vicious circle of inertia and depression. Just as dwelling as a place may imply for some a prison, dwelling as a practice might represent paralysis. Dwelling is not automatically associated with creative self-expression. Actually, it is often presented in opposition to creativity. The monotony of Penelope's weaving and unweaving of her tapestry while waiting for Odysseus' return seems to be dull habit that creates nothing.[89]

Nor does dwelling seem to be an appropriate metaphor for the experience of women who gain strength from envisioning life as a struggle that we "can and should relish."[90] For these women, being realistic about their hardship provides the driving force to stand against their oppression. The serenity of dwelling does not resonate with their orienting vision. It bears repeating that my point is not to insist on dwelling as a fitting metaphor for some universal experience. As Susan Thistlethwaite so aptly reminds us, our differences must always be located in "particular dwellings."[91] At the same time, however, these particularities and anomalies point to aspects of the metaphor that can suggest refinements to our theories. Hence, the danger of paralysis challenges us to dwell *richly* and *with intentionality* rather than just become immobilized. Sanders acknowledges this tension and tries to distinguish the two: "By sitting still I do not mean the paralysis of dread, like that of a rabbit frozen beneath the dive of a hawk. I mean something like reverence, a respectful waiting, a deep attentiveness to forces much greater than our own."[92] Dwelling as a practice has undeniable associations with receptivity and patience. Nevertheless, these should not be confused with the old stereotypes of female passivity. Instead, consider dwelling as more indicative of a wild and radical patience, untamed and elemental, a form of courage because it "requires a dauntless trust in the creative process, wherever we encounter it."[93] Dwelling as a metaphor for improvising

Conclusion

I have proposed dwelling as a new metaphor for the self particularly because it challenges "journey" as the "root metaphor" for human development. There are many other metaphors whose iconoclastic promise has been similarly explored, ranging from metaphors focusing on movement and process, like "walk" and "dance," to more organic ones like "garden," to those emphasizing interconnection, like "web" and "Indra's net." As metaphors, none of these images are perfect representations of the complex phenomenon to which they point. It is the nature and power of metaphor to concurrently confirm, extend, and contradict our theorizing. This chapter is only a beginning exploration of the rich imagery of dwelling and makes no claim to exhaust its metaphoric meaning for human selfhood. Rather, it is an invitation for others to continue to weave connections in both theory and image.[94]

Like many recently proposed metaphors, dwelling has been intentionally taken from women's experiences as an attempt to break out of the masculine bias of the ruling metaphors of modernity. Using women's experiences in this way invites the misunderstanding that one is making historically oppressive stereotypes appear virtuous. Some women are highly resistant to the work of uncovering and articulating skills that women have developed while carrying out their subordinate tasks, fearing that such valorization consigns women to role bondage. "It feels like a prison closing back over us again," one woman protests.[95] Dwelling is not proposed as a metaphor to confirm some stereotypical, universalized feminine self. At the same time, it is too simplistic to say that we merely need to balance the twofold dynamic of dwelling and journey, connection and separation, or social and individual. Maintaining these dichotomies will not dislodge a worldview that favors one pole.

In spite of such difficulties, dwelling can portray selfhood as relational, complex, and processive. It helpfully highlights certain areas of weakness in process thought as it has been interpreted. There remains some ambiguity because it can be polarized, but it does capture something of the radical paradigm shift away from identity through separation. Dwelling effectively pictures creativity as composition from multiple elements and harmony without sameness, in addition to highlighting a much-needed affirmation of rest, contentment, and acceptance.

NOTES

1. Gibson Winter, *Liberating Creation: Foundations of Religious Social Ethics* (New York: Crossroad, 1981), xii.

2. Sallie McFague, *Models of God: Theology for an Ecological, Nuclear Age* (Philadelphia: Fortress Press, 1987), 38.

3. The amount of literature on metaphor is enormous. For this work, I have relied substantially upon the following: Sallie McFague, *Models of God*; *Speaking in Parables* (Philadelphia: Fortress Press, 1975); and *Metaphorical Theology* (Philadelphia: Fortress Press, 1982); Linda E. Olds, *Metaphors of Interrelatedness* (Albany: State University of New York Press, 1992); and Frank Burch Brown, *Transfiguration: Poetic Metaphor and the Languages of Religious Belief* (Chapel Hill: University of North Carolina Press, 1983). Their bibliographies provide an abundance of resources for further study.

4. The terms "epiphor" and "diaphor" have been used to distinguish the two ways that metaphors function. The epiphoric aspect expresses the similarity of two experiences, or the "is-ness" of a comparison. The diaphoric element of metaphor is suggestive of possible meanings, generating new connections from the "is-notness" of the comparison. See Earl R. MacCormac, *Metaphor and Myth in Science and Religion* (Durham, N.C.: Duke University Press, 1976), 84–91.

5. Sallie McFague argues this point most convincingly in her three books, cited above. See especially *Metaphorical Theology*, 32–37.

6. McFague, *Metaphorical Theology*, 15.

7. Ibid., 26.

8. Frank Burch Brown, 181. See also Olds, 21.

9. Morton, 20, 31.

10. Winter, 8.

11. MacCormac, xii–xvi, 93–96.

12. Freire, *Pedagogy of the Oppressed*.

13. Don S. Browning, *Religious Thought and the Modern Psychologies* (Philadelphia: Fortress Press, 1987), 120–21.

14. McFague, *Parables*, 44.

15. Kenneth J. Gergen, "Metaphor, Metatheory, and the Social World," in *Metaphors in the History of Psychology*, ed. David E. Leary (Cambridge: Cambridge University Press, 1990), 275–76. See also Scott F. Gilbert, "The Metaphorical Structuring of Social Perceptions," *Soundings* 62, no. 2 (Summer 1979): 166–86; and Daniel Rothbart, *Explaining the Growth of Scientific Knowledge: Metaphors, Models and Meanings* (Lampeter, UK: Edwin Mellen Press, 1997).

16. Morton, xxiii–xxiv, 155. Catherine Keller discusses Morton's conception of metaphor, its power to bind and liberate, and its connection to concrete life in "Goddess, Ear, and Metaphor: On the Journey of Nelle Morton," *Journal of Feminist Studies in Religion* 4, no. 2 (Fall 1988): 51–67.

17. Sharon Daloz Parks, "Home and Pilgrimage: Companion Metaphors for Personal and Social Transformation," *Soundings* 72, nos. 2–3 (Summer/Fall 1989): 297–315. Other examples that explore alternative metaphors taken from women's experiences include Kathryn Allen Rabuzzi, *The Sacred and the Feminine: Toward a Theology of Housework* (New York: Seabury Press, 1982); Wendy M. Wright, *Sacred Dwelling: A Spirituality of Family Life* (New York: Crossroad, 1990); Sherry Ruth Anderson and Patricia Hopkins, *The Feminine Face of God: The Unfolding of the Sacred in Women* (New York: Bantam Books, 1991); Harriet Crabtree, *The Christian Life: Traditional Metaphors and Contemporary Theologies* (Minneapolis: Fortress Press, 1991); and Maria Harris, *Dance of the Spirit*.

18. Parks, "Home and Pilgrimage," 303–4.

19. Ibid., 301. An excellent discussion of the benefits and problems of the journey metaphor can also be found in Harriet Crabtree, *The Christian Life*, 131–62, and Carol Ochs, *Women and Spirituality* (Totowa, N.J.: Rowman & Allanheld, 1983), 117–23.

20. This is not intended to be a comprehensive description of the characteristics of the archetypal hero's journey. A more accurate account can be found in Joseph Campbell's *The Hero with a Thousand Faces* (Princeton: Princeton University Press, 1973, 1972, 1968, 1949). An addition to Campbell's portrayal that is especially significant for feminist discussion is Jean and Wallace Clift's emphasis on the social significance of the hero's return to share his boon with the community in *The Hero Journey in Dreams* (New York: Crossroad, 1988), 126–42.

21. Winter, x, 116–17. See also Margaret Miles, "Pilgrimage as Metaphor in a Nuclear Age," *Theology Today* 45, no. 2 (July 1988): 166–79. Gabriel Moran offers an insightful critique of development and its imagery in "Alternative Developmental Images," in *Stages of Faith and Religious Development*, ed. James W. Fowler, Karl Ernst Nipkow, and Friedrich Schweitzer (New York: Crossroad, 1991), 149–61.

22. Parks, "Home and Pilgrimage," 305.

23. Ibid., 301.

24. Ibid., 302. Catherine Keller develops a comprehensive argument that links the traditional western model of development through separation with the archetypal hero journey. "In the classic Western epic, Penelope waits while Odysseus wanders. As he intrudes, escapes and seduces his way through time and space, he creates an ego of epic independence....[Others] exist only to strengthen his self-identity and to test the powers of his autonomy" (*From a Broken Web*, 7). On the other hand, a more positive presentation of gender characteristics of the hero journey is that of Jean and Wallace Clift in *The Hero Journey in Dreams*, 29–36.

25. Monica Furlong, *Travelling In* (Boston: Cowley Publications, 1971, 1984), 60.

26. Parks, "Home and Pilgrimage," 310.

27. Ibid.

28. Maria Harris prefers "completion" in "Completion and Faith Development," in *Faith Development and Fowler*, ed. Craig Dykstra and Sharon Parks (Birmingham: Religious Education Press, 1986), 115–33. Sally Johnston opts for personal "formation" in "Exploring the Development/Formation Connection: A Participation in Cultural Critique and Reformation," unpublished paper, Presbyterian School of Christian Education, Richmond, Va., January 1988. John B. Cobb, Jr., struggles similarly to redefine "growth" in "From Individualism to

Persons in Community: A Postmodern Economic Theory," in *Sacred Interconnections*, ed. David Ray Griffin, 123–42.

29. Parks, "Home and Pilgrimage," 309. Parks does an excellent job of balancing the virtues and vices of these conflicting forces in her article. However, feminist theologian Kathryn Tanner has issued an important warning to beware of a patriarchal system's appropriation of "feminine" symbols without allowing them to impact and transform deeper patriarchal logic, organizing principles, and values ("Social Theory Concerning the 'New Social Movements' and the Practice of Feminist Theology," in *Horizons in Feminist Theology: Identity, Tradition, and Norms*, edited by Rebecca S. Chopp and Sheila Greeve Davaney, Minneapolis: Fortress Press, 1997). Gibson Winter, who describes the struggle over sexism as a clash of root metaphors, writes, "This is a war of worlds, for it is a contention between total views of life and foundational symbolizations of the world" (5). We should be wary of relinquishing the spotlight on women's voices too soon—before the images can be thoroughly excavated for their deepest implications—lest lip service be paid to inclusion while the underlying root metaphors of patriarchy remain. For an example of appropriating the image of home without challenging traditional assumptions of separation and maternal hindrance, see Herbert Anderson and Kenneth R. Mitchell, *Leaving Home* (Louisville: Westminster/John Knox, 1993).

30. Morton, 127.

31. Richard R. Niebuhr, "Pilgrims and Pioneers," *Parabola* 9, no. 3 (August 1984): 8.

32. Highlighting these activities that the dominant culture has treated as insignificant becomes a means for presenting alternative worldviews. See bell hooks, 102–5; Marialisa Calta, "Women's Novels Tell Stories Through Cooking, Recipes," *Boulder Daily Camera* (Wednesday, June 23, 1993), 2(D); and Thistlethwaite, *Sex, Race, and God*, 4.

33. Regarding the association of male with structure and female with interior space, see Erik Erikson, *Childhood and Society* (New York: W.W. Norton & Co., 1950, 1963), especially 97–108. Jean Paul Filiod and Daniel Welzer-Lang have examined how interior domestic space is changing as a result of the shifting cultural patterns of the relationships between the sexes. "L'Èmergence du Masculin dans L'Espace Domestique," *Architecture and Behavior* 8, no. 2 (1992): 159–80.

34. C. A. Bowers sets forth "making special" as an ecological understanding of creativity that is both transforming and conserving/preserving (66ff). It is an understanding that I identify with "constructive" (rather than "generative") creativity, as I have defined them.

35. Alice Walker, *In Search of Our Mothers' Gardens*, (San Diego: Harcourt Brace Jovanovich, 1983), 241. Elizabeth Dodson Gray has collected dozens of essays about women's self-perceptions of creativity expressed through daily acts of caregiving in *Sacred Dimensions of Women's Experience*.

36. Parks, "Home and Pilgrimage," 307.

37. Florian G. Kaiser, "Dwelling: Speaking of an Unnoticed Universal Language," *New Ideas in Psychology* 14, no. 3 (1996): 225–36.

38. This passage from Nora Ephron's *Heartburn* is quoted by Marialisa Calta.

39. Rosalie Ann Wells, "Between Earth and Sky: Toward a Psychology of Homecoming" (Ph.D. diss., University of Dallas, 1983), 34. Wells points out that

historical anthropologists associate female dominance with the development of techniques for containing and preserving resources—vases, jars, barns, houses—and that the possibility of storage then provided for the continuity and surplus that gave life stability (p. 269).

40. Scott Russell Sanders, *Staying Put: Making a Home in a Restless World* (Boston: Beacon Press, 1993), 23.

41. William E. McConville, "The Dwelling and the Journey: The Early Christian Experience of Mission," Proceedings from the Annual Federation Council Conference (Pittsburgh: Franciscan Federation, 1989), 12–13.

42. John Koenig, *New Testament Hospitality: Partnership with Strangers as Promise and Mission* (Philadelphia: Fortress Press, 1985), 5. Koenig continues, "It is no accident, I think, that the three major festivals of the church—Christmas, Easter, and Pentecost—all have to do with the advent of a divine stranger....The child in the manger, the traveler on the road to Emmaus, and the mighty wind of the Spirit all meet us as mysterious visitors, challenging our belief systems even as they welcome us to new worlds." For further discussions of hospitality see Ogletree; Hauerwas; Parker J. Palmer, *The Company of Strangers* (New York: Crossroad, 1981); and Henri J. M. Nouwen, *Reaching Out* (Garden City, N.Y.: Image Books, 1975, 1986). The November 1990 issue of *Parabola* (Vol. 15, no. 4) is devoted to myths and traditions of hospitality.

43. Letty M. Russell, *Church in the Round: Feminist Interpretation of the Church* (Louisville: Westminster Press, 1993), 173. For William Schweiker also, "dwelling" represents plurality and interdependence ("To Dwell On the Earth: Authority and Ecumenical Theology," in *Worldviews and Warrants: Plurality and Authority in Theology*, ed. William Schweiker and Per M. Anderson (Lanham, Md.: University Press of America, 1987), 89–112).

44. Judith A. Berling, *A Pilgrim in Chinese Culture: Negotiating Religious Diversity* (Maryknoll, N.Y.: Orbis Books, 1997), 131–32.

45. Esteva, Gustavo. "From 'Development' to 'Hospitality' of the Hammock: Regenerating People's Place," *Interculture* 20 (April–June 1987): 25. This issue of *Interculture*, entitled "Should We Say No to Development?", examines development as a western notion that is imposed evaluatively on other cultures.

46. Regarding the Native American reverence for space, see George Tinker, "Native Americans and the Land," in *Lift Every Voice: Constructing Christian Theologies from the Underside*, ed. Susan Brooks Thistlethwaite and Mary Potter Engel, 141–51, and the interview with Twylah Nitsch in Anderson and Hopkins, 33–38.

47. McFague, "Cosmology and Christianity," 39, and *The Body of God* (Minneapolis: Fortress Press, 1993). See also Martin Heidegger, "Building Dwelling Thinking" and "...Poetically Man Dwells...", in *Poetry, Language, Thought*, trans. Albert Hofstadter (New York: Harper & Row, 1971), 143–62, 211–29.

48. However, as Thistlethwaite cautions, women of color and white women view our embodied identities differently. Whereas white women often want to reclaim their biological connections, women of color have been stereotyped by their biological connections and insist on being "more than a body." See *Sex, Race, and God*, 42–43, 60, 85.

49. Sanders, 106.

50. I am thinking particularly of object relation theorists following D. W. Winnicott (*The Maturational Processes and the Facilitating Environment*, New York:

International Universities Press, 1965). Robert Kegan, who builds on Piaget and the constructive-developmentalists, extends this discussion to "cultures of embeddedness" (*The Evolving Self*).

51. Thomas H. Groome, "The Spirituality of the Religious Educator," *Religious Education* 83, no. 1 (Winter 1988): 9–20. Carter Heyward writes that her friend's compassion toward her is "a resting place" in *Passion for Justice*, 240–41.

52. Schlauch, 82–83.

53. For example, Rom. 3:11; 2 Cor. 6:16; Eph. 2:22, and 3:17.

54. The phrase is used by Thandeka to describe clarity of selfhood in "The Self Between Feminist Theory and Theology" (In *Horizons in Feminist Theology: Identity, Tradition, and Norms*, edited by Rebecca S. Chopp and Sheila Greeve Davaney, Minneapolis: Fortress Press, 1997). It is echoed by others writing in the same volume as, for example, syncretistic selves, the multiple/shifting self, and the negotiation of divergent currents that constitute the self. These represent efforts to articulate a postmodern understanding of identity as multiple, fluid, and shifting, yet still limited in ways that provide coherence.

55. Parks, "Home and Pilgrimage," 304.

56. Wells, 149. "Human dwelling seems to call for centering, the discovery or creation of a place particularly one's own.... To dwell upon the earth requires a *focus*, a hearth around which the diverse patterns of life can be woven together" (p. 168).

57. Sanders, 121.

58. This is how monastic communities have understood the dialectic of retreat and mission (McConville, 16).

59. Emmanuel Levinas, "I and Dependence" and "The Dwelling," in *Totality and Infinity*, trans. Alphonso Lingis (Pittsburgh: Duquesne University Press, 1969), 143–74. Levinas' writing portrays both the traditional view of identity gained through separation and the feminine identified with welcome, dependence, intimacy, gentleness, and dwelling.

60. Parks, "Home and Pilgrimage," 308–9. Being confined to a dwelling and to the so-called "private sphere" of life has even been linked with such things as women's underdeveloped ego-strength and comparatively poorer math skills! See Keller, "Toward a Postpatriarchal Postmodernity," 73, and Coser, 160.

61. I am thinking here of deconstructionists' critiques of our "houses of language" and the "metaphysics of presence" by which we would escape from our uncertainty and relativity. See Sallie McFague's discussion of theological construction in *Models of God*, 21–28.

62. Dwelling as both a place and a condition of the spirit is explored in numerous essays in Leroy S. Rouner, ed., *The Longing for Home*, Boston University Studies in Philosophy and Religion, no. 17 (Notre Dame, Ind.: University of Notre Dame Press, 1997).

63. Keller, *From a Broken Web*, 195.

64. Morton, 227.

65. Harris, *Dance of the Spirit*, 87.

66. Kathryn Allen Rabuzzi, "Women's Work and the Sense of Time in Women's Lives," in *Sacred Dimensions of Women's Experience*, ed. Elizabeth Dodson Gray (Wellesley, MA: Roundtable Press, 1988), 153.

67. Elizabeth Dodson Gray, "Women's Creativity," in *Sacred Dimensions of Women's Experience*, ed. Elizabeth Dodson Gray (Wellesley, Mass.: Roundtable Press, 1988), 9.

68. Rabuzzi, "Women's Work," 153. Monica Furlong also objects to overemphasizing activity: "It is now a truism that this is a period which devalues the feminine....What frightens me most is the glorification of activity, especially when it happens in the Church. How can anything grow in us without passivity, the long, dull wait for birth?" (p. 59).

69. Esther de Waal, *Seeking God: The Way of St. Benedict* (Collegeville, Minn.: The Liturgical Press, 1984).

70. Ibid., 57. See also Henri J. M. Nouwen, *The Genesee Diary: Report from a Trappist Monastery* (Garden City, N.Y.: Image Books, 1981).

71. Niebuhr, 10, 12.

72. Charles S. Milligan, "Ethics, Ethos and Habitat—Part One," *Iliff Review* 33, no. 3 (Fall 1976): 27.

73. Ibid., 21.

74. Harris, "Completion and Faith Development," 128. Dorothy C. Bass notes that "we the harried citizens of late modernity yearn for...Sabbath" in "Keeping Sabbath: Reviving a Christian Practice," *The Christian Century* (Jan 1–8, 1997): 12.

75. Richard H. Lowery, "Sabbath and Survival: Abundance and Self-Restraint in a Culture of Excess," *Encounter* 54, no. 2 (Spring 1993): 155. For an enlightening discussion of acceptance of one's finitude as one aspect of healthy human dwelling, see Charles S. Milligan, "Ethics, Ethos and Habitat—Part Two," *Iliff Review* 34, no. 2 (Spring 1977): 48–52.

76. Sanders, 105.

77. Eugene H. Peterson, "Rhythms of Grace," *Weavings* 8, no. 2 (March/April 1993): 17. This issue of *Weavings* ("And God Rested") is devoted to the exploration of the sacredness of rest.

78. John B. Cobb, Jr., "Response to Loomer," in *The Size of God: The Theology of Bernard Loomer in Context*, ed. William Dean and Larry E. Axel (Macon, GA: Mercer University Press, 1987), 54.

79. Margaret Pamment, "Path and Residence Metaphors in the Fourth Gospel," *Theology* 88, no. 722 (March 1985): 121. John 15 and 1 John 2 are especially pertinent passages.

80. Sanders, xv.

81. Milligan, "Ethics—Part Two," 49.

82. McConville, 30.

83. Anderson and Hopkins, 124.

84. de Waal, 58. I do not mean to suggest that there are never valid reasons for escape from some situations. For example, victims of domestic violence often need to be encouraged and empowered to leave an abusive situation. Exhortations like de Waal's for "a readiness to accept suffering" can be particularly dangerous and offensive when employed in a nonredemptive context. De Waal's point (and mine) is simply that sometimes creativity is stifled by dissatisfaction and distractive grumbling and could be better served by commitment to the materials at hand and faith in the process.

85. Milligan, "Ethics—Part One," 24.

86. Robert Kegan uses this phrase when he critiques our tendency to abandon a particular context in which we are uncomfortable rather than rework our relationship to it ("There the Dance Is," 403–40).

87. Sanders, 121.

88. Carter Heyward, "The Power of God-With-Us: How My Mind Has Changed," *The Christian Century* 107 (March 14, 1990): 277.
89. Keller, *From a Broken Web*, 14.
90. Ada Maria Isasi-Diaz, "A Hispanic Garden in a Foreign Land," in *Inheriting Our Mothers' Gardens: Feminist Theology in Third World Perspective*, ed. Letty M. Russell, Kwok Pui-lan, Ada Maria Isasi-Diaz, Katie Geneva Cannon (Louisville: Westminster Press, 1988), 99.
91. Thistlethwaite, *Sex, Race, and God*, 9.
92. Sanders, 102.
93. Keller, *From a Broken Web*, 224.
94. For example, I encourage readers to examine the collection of essays in *The Longing for Home*, edited by Leroy S. Rouner. These essays from the Boston University Institute lecture series (including essays by Elie Wiesel, Frederick Buechner, Wendy Doniger, Jürgen Moltmann, and Martin Marty) explore the ambiguities of "home" and our longings for it.
95. Elizabeth Dodson Gray, "Doing Housework," in *Sacred Dimensions of Women's Experience*, ed. Elizabeth Dodson Gray (Wellesley, Mass.: Roundtable Press, 1988), 139.

SIX

CONCLUSION

Postlude as Prelude

Over the past twenty or thirty years, feminist researchers and writers have identified a gender bias in traditional models of human development and have taken steps to balance them by attending to the voices of women's experiences of selfhood. The context of their inquiry is circumscribed by a postmodern questioning of any appeal to universal norms and a recognition of the local and plural nature of all truth claims. Hence alternative models of selfhood are tentative and multiple but nevertheless an essential element in the pursuit of more inclusive and adequate representations of what is "human." Feminist perspectives have made significant contributions, especially toward the appreciation of human interrelatedness, but often these observations and insights could benefit from better conceptual grounding.

At the same time, theologians face the task of relating evolving psychological models of the self to theological understandings of the nature of humanity and divinity. Such ongoing reformulations of our theological constructions are necessary if theology is to remain relevant, credible, and convincing in public dialogues about the nature of reality and our human resources for coping with it. That is, advances in the understanding and appreciation of the psychology of women must be met with theological interpretations that are attuned to the new meanings emerging from women's experiences.

In this book I have argued that a process philosophical framework accessed through the overarching concept of creativity provides a cohesive and comprehensive context within which to clarify feminist insights about the nature of selfhood and their theological implications. Creativity, as it is defined in process philosophy and theology, encompasses openness to the world, the synthesis of the many into something new, and the interplay of complexity and contrast as components of beauty. These dimensions of the process notion of creativity are represented in a less technical form in theological discussions about the tension between notions of human and divine creativity, creativity as transformative erotic power, and creativity as a lifestyle attuned to the divine harmony in the universe. Likewise, psychological studies of creativity highlight attributes that correlate with process notions about creativity, for example, value and social influences, openness, tension, synthesis, satisfaction, and contribution. These common elements make creativity a fruitful conceptual bridge among the disciplines of philosophy, theology, and psychology, and therefore a promising framework for wholistic feminist models of selfhood. Receptivity, relational mutuality, and the capability of adjudicating multiplicity are the manifestations of the creative process that we recognize as the self.

In particular, grounding the developmental role of empathy as it has been outlined in feminist psychology in a cosmological theory that places aspects of empathy (that is, feeling and openness) at the center of reality suggests a rationale for allaying our fears of difference. The "modern bourgeois concept of personality," which conceives selfhood as an isolated, encapsulated entity, resists diversity because it is "understood as a threat to the integrity of personality."[1] A new vision of openness as self-empowering rather than endangering the self generates considerably greater creative possibilities than mere tolerance of differences. The role of empathy in defining and creating our self-understanding is illuminated by our realization that both *receptive* and *revelatory* openness are necessary for the mutual empowerment of life-giving relationships. The process notion of creativity portrays this mutuality in the subject-superject of simultaneously being for self and being for others.

Realizing the importance of mutuality in human relationships leads us to question the traditional theistic emphasis on God's transcendence and separation from humanity. An alternative interpretation that finds expression in process theology proposes an openness and mutuality in God as aspects of God's consequent nature. This *receptive* openness in God is complemented by the *revelatory* self-disclosure that Christians know as the Incarnation. Other theological implications drawn from the correlation of process categories with mutually empathic relationships include a picture of sin as the rejection or denial of relationship, justice as right-relationship, and spirituality as compassion that makes us co-workers with God to create good (beauty) in the world.

In conjunction with the importance of openness and receptivity, drawing upon the patterns of women's development leads to new ways of understanding identity as the clarity that emerges from multiple relationships. Instead of a dynamic of detaching to maintain purity, what emerges is the dynamic of integrating through contrasts, a process that challenges the deeply rooted western understanding of individuality as being established through separation. Supported by recent research in infant development, this description of self-identity also correlates with Whitehead's explanation of concrescence. That is, creativity is actualized as the process of bringing disparate elements together in new relationships that produce something of beauty—something new and unique but not able to be divorced from the elements that compose it. Discerning how clarity is achieved *as a result of* increasing complexity—a complexity characterizing every interrelated level of reality—promises to contribute significantly to our attempts to live creatively in a complex, interrelated world without feeling fragmented.

The clarity of selfhood that results from mutually empathic connections and through the composition of multiplicity can be linked with process theology's understanding of God's primordial nature. As the ordering principle that introduces the possibility of transformation into the world, God's primordial nature enables each of us to transcend our past by choosing beauty and justice in the present moment. Sin is characterized by the fragmentation, diffuseness, and triviality that results when we do not respond to God's initial aim for the maximum achievement of good in our next moment. The multiplicity that is enriched by our openness is unsuccessfully integrated. Centering as a spiritual practice illustrates the intentionality that facilitates the focus and clarity that imitates the activity of God's primordial nature in the world.

The concept of creativity extends the familiar arguments for a relational self by illuminating empathy as a crucial feature of human emergence and clarity of self as it is achieved through increasing complexity and contrast. Theological themes like immanence and transcendence, the divine nature, sin, and spirituality are helpfully reframed from the perspective of these two facets of selfhood. Process thought in its contemporary refinements, adaptations, and theological extensions provides a vehicle for supporting and interpreting the psychological data within a particular comprehensive interpretation of the nature of reality. Such a linkage lends greater clarity, consistency, and cohesiveness to several aspects of relational selfhood, but this appropriation is best made through critical dialogue between Whiteheadian process categories and feminist and postmodern sensibilities. For example, I have argued that there exists a bias toward progressivism in much of process thought along with an untapped potential for greater development of the notion of God's consequent nature.

As an experiment in applying the above conceptual framework, dwelling, as it depicts both a place and a practice, is a metaphor that reveals creativity in the concrete activities that have occupied women for centuries. It is linked with skills that women have developed as a result of their social roles and location. In contrast to the popular treatments of journey and pilgrimage, dwelling accentuates presence, acceptance, and peace within self and with God. It augments the qualities of self investigated here by balancing the more traditional emphasis on struggle, development, and progress as representative of self-emergence. This contribution is congruent with feminists' attempts to dissemble metaphors that promote separation, independence, power over others, and victory at all costs. It is another alternative metaphor for selfhood that enlarges our vision to include more of the diversity of human experience. Dwelling is both like and unlike the self that receives the other, offering hospitality to the stranger, and becoming more unique and beautiful because of that relationship. It is an image that attends to the unrecognized strength required to hold in a nurturing way the chaos and fragmentation that characterizes many contemporary lives.

Any appeal to women's historical experiences is vulnerable to several types of misinterpretation. Therefore, it is important to reiterate here that, while I have pointed to traditional dichotomies of gendered experience, the goal is emphatically *not* to reinforce those dichotomies nor to further imprison women in them by valorizing one pole. I am not prescribing a particular female lifestyle, nor do I claim to describe a universalized or generic "woman's experience." I do attempt to reframe the identity of women in positive terms that are not based on their victimization. My views, I believe, are strengthened by their ontological grounding in process philosophy and by an attempt to recognize and include other perspectives. However, it must remain for spokespersons of other perspectives to evaluate the relevance and adequacy of my particular concepts and metaphors for embodying their own experiences.

Because I only investigate certain aspects of personhood that have received less attention in the literature, I view this book as a contribution to a more extensive dialogue between feminism and other modes of inquiry about the construction of more adequate models of the human self. While I utilize valuable resources in feminist and process thought, I nevertheless recognize that other philosophical and theological frameworks might also make valid contributions.[2] Ongoing conversations about selfhood will continue to profit from the interplay of multifarious worldviews. Indeed, the most propitious conclusion will necessarily be a forward-looking one that suggests possible connections, ramifications, and bases for testing or extending the expressed views in other domains. Making the postlude a prelude is the task to which we now proceed.

Plural Selves, Plural Traditions, and Pluralism

When we envision the self as composed or improvised from an abundance of relationships, the multiplistic nature of the self is revealed. No longer is it feasible to think of some monolithic identity that is unchanging—a "self-homunculus" existing independently secure from all "others."[3] Instead, we arrive at a picture consistent with postmodern descriptions of the fluid, local, multiple, and historical nature of truth. Contrary to knowing all others as the objects to our univocal subjectivity, we are confronted with the plural nature of self and world and must consider how we should now reconstrue things that once seemed so singular. Such recastings would include Delwin Brown's treatment of the character of religious tradition as it is canalized from multiple traditions and contexts into an "integration of inheritance and imagination" that funds our theological constructions.[4] Tradition is reframed as a dynamic creative synthesis of past, present and future vision rather than a static, encapsulated version of truth.

Education is another arena that is experiencing the transforming impact of increasing multiplicity and complexity in ways that require new principles of cohesion. The information explosion threatens long-standing values and ideals and the identities that we have erected upon them. Traditional views of how identity is created would have us shore up the boundaries between "us" and "them"—between academic disciplines, between ethnic groups, between religious denominations—even as we do lip service to undoing the boundaries of race, class, and gender. This contradiction does not bode well as a developmental or educational model that will equip us to thrive in global community. Rather, the clarity that is created from concrescing complexity suggests a basis on which we might reevaluate our defenses and develop trust in the potential growth that encountering difference offers us.

"The North American contradiction—a universalism made up of ethnic, cultural, religious and sexual exclusions—"[5] has been exposed; pluralism has staked its claim to the validity of multiple worldviews. What educational practices help or hinder our efforts to bridge the boundaries of difference? The dynamics of empathy and clarity in connection help us enter other traditions with "epistemic humility" without losing our identity.[6] Border pedagogies make certain that all voices in the classroom are heard, and we gain keener awareness of, and mutual respect for our commonalities and differences. Hospitality becomes a new educational paradigm that shows us the value of de-centering our private perspectives in order to learn a more adequate representation of communal truth.[7] When we study the fluidity of boundaries and learn to evaluate various degrees and types of "elasticity" and "border-crossings," then we will be better able to articulate an integrity that is not compromised by porous perimeters.

Bridging differences has become increasingly central to our attempts to create some form of togetherness in the midst of the burgeoning multiplicity. The promise of a planetary community depends on our ability to welcome the "ever-increasing number of 'foreign invaders' coming across the frontiers of our personal and our collective frames of mind."[8] The role of empathy in developing individual "stature" and in cultivating "hospitality to the stranger" recommends empathy and forgiveness as political as well as religious virtues that can contribute to the pluralism of a comprehensive human community.

From Judith Jordan's work on mutually empathic relationships, we know that empathy is much more than the mushy, mindless absorption of some oversimplified version of another person's feelings. Its highly complex cognitive-emotional interaction translates well, according to Marie McCarthy,[9] into the intercultural experience that characterizes the mutually transformative power of ministry in a world church. Jordan's emphasis on the mutuality that characterizes growth-producing empathic connections finds resonance with other feminists' spotlighting of reciprocity as the key to genuine dialogue about differences among white women and women of color.[10] It is mutual dialogue that does not reduce either side to abstraction that enables us to place trust in some degree of common experience. It is mutual "hospitality" that mitigates unilateral power, allowing us to be "both outsider and insider with respect to each other."[11]

But how should we understand this advocacy for mutuality, empathy, and bridging differences in our plural religious contexts? How can faithful commitment and a sense of Christian identity be instilled in people without inculcating attitudes of opposition and superiority toward other faith perspectives? In a publication that advances an understanding of Christian nurture for a pluralistic age, the British Council of Churches encourages an attitude of "critical openness." It is an attitude that unites attentive receptivity to the world with commitment to ongoing inquiry—inquiry that seeks the true over the merely plausible.[12] Susanne Johnson calls it "critical pluralism" and points to reflexive analysis as the distinguishing mark that keeps us open to difference and diversity in interreligious dialogue, dialogue among hermeneutical options within a single religious tradition, or dialogue among diverse ethnic cultures.[13] In this book, the dynamics of empathy and clarity through contrast describe the same characteristics and demonstrate how they equip individuals for negotiating plurality into identity.

Pushing the Edges: Relation, Separation, and Self-Critique

I have pushed against the edges of some longstanding and powerful assumptions. It has been beyond the scope of this project to dialogue in depth with particular dissidents, but such dialogue is essential to uncover and correct the myopia of my own immediate life-context as well as the blinding effects of my particular privilege.[14] "Our visions of what is better are always informed by our perception of what is bad about our present situation."[15] Nevertheless, this does not mean that we are silenced by our imperfections—only humbled. Here I will mention just three "edges" that seem to especially warrant further conversation.

A particularly strong contrast exists between the views expressed here and those of feminists who speak from a psychoanalytic perspective. The latter hold as a fundamental assumption that humans begin life psychologically fused with their primary caregiver. As we have seen, this model has been seriously challenged by recent infant research, but the model continues to fund the vast network of theorists who place their roots in Freud's genius. Hence, even though the context has been shifted from biological to linguistic categories, French feminist Julia Kristeva retains the theme of separation as the necessity from which the subject is born.[16] In spite of much common ground with respect to reconstructing the subject, Kristeva's dichotomies of semiotic and symbolic challenge my insistence on converging multiplicity as the means by which articulation of self is accomplished. Citing the "thetic phase" where the subject breaks from the object, Kristeva continues to base development of personhood on repression of the mother (*jouissance*) and rupture with the other as the separation that is necessary for meaning.[17] The influential works of the French feminists like Kristeva offer provocative contrasts with claims made here that such models perpetuate sexism by making women/mothers the disruptive force or enemy that stands in the way of development.

Dismantling the traditional trajectory of development not only pushes against the edges of accepted patterns and measures of advancement; it also lays challenge to the very process of measurement and the ideal of progress. The door is opened to a renewed appreciation of contentment to balance the voracious ambition that can ravage our environment as well as our relationships. Shifting the focus from linear movement toward a goal to one of mutual interaction and relationship prevents us from treating caregivers as extensions or blank objects of the "developing" subject. It introduces a space for mothers to be more complex subjects who perform less than perfectly, a way to take seriously the moral ambiguity in women's subjectivity.[18]

Finally, pushing the edge of currently accepted points of view also describes the intellectual climate for utilizing Whitehead and process thought as a philosophical framework. The viability of such a framework is supported by its explanatory power, but critiques of its esoteric linguistic elitism and androcentric bias are well-founded. A more focused engagement of these problems, like that undertaken by Thistlethwaite, Olds, and Howell for their own specific inquiries,[19] will contribute to contemporary adaptations of process thought. It is a worthwhile effort because the cross-disciplinary connections that were fundamental among Whitehead's criteria for adequacy continue to serve in the postmodern era of relativized norms.

Accountability

Feminists writing in both psychology and theology have exposed the "destructiveness of others presuming to speak about us or for us."[20] From this observation arises the commitment to keep theory firmly grounded in the experiences of women. Does it make a difference there? The application of theory to real lives may ultimately be more important as a test of its adequacy than its coherency and comprehensiveness. However, its accountability to academic settings and to long-established methods of discourse can easily make theory esoteric and irrelevant. At the same time, the privilege that determines who is educated and writing further distances theory from its roots in underrepresented lives.

Nevertheless, theory-building like that undertaken here can be justified as helpful "if it enables one to see how parts of one's life fit together, for example, to see connections among parts of one's life one hasn't seen before."[21] If it can help one locate oneself accurately and concretely in the world and enable one to discern the extent of one's responsibility for being in that location, then theory can claim validity by means of its applications. So the link between theory and practice is an essential extension of theory in general and this exercise in particular. For example, if we begin to view the self as articulated through multiple and shifting relationships rather than increasingly independent and autonomous, it makes sense to question, as Pamela Couture has done, the wisdom of public policy forcing single parents and their children to prove their self-sufficiency rather than supporting "shared responsibility or interdependence" through networks of care.²² Such significant and timely applications remind us that, ultimately, the goal must be to make theory accountable to the people whose lives it presumes to describe.²³

Chasing Rabbits

This brief foray into some implications and cross-disciplinary associations reminds me of one professor's favorite observation when his class discussions strayed far from the course syllabus. He called students back to the day's topic, saying that they had "chased enough rabbits." The image is of a husk of hares surprised by some intruder and scattering in all directions to wooded safety. The connections our students make between course content and lived experience might lead anywhere—their connections are unfocused, yet they build upon one another; they are often irreverent (sometimes irrelevant). This is creativity at work in the generative chaos of diverse minds interacting around a common inquiry. Interestingly, "chasing rabbits" is also what Alice did in Wonderland. Chasing rabbits introduced Alice to a new way of experiencing the world.

There are, therefore, and in accordance with postmodern sensibilities, no tidy and singular conclusions. There is no comprehensive model of the postmodern self advanced; the locality of the discussion disallows final and complete solutions. There are only possibilities, questions, and implications multiplying one on top of another into distant arenas of application and verification. Just so do we learn to deal with the fluidity of our truth claims. It does not mean that they are trivial or apologetic, only provisional.

Until we come to terms with the radical relatedness of human selfhood and allow that relatedness to transform our life philosophies and their social constructions, our obsession with separation will continue to fog our self-perceptions and pollute any hopeful vision of a communal future. Investigating the nature of our interconnections and doggedly tracing them through every aspect of thought and life will enable us to shake off the tenacious lenses of the favored western interpretive paradigm that creates individualism through its fear and objectification of difference. If I have succeeded in this book's particular venture, then I will have scattered a slew of rabbits scampering across the ideological landscape. Perhaps a reader will chase a few into the wonderland of a different worldview. Perhaps a few will emerge as contributors to a more just and adequate human equation as we explore and learn to nurture the creative dwelling that is the postmodern self.

NOTES

1. Susan Brooks Thistlethwaite, "'I Am Become Death': God In the Nuclear Age," in *Lift Every Voice: Constructing Christian Theologies from the Underside*, ed. by Susan Brooks Thistlethwaite and Mary Potter Engel (San Francisco: Harper San Francisco, 1990), 101.
2. One excellent excellent example is Carol Lakey Hess's exploration of the interplay of theology and women's development within the framework of the Reformed tradition and the practices of the church (*Caretakers of Our Common House: Women's Development in Communities of Faith*, Nashville: Abingdon Press, 1997). Hess also draws extensively from the Stone Center model of women's development.
3. Fogel, 124.
4. Delwin Brown, *Boundaries of Our Habitations: Tradition and Theological Construction* (Albany: State University of New York Press, 1994), 7.
5. William Greenbaum, "America in Search of a New Ideal: An Essay on the Rise of Pluralism," *Harvard Educational Review* (August 1974), quoted by Donald W. Shriver, Jr., "The Pain and Promise of Pluralism," *Christian Century* 97, no. 11 (March 26, 1980): 345.
6. Charles R. Foster, "Teaching for Belief: Power and Pedagogical Practice," paper presented at the Association of Professors and Researchers in Religious Education, Chicago, 1995.
7. Jane McAvoy, "Hospitality: A Feminist Theology of Education," *Teaching Theology and Religion* 1, no. 1 (February 1998): 20-26. See also Parker J. Palmer, *The Courage to Teach:Exploring the Inner Landscape of a Teacher's Life* (San Francisco: Jossey-Bass Publishers, 1998), 74-75.
8. Shriver, 348.
9. McCarthy, 120.
10. Maria C. Lugones and Elizabeth V. Spelman, "Have We Got a Theory for You! Feminist Theory, Cultural Imperialism and the Demand for 'The Woman's Voice,'" *Women's Studies International Forum* 6, no. 6 (1983): 577.
11. Ibid.
12. British Council of Churches, *The Child in the Church and Understanding Christian Nurture* (Cheshire, England: W. Hutson Print Ltd., 1984), 64.
13. Susanne Johnson, "Reshaping Religious and Theological Education in the 90's: Toward a Critical Pluralism, *Religious Education* 88, no. 3 (Summer 1993): 335-49.
14. An especially relevant and powerful example of such dialogue is one between Carter Heyward and Marie Fortune centering on Heyward's most recent book, *When Boundaries Betray Us: Beyond What Is Ethical in Therapy and Life* (San Francisco: Harper, 1993). Fortune's review and Heyward's response are

found in *The Christian Century* 3, no. 17 (May 18-25, 1994): 524-26 and no. 18 (June 1-8, 1994): 579-82.

15. Lugones and Spelman, 579.

16. Julia Kristeva, *The Kristeva Reader*, ed. Toril Moi (New York: Columbia University Press, 1986), 99, 101, 198.

17. Ibid., 101. However, in other places Kristeva seems to argue the opposite, that is, that we must challenge the myth of the totally englobing archaic mother, such a challenge being "an unbelievable force for subversion in the modern world!" (p. 205). See Catherine Keller's discussion of Kristeva's antiessentialism in "Seeing and Sucking: On Relation and Essence in Feminist Theology," in *Horizons in Feminist Theology*, ed. Rebecca Chopp and Sheila Greeve Davaney (Minneapolis: Fortress Press, 1997), 64-65.

18. Paula Cooey, "Bad Women: The Limits of Theory and Theology," in *Horizons in Feminist Theology*, ed. Rebecca Chopp and Sheila Greeve Davaney (Minneapolis: Fortress Press, 1997), 137-53.

19. Thistlethwaite, *Sex, Race, and God*, 87-91; Olds, 126-129; Howell, "A Feminist Theory of Relations," 135-43.

20. Lugones and Spelman, 574.

21. Ibid., 578.

22. Couture, *Blessed Are the Poor?*, 135, and "Weaving the Web: Pastoral Care in an Individualistic Society," in *Through the Eyes of Women*, ed. Jeanne Stevenson Moessner (Minneapolis: Fortress Press, 1996), 94-104.

23. Lugones and Spelman, 580.

BIBLIOGRAPHY

Abra, Jock. *Assaulting Parnassus: Theoretical Views of Creativity.* Lanham, Md.: University Press of America, 1988.
_____, and Suzanne Valentine-French. "Gender Differences in Creative Achievement: A Survey of Explanations." *Genetic, Social, and General Psychology Monographs* 117, no. 3 (1991): 233–84.
Anderson, Harold H., ed. *Creativity and Its Cultivation.* New York: Harper, 1959.
Anderson, Herbert, and Kenneth R. Mitchell. *Leaving Home.* Louisville, Ky.: Westminster/John Knox Press, 1993.
Anderson, Sherry Ruth, and Patricia Hopkins. *The Feminine Face of God: The Unfolding of the Sacred in Women.* New York: Bantam Books, 1991.
Arieti, Silvano. *Creativity: The Magic Synthesis.* New York: Basic Books, 1976.
Arnold, Karen, Kathleen D. Noble, and Rena F. Subotnik, ed. *Remarkable Women: Perspectives on Female Talent Development.* Cresskill, N.J.: Hampton Press, Inc., 1996.
Assagioli, Roberto. *Psychosynthesis.* New York: Penguin Books, 1976; Hobbs, Dorman & Co., 1965.
Bamberger, John Eudes. "Defining the Center: A Monastic Point of View." *Criterion* 20, no. 2 (Spring 1981): 4–11.
Barnhart, J. E. "Incarnation and Process Philosophy." *Religious Studies* 2 (1967): 225–32.
Bartky, Sandra Lee. "Sympathy and Solidarity." In *Feminists Rethink the Self,* ed. Diana Tietjens Meyers, 177–96. Boulder, Colo.: Westview Press, 1997.
Bass, Dorothy C. "Keeping Sabbath: Reviving a Christian Practice." *The Christian Century* (January 1–8, 1997): 12–16.
Bateson, Mary Catherine. *Composing a Life.* New York: Atlantic Monthly Press, 1989.
Belenky, Mary, Blythe Clynchy, Nancy Goldberger, and Jill Tarule. *Women's Ways of Knowing: The Development of Self, Voice, and Mind.* New York: Basic Books, 1986.
Benjamin, Jessica. *The Bonds of Love: Psychoanalysis, Feminism, and the Problem of Domination.* New York: Pantheon Books, 1988.
Bennett, Paula. *My Life a Loaded Gun: Female Creativity and Feminist Poetics.* Boston: Beacon Press, 1986.
Berling, Judith A. *A Pilgrim in Chinese Culture: Negotiating Religious Diversity.* Maryknoll, N.Y.: Orbis Books, 1997.
Berman, Morris. "The Two Faces of Creativity." Chapter 10 in *Coming to Our Senses: Body and Spirit in the Hidden History of the West.* New York: Simon and Schuster, 1989.

Berryman, Jerome. *Godly Play: A Way of Religious Education.* San Francisco: Harper, 1991.

Bograd, Michele. "Enmeshment, Fusion or Relatedness? A Conceptual Analysis." *Journal of Psychotherapy and the Family* 3 (Winter 1987): 65–80.

Bohart, Arthur C., and Leslie S. Greenbert. "Empathy and Psychotherapy: An Introductory Overview." In *Empathy Reconsidered: New Directions in Psychotherapy,* ed. Arthur C. Bohart and Leslie S. Greenbert, 3–31. Washington, D.C.: American Psychological Association, 1997.

Boler, Megan. "The Risks of Empathy: Interrogating Multiculturalism's Gaze." *Cultural Studies* 11, no. 2 (1997): 253–73.

Boston Lesbian Psychologies Collective. "Introduction." In *Lesbian Psychologies: Explorations and Challenges,* ed. Boston Lesbian Psychologies Collective, 1–16. Urbana, Ill.: University of Illinois Press, 1987.

Bowers, C. A. *Education for an Ecologically Sustainable Culture: Rethinking Moral Education, Creativity, Intelligence, and Other Modern Orthodoxies.* Albany: State University of New York Press, 1995.

Brison, Susan J. "Outliving Oneself: Trauma, Memory, and Personal Identity." In *Feminists Rethink the Self,* ed. Diana Tietjens Meyers, 12–39. Boulder, Colo.: Westview Press, 1997.

British Council of Churches. *The Child in the Church and Understanding Christian Nurture.* Cheshire, England: W. Hutson Print Ltd., 1984.

Brock, Rita Nakashima. "Power, Peace, and the Possibility of Survival." In *God and Global Justice: Religion and Poverty in an Unequal World,* ed. Frederick Ferre and Rita H. Mataragnon, 17–35. New York: Paragon House, 1985.

──────. *Journeys by Heart: A Christology of Erotic Power.* New York: Crossroad, 1991.

Brown, Delwin. *To Set At Liberty: Christian Faith and Human Freedom.* Maryknoll, N.Y.: Orbis Books, 1981.

──────. *Boundaries of Our Habitations: Tradition and Theological Construction.* Albany: State University of New York Press, 1994.

Brown, Frank Burch. *Transfiguration: Poetic Metaphor and the Languages of Religious Belief.* Chapel Hill, N.C.: University of North Carolina Press, 1983.

Brown, Laura S. "Cultural Diversity in Feminist Therapy: Theory and Practice." In *Bringing Cultural Diversity to Feminist Psychology,* ed. Hope Landrine, 143–61. Washington: American Psychological Association, 1995.

Browning, Don S. *The Atonement and Psychotherapy.* Philadelphia: Westminster Press, 1966.

──────. *Religious Thought and the Modern Psychologies.* Philadelphia: Fortress Press, 1987.

Brunel, Marie-Lise. "Empathie, Femmes, Fèminisme et Prèfèrence de Genre en Psychothèrapie." *Revue Quèbècoise de Psychologie* 8, no. 3 (1987): 89–118.

Burch, Beverly. "Barriers to Intimacy: Conflicts over Power, Dependency, and Nurturing in Lesbian Relationships." In *Lesbian Psychologies: Explorations and Challenges,* ed. Boston Lesbian Psychologies Collective, 126–41. Urbana, Ill.: University of Illinois Press, 1987.

Cady, Linell E. "Relational Love: A Feminist Christian Vision." In *Embodied Love: Sensuality and Relationship as Feminist Values,* ed. Paula M. Cooey, Sharon A. Farmer, and Mary Ellen Ross, 135–50. San Francisco: Harper & Row, 1987.

Calta, Marialisa. "Women's Novels Tell Stories Through Cooking, Recipes." *Boulder Daily Camera,* 23 June 1993, 2(D).

Campbell, Joseph. *The Hero with a Thousand Faces.* Princeton: Princeton University Press, 1973, 1972, 1968, 1949.

Caplan, Paula J. "Driving Us Crazy: How Oppression Damages Women's Mental Health and What We Can Do About It." *Women & Therapy* 12, no. 3 (1992): 5–28.

Carlozzi, Alfred F., Kay S. Bull, Gregory T. Eells, and John D. Hurlburt. "Empathy as Related to Creativity, Dogmatism, and Expressiveness." *Journal of Psychology* 129, no. 4 (1995): 365–73.

Carter, Betty. "Fathers and Daughters." In *The Invisible Web: Gender Patterns in Family Relationships*, ed. Marianne Walters, Betty Carter, Peggy Papp, and Olga Silverstein, 90–114. New York: Guilford Press, 1988.

Chodorow, Nancy J. *Feminism and Psychoanalytic Theory.* New Haven: Yale University Press, 1989.

Chopp, Rebecca S., and Sheila Greeve Davaney. *Horizons in Feminist Theology.* Minneapolis: Fortress Press, 1997.

Christ, Carol P., and Judith Plaskow. *Womanspirit Rising: A Feminist Reader in Religion.* San Francisco: Harper & Row, 1979, 1992.

Clift, Jean Dalby, and Wallace B. Clift. *The Hero Journey in Dreams.* New York: Crossroad, 1988.

Cobb, John B., Jr. *God and the World.* Philadelphia: Westminster Press, 1969.

―――. "Feminism and Process Thought: A Two-Way Relationship." In *Feminism and Process Thought*, ed. Sheila Greeve Davaney, 32–61. New York: Edwin Mellen Press, 1981.

―――. "Response to Loomer." In *The Size of God: The Theology of Bernard Loomer in Context*, ed. William Dean and Larry E. Axel, 52–55. Macon, Ga.: Mercer University Press, 1987.

―――. "From Individualism to Persons in Community: A Postmodern Economic Theory." In *Sacred Interconnections: Postmodern Spirituality, Political Economy, and Art*, ed. David Ray Griffin, 123–42. Albany: State University of New York Press, 1990.

―――, and David Ray Griffin. *Process Theology: An Introductory Exposition.* Philadelphia: Westminster Press, 1976.

Cooey, Paula M. "Bad Women: The Limits of Theory and Theology." In *Horizons in Feminist Theology*, ed. Rebecca S. Chopp and Sheila Greeve Davaney, 137–53. Minneapolis: Fortress Press, 1997.

Cooey, Paula M., Sharon A. Farmer, and Mary Ellen Ross, eds. *Embodied Love: Sensuality and Relationship as Feminist Values.* San Francisco: Harper & Row, 1987.

Cook, Ellen Piel. "Role Salience and Multiple Roles: A Gender Perspective." *Career Development Quarterly* 43 (September 1994): 85–95.

Coser, Rose Laub. *In Defense of Modernity: Role Complexity and Individual Autonomy.* Stanford, Calif.: Stanford University Press, 1991.

Couture, Pamela D. *Blessed Are The Poor? Women's Poverty, Family Policy, and Practical Theology.* Nashville: Abingdon Press, 1991.

―――. "Weaving the Web: Pastoral Care in an Individualistic Society." In *Through the Eyes of Women*, ed. Jeanne Stevenson Moessner, 94–104. Minneapolis: Fortress Press, 1996.

Crabtree, Harriet. *The Christian Life: Traditional Metaphors and Contemporary Theologies.* Minneapolis: Fortress Press, 1991.

Crosby, Faye J., ed. *Spouse, Parent, Worker: On Gender and Multiple Roles.* New Haven: Yale University Press, 1987.

Curtis, Rebecca C., ed. *The Relational Self: Theoretical Convergences in Psychoanalysis and Social Psychology*. New York: Guilford Press, 1991.

Cyr, Mireille, and Helene David. "L'Adaptation de Femmes Professionnelles à la Carrière, à la Maternitè et aux Responsabilitès Familiales." *Canadian Journal of Counselling* 25, no. 4 (1991): 520–30.

Daly, Mary. *Beyond God the Father: Toward a Philosophy of Women's Liberation*. Boston: Beacon Press, 1973.

―――. *Gyn/Ecology: The Metaethics of Radical Feminism*. Boston: Beacon Press, 1978.

Davaney, Sheila Greeve, ed. *Feminism and Process Thought*. New York: Edwin Mellen Press, 1981.

―――. "The Limits of the Appeal to Women's Experience." In *Shaping New Visions: Gender and Values in American Culture*, ed. Clarissa W. Atkinson, Constance H. Buchanan, and Margaret R. Miles, 31–49. Ann Arbor: UMI Research Press, 1987.

Davis, Mark H. *Empathy: A Social Psychological Approach*. Boulder, Colo.: Westview Press, 1996.

De Waal, Esther. *Seeking God: The Way of St. Benedict*. Collegeville, Minn.: The Liturgical Press, 1984.

Dean, William D. *History Making History: The New Historicism in American Religious Thought*. Albany: State University of New York Press, 1988.

di Zerega, Gus. "Empathy, Society, Nature, and the Relational Self: Deep Ecology and Liberal Modernity." *Social Theory and Practice* 21, no. 2 (Summer 1995): 239–69.

Doehring, Carrie. *Taking Care: Monitoring Power Dynamics and Relational Boundaries in Pastoral Care & Counseling*. Nashville: Abingdon Press, 1995.

Driver, Tom F. *Patterns of Grace: Human Experience as Word of God*. San Francisco: Harper & Row, 1977.

Duan, Changming, and Hill, Clara E. "The Current State of Empathy Research." *Journal of Counseling Psychology* 43, no. 3 (1996): 261–74.

Eisenberg, Nancy, and Janet Strayer, eds. *Empathy and Its Development*. Cambridge, Mass.: Cambridge University Press, 1987.

Ellsworth, Elizabeth. "Claiming the Tenured Body." In *The Center of the Web: Women and Solitude*, ed. Delese Wear, 63–74. Albany: State University of New York Press, 1993.

Epstein, Cynthia Fuchs. "Multiple Demands and Multiple Roles: The Conditions of Successful Management." In *Spouse, Parent, Worker: On Gender and Multiple Roles*, ed. Fay J. Crosby, 23–35. New Haven: Yale University Press, 1987.

Erikson, Erik H. *Childhood and Society*. New York: W.W. Norton & Co., 1950, 1963.

―――. *Identity and the Life Cycle*. New York: W.W. Norton & Co., 1980; International Universities Press, 1959.

Esteva, Gustavo. "From 'Development' to 'Hospitality' of the Hammock: Regenerating People's Place." *Interculture* 20 (April–June 1987): 25.

Farley, Edward. *Divine Empathy: A Theology of God*. Minneapolis: Fortress Press, 1996.

Filiod, Jean Paul, and Daniel Welzer-Lang. "L'Èmergence du Masculin dans L'Espace Domestique." *Architecture and Behavior* 8, no. 2 (1992): 159–80.

Fine, Michelle, and Susan Merle Gordon. "Feminist Transformations of/Despite Psychology." In *Gender and Thought: Psychological Perspectives*, ed. Mary Crawford and Margaret Gentry, 146–74. New York: Springer-Verlag, 1989.

Bibliography

Fogel, Alan. "Relational Narratives of the Prelinguistic Self." In *The Self in Infancy: Theory and Research*, ed. Phillipe Rochat, 117–39. New York: Elsevier Science, 1995.
Ford, Lewis S. "Tillich, Whitehead and Creativity." In *Paul Tillich on Creativity*, ed. Jacquelyn Ann K. Kegley, 121–30. Lanham, Md.: University Press of America, 1989.
Fortune, Marie. "Therapy and Intimacy: Confused About Boundaries." *The Christian Century* 3, no. 17 (May 18–25, 1994): 524–26.
Foster, Charles R. "Teaching for Belief: Power and Pedagogical Practice." Paper presented at the Association of Professors and Researchers in Religious Education, Chicago, 1995.
Fox, Matthew. *A Spirituality Named Compassion*. San Francisco: Harper & Row, 1979.
———. *Original Blessing*. Santa Fe: Bear & Company, 1983.
———. *The Coming of the Cosmic Christ*. San Francisco: Harper & Row, 1988.
———. "Creation Spirituality: A Personal Retrospective." *Listening* 24, no. 2 (1989): 116–36.
———. "A Mystical Cosmology: Toward a Postmodern Spirituality." In *Sacred Interconnections: Postmodern Spirituality, Political Economy, and Art*, ed. David Ray Griffin, 15–34. Albany: State University of New York Press, 1990.
Frankenberry, Nancy K. *Religion and Radical Empiricism*. Albany: State University of New York Press, 1987.
———. "Pragmatism, Truth, and Objectivity." *Soundings* 74, nos. 3–4 (Fall/Winter 1991): 509–24.
Freire, Paulo. *Pedagogy of the Oppressed*. Trans. Myra Bergman Ramos. New York: Seabury Press, 1974, 1970.
Fulkerson, Mary McClintock. *Changing the Subject: Women's Discourses and Feminist Theology*. Minneapolis: Fortress Press, 1994.
Furlong, Monica. *Travelling In*. Boston: Cowley Publications, 1971, 1984.
Geertz, Clifford. "Thick Description: Toward an Interpretive Theory of Culture." In *The Interpretation of Culture*, ed. Clifford Geertz, 3–30. New York: Basic Books, 1973.
Gentry, Margaret. "Feminist Perspectives on Gender and Thought: Paradox and Potential." In *Gender and Thought: Psychological Perspectives*, ed. Mary Crawford and Margaret Gentry, 1–16. New York: Springer-Verlag, 1989.
Gergen, Kenneth J. "Metaphor, Metatheory, and the Social World." In *Metaphors in the History of Psychology*, ed. David E. Leary, 267–99. Cambridge: Cambridge University Press, 1990.
Gilbert, Scott F. "The Metaphorical Structuring of Social Perceptions." *Soundings* 62, no. 2 (Summer 1979): 166–86.
Gilligan, Carol. *In a Different Voice: Psychological Theory and Women's Development*. Cambridge, Mass.: Harvard University Press, 1982.
Gordon, Beverly M. "Speaking in Tongues: An African-American Woman in the World and the Academy." In *The Center of the Web: Women and Solitude*, ed. Delese Wear, 153–69. Albany: State University of New York Press, 1993.
Graham, Larry Kent. *Care of Persons, Care of Worlds: A Psychosystems Approach to Pastoral Care and Counseling*. Nashville: Abingdon, 1992.
Grant, Jacquelyn. *White Women's Christ and Black Women's Jesus: Feminist Christology and Womanist Response*. Atlanta: Scholars Press, 1989.

Graves, Thomas H. "A Critique of Process Theodicy from an African Perspective." *Process Studies* 17, no. 2 (Summer 1988): 103–11.
Gray, Elizabeth Dodson. "Doing Housework—Introduction." In *Sacred Dimensions of Women's Experience*, ed. Elizabeth Dodson Gray, 138–41. Wellesley, Mass.: Roundtable Press, 1988.
──────. "Women's Creativity—Introduction." In *Sacred Dimensions of Women's Experience*, ed. Elizabeth Dodson Gray, 8–11. Wellesley, Mass.: Roundtable Press, 1988.
──────, ed. *Sacred Dimensions of Women's Experience*. Wellesley, Mass.: Roundtable Press, 1988.
Grey, Mary. *Towards a Christian Feminist Spirituality of Redemption as Mutuality in Relation*. Ann Arbor: University Microfilms International, 1987.
Griffin, David Ray. "Creativity in Post-Modern Religion." In *Creativity in Art, Religion, and Culture*, ed. Michael H. Mitias, 64–85. Amsterdam: Rodopi, 1985.
──────. *God and Religion in the Postmodern World: Essays in Postmodern Theology*. Albany: State University of New York Press, 1989.
──────, ed. *Sacred Interconnections: Postmodern Spirituality, Political Economy, and Art*. Albany: State University of New York Press, 1990.
Groome, Thomas H. "The Spirituality of the Religious Educator," *Religious Education* 83, no. 1 (Winter 1988): 9–20.
Gunter, Pete A.Y. "Creativity and Ecology." In *Creativity in Art, Religion, and Culture*, ed. Michael H. Mitias, 107–16. Amsterdam: Rodopi, 1985.
Harding, Sandra. "The Instability of the Analytical Categories of Feminist Theory." *Signs* 11, no. 4 (1986): 645–64.
──────. *Whose Science? Whose Knowledge? Thinking from Women's Lives*. Ithaca, N.Y.: Cornell University Press, 1991.
Harris, Maria. "Completion and Faith Development." In *Faith Development and Fowler*, ed. Craig Dykstra and Sharon Parks, 115–33. Birmingham, Ala.: Religious Education Press, 1986.
──────. *Dance of the Spirit: The Seven Steps of Women's Spirituality*. New York: Bantam Books, 1989.
Harrison, Beverly Wildung. *Our Right to Choose: Toward a New Ethic of Abortion*. Boston: Beacon Press, 1983.
──────. "The Power of Anger in the Work of Love." In *Weaving the Visions: New Patterns in Feminist Spirituality*, ed. Judith Plaskow and Carol P. Christ, 214–25. San Francisco: Harper & Row, 1989.
Hartshorne, Charles. "The Idea of Creativity in American Philosophy." *Journal of Karnatak University—Social Sciences* 2 (1966): 1–13.
──────. *Creative Synthesis and Philosophic Method*. La Salle, Ill.: Open Court Publishing, 1970.
──────. "Creativity as a Value and Creativity as a Transcendental Category." In *Creativity in Art, Religion, and Culture*, ed. Michael H. Mitias, 3–11. Amsterdam: Rodopi, 1985.
Hauerwas, Stanley. *The Peaceable Kingdom*. Notre Dame: University of Notre Dame Press, 1983.
Hausman, Carl R. "Originality as a Criterion for Creativity." In *Creativity in Art, Religion, and Culture*, ed. Michael H. Mitias, 26–41. Amsterdam: Rodopi, 1985.
Heidegger, Martin. *Poetry, Language, Thought*. Trans. Albert Hofstadter. New York: Harper & Row, 1971.

Hekman, Susan J. *Gender and Knowledge: Elements of a Postmodern Feminism.* Boston: Northeastern University Press, 1990.

―――. "Truth and Method: Feminist Standpoint Theory Revisited." *Signs* 22, no. 2 (Winter 1997): 341–366.

Helson, Ravenna, Teresa Elliott, and Janet Leigh. "Number and Quality of Roles." *Psychology of Women Quarterly* 14, no. 1 (March 1990): 83–101.

Hess, Carol Lakey. *Caretakers of Our Common House: Women's Development in Communities of Faith.* Nashville: Abingdon Press, 1997.

Heyward, Carter. *The Redemption of God: A Theology of Mutual Relation.* Washington, D.C.: University Press of America, 1982.

―――. *Our Passion for Justice: Images of Power, Sexuality, and Liberation.* New York: Pilgrim Press, 1984.

―――. "The Radicalization of Christian Feminism Among White U.S. Women." *Journal of Feminist Studies in Religion* 1, no. 1 (1985): 99–117.

―――. *Coming Out and Relational Empowerment: A Lesbian Feminist Theological Perspective.* Work in Progress, no. 38. Wellesley, Mass.: Stone Center, 1989.

―――. *Touching Our Strength: The Erotic as Power and the Love of God.* San Francisco: Harper & Row, 1989.

―――. "The Power of God-With-Us." *The Christian Century* 107 (March 14, 1990): 275–78.

―――. *When Boundaries Betray Us: Beyond What Is Ethical In Therapy and Life.* San Francisco: Harper, 1993.

―――. "Boundaries or Barriers?" *The Christian Century* 3, no. 18 (June 1–8, 1994): 579–82.

Hillman, James. *Re-Visioning Psychology.* New York: Harper & Row, 1977, 1975.

Hochschild, Arlie Russell. *The Second Shift: Working Parents and the Revolution at Home.* New York: Viking, 1989.

hooks, bell. *Feminist Theory: From Margin to Center.* Boston: South End Press, 1984.

Howell, Nancy R. "The Promise of a Process Feminist Theory of Relations." *Process Studies* 17, no. 2 (Summer 1988): 78–87.

―――. "A Feminist Theory of Relations." Ph.D. diss., Claremont Graduate School, 1991.

Hunter, Anne Marie. "Numbering the Hairs of Our Heads: Male Social Control and the All-Seeing Male God." *Journal of Feminist Studies in Religion* 8, no. 2 (1992): 7–26.

Ickes, William, ed. *Empathic Accuracy.* New York: The Guilford Press, 1997.

Interculture 20. "Should We Say No to Development?" (Spring/April 1987): 1–48.

Isasi-Diaz, Ada Maria. "A Hispanic Garden in a Foreign Land." In *Inheriting Our Mothers' Gardens: Feminist Theology in Third World Perspective,* ed. Letty M. Russell, Kwok Pui-lan, Ada Maria Isasi-Diaz, and Katie Geneva Cannon, 91–106. Louisville: Westminster Press, 1988.

James, William. "The Consciousness of Self." In *The Principles of Psychology,* Vol. 1. New York: Dover Publications, Inc., 1950; Henry Holt & Co., 1890.

Johnson, Susanne. "Reshaping Religious and Theological Education in the 90's: Toward a Critical Pluralism." *Religious Education* 88, no. 3 (Summer 1993): 335–49.

Johnston, Sally. "Exploring the Development/Formation Connection: A Participation in Cultural Critique and Reformation." Unpublished paper, Presbyterian School of Christian Education, Richmond, Va., January 1988.

Jones, James W. *Contemporary Psychoanalysis and Religion.* New Haven: Yale University Press, 1991.

Jordan, Judith V. *Empathy and Self Boundaries.* Work in Progress, no. 16. Wellesley, Mass.: Stone Center, 1984.
_____. *The Meaning of Mutuality.* Work in Progress, no. 23. Wellesley, Mass.: Stone Center, 1986.
_____. *Clarity in Connection: Empathic Knowing, Desire and Sexuality.* Work in Progress, no. 29. Wellesley, Mass.: Stone Center, 1987.
_____. *Relational Development: Therapeutic Implications of Empathy and Shame.* Work in Progress, no. 39. Wellesley, Mass.: Stone Center, 1989.
_____. *Courage in Connection: Conflict, Compassion, Creativity.* Work in Progress, no. 45. Wellesley, Mass.: Stone Center, 1990.
_____. "Relational Development Through Mutual Empathy." In *Empathy Reconsidered: New Directions in Psychotherapy,* ed. Arthur C. Bohart and Leslie S. Greenberg, 343–51. Washington, D.C.: American Psychological Association, 1997.
_____, ed. *Women's Growth in Diversity: More Writings from the Stone Center.* New York: Guilford Press, 1997.
_____, Alexandra G. Kaplan, Jean Baker Miller, and Irene Stiver. *Women's Growth in Connection: Writings from the Stone Center.* New York: Guilford Press, 1991.
_____, and Janet L. Surrey. "The Self-in-Relation: Empathy and the Mother-Daughter Relationship." In *The Psychology of Today's Woman: New Psychoanalytic Visions,* ed. Toni Bernay and Dorothy W. Cantor, 81–104. Hillsdale, N.J.: The Analytic Press/Earlbaum Associates, 1986.
_____, Janet L. Surrey, and Alexandra G. Kaplan. *Women and Empathy: Implications for Psychological Development and Psychotherapy.* Work in Progress, no. 2. Wellesley, Mass.: Stone Center, 1983.
Josselson, Ruthellen. "The Embedded Self: I and Thou Revisited." In *Self, Ego, and Identity: Integrative Approaches,* ed. Daniel K. Lapsley and F. Clark Power, 91–106. New York: Springer-Verlag, 1988.
Jung, C. G. "The Transcendent Function." In *The Portable Jung,* ed., trans. R. F. C. Hull, 273–300. New York: Viking Press, 1984, 1971.
Kaiser, Florian G. "Dwelling: Speaking of an Unnoticed Universal Language." *New Ideas in Psychology* 14, no. 3 (1996): 225–36.
Kaplan, Alexandra, and Nancy Gleason. *Women's Self Development in Late Adolescence.* Work in Progress, no. 17. Wellesley, Mass.: Stone Center, 1985.
Kegan, Robert. "There the Dance Is: Religious Dimensions of a Developmental Framework." In *Toward Moral and Religious Maturity, First International Conference on Moral and Religious Development,* 403–40. Morristown, N.J.: Silver Burdett Co., 1980.
_____. *The Evolving Self: Problem and Process in Human Development.* Cambridge: Harvard University Press, 1982.
Keller, Catherine. *From a Broken Web: Separation, Sexism, and Self.* Boston: Beacon Press, 1986.
_____. "Goddess, Ear, and Metaphor: On the Journey of Nelle Morton." *Journal of Feminist Studies in Religion* 4, no. 2 (Fall 1988): 51–67.
_____. "Toward a Postpatriarchal Postmodernity." In *Spirituality and Society: Postmodern Visions,* ed. David Ray Griffin, 63–80. Albany: State University of New York Press, 1988.
_____. "Seeing and Sucking: On Relation and Essence in Feminist Theology." In *Horizons in Feminist Theology,* ed. Rebecca S. Chopp and Sheila Greeve Davaney, 54–78. Minneapolis: Fortress Press, 1997.

Koenig, John. *New Testament Hospitality: Partnership with Strangers as Promise and Mission*. Philadelphia: Fortress Press, 1985.

Koestler, Arthur. *The Act of Creation*. New York: Macmillan, 1964, 1969.

Kohut, Heinz. *Analysis of the Self*. New York: International Universities Press, 1971.

Kollias, Karen. "Class Realities: Create a New Power Base." *Quest, a Feminist Quarterly* 1, no. 3 (Winter 1975): 28–43.

Kramer, Deirdre A., and Jacqueline Melchior. "Gender, Role Conflict and the Development of Relativistic and Dialectical Thinking." *Sex Roles* 23, no. 9/10 (November 1990): 553–75.

Kristeva, Julia. *The Kristeva Reader*. Edited by Toril Moi. New York: Columbia University Press, 1986.

Lambert, Jean. "Becoming Human: A Contextual Approach to Decisions About Pregnancy and Abortion." In *Feminism and Process Thought*, ed. Sheila Greeve Davaney, 106–37. New York: Edwin Mellen Press, 1981.

LeClerc, Ivor. *Whitehead's Metaphysics: An Introductory Exposition*. London: George Allen and Unwin, 1958.

Lerner, Harriet Goldhor. *Women in Therapy*. Northvale, N.J.: Jason Aronson Inc., 1988.

Levinas, Emmanuel. *Totality and Infinity*. Trans. Alphonso Lingis. Pittsburgh: Duquesne University Press, 1969.

Levine, Ellen G. "Women and Creativity: Art-In-Relationship." *The Arts in Psychotherapy* 16, no. 4 (1989): 309–25.

Loder, James E. "Creativity In and Beyond Human Development." In *Aesthetic Dimensions of Religious Education*, ed. Gloria Durka and Joanmarie Smith, 219–35. New York: Paulist Press, 1979.

_____. "Transformation in Christian Education." *Religious Education* 76, no. 2 (1981): 204–21.

_____. *The Transforming Moment*. 2d ed. Colorado Springs: Helmers & Howard, 1989; Harper & Row, 1981.

Loomer, Bernard M. "S-I-Z-E Is the Measure." In *Religious Experience and Process Theology: The Pastoral Implications of a Major Modern Movement*, ed. Harry James Cargas and Bernard Lee, 69–76. New York: Paulist Press, 1976.

_____. "Two Conceptions of Power." *Process Studies* 6, no. 1 (Spring 1976): 5–32.

_____. "The Size of God." In *The Size of God: Bernard Loomer's Theology in Context*, ed. William Dean and Larry E. Axel, 20–51. Macon, Ga.: Mercer University Press, 1987.

Lorde, Audre. *Sister Outsider*. Freedom, Calif.: The Crossing Press, 1984.

Lowery, Richard H. "Sabbath and Survival: Abundance and Self-Restraint in a Culture of Excess." *Encounter* 54, no. 2 (Spring 1993): 143–67.

Lugones, Maria C., and Elizabeth V. Spelman. "Have We Got a Theory for You! Feminist Theory, Cultural Imperialism and the Demand for 'The Woman's Voice.'" *Women's Studies International Forum* 6, no. 6 (1983): 573–81.

MacCormac, Earl R. *Metaphor and Myth in Science and Religion*. Durham, N.C.: Duke University Press, 1976.

Macy, Joanna. "The Ecological Self: Postmodern Ground for Right Action." In *Sacred Interconnections*, ed. David Ray Griffin, 35–48. Albany: State University of New York Press, 1990.

Martire, Lynn M., Mary Ann Parris Stephens, Melissa M. Franks. "Multiple Roles of Women Caregivers: Feelings of Mastery and Self-Esteem as Predictors

of Psychosocial Well-Being." *Journal of Women & Aging* 9, no. 1/2 (1997): 117–31.
McAvoy, Jane. "Hospitality: A Feminist Theology of Education." *Teaching Theology and Religion* 1, no. 1 (February 1998): 20–26.
McCarthy, Marie. "Empathy: A Bridge Between." *Journal of Pastoral Care* 46, no. 2 (Summer 1992): 119–28.
McConville, William E. "The Dwelling and the Journey: The Early Christian Experience of Mission." Proceedings from the Annual Federation Council Conference. Pittsburgh: Franciscan Federation, 1989.
McFague, Sallie. *Speaking in Parables*. Philadelphia: Fortress Press, 1975.
―――――. *Metaphorical Theology: Models of God in Religious Language*. Philadelphia: Fortress Press, 1982.
―――――. *Models of God: Theology for an Ecological, Nuclear Age*. Philadelphia: Fortress Press, 1987.
―――――. "Cosmology and Christianity: Implications of the Common Creation Story for Theology." In *Theology at the End of Modernity*, ed. Sheila Greeve Davaney, 19–40. Philadelphia: Trinity Press International, 1991.
―――――. *The Body of God: An Ecological Theology*. Minneapolis: Fortress Press, 1993.
Mencher, Julie. *Intimacy in Lesbian Relationships: A Critical Re-Examination of Fusion*. Work in Progress, no. 42. Wellesley, Mass.: Stone Center, 1990.
Miles, Margaret. "Pilgrimage as Metaphor in a Nuclear Age." *Theology Today* 45, no. 2 (July 1988): 166–79.
Miller, Alice. *The Drama of the Gifted Child*. New York: Basic Books, 1981.
―――――. *For Your Own Good: Hidden Cruelty in Child-Rearing and the Roots of Violence*. New York: Farrar, Strauss, and Giroux, 1983.
―――――. *Thou Shalt Not Be Aware: Society's Betrayal of the Child*. New York: Farrar, Strauss, and Giroux, 1984.
Miller, Jean Baker. *Toward a New Psychology of Women*. Boston: Beacon Press, 1976.
―――――. *The Construction of Anger in Women and Men*. Work in Progress, no. 4. Wellesley, Mass.: Stone Center, 1983.
―――――. *The Development of Women's Sense of Self*. Work in Progress, no. 12. Wellesley, Mass.: Stone Center, 1984.
―――――. *What Do We Mean by Relationships?* Work in Progress, no. 22. Wellesley, Mass.: Stone Center, 1986.
Miller-McLemore, Bonnie. *Also a Mother: Work and Family as Theological Dilemma*. Nashville: Abingdon Press, 1994.
Milligan, Charles S. "Ethics, Ethos and Habitat—Part One." *Iliff Review* 33, no. 3 (Fall 1976): 21–35.
―――――. "Ethics, Ethos and Habitat—Part Two." *Iliff Review* 34, no. 2 (Spring 1977): 39–52.
Moran, Gabriel. "Alternative Developmental Images." In *Stages of Faith and Religious Development*, ed. James W. Fowler, Karl Ernst Nipkow, and Friedrich Schweitzer, 149–61. New York: Crossroad, 1991.
Morawski, Jill G. *Practicing Feminisms, Reconstructing Psychology: Notes on a Liminal Science*. Ann Arbor, Mich.: University of Michigan Press, 1994.
More, Ellen S. "Empathy as a Hermeneutic Practice." *Theoretical Medicine* 17 (1996): 243–54.
Morton, Nelle. *The Journey Is Home*. Boston: Beacon Press, 1985.
Moseley, Romney M. *Becoming a Self Before God: Critical Transformations*. Nashville: Abingdon, 1991.

Bibliography

Narayan, Una. "Working Together Across Difference." *Hypatia* 3, no. 2 (1988): 31–48.
Neville, Robert C. *Creativity and God: A Challenge to Process Theology.* New York: Seabury Press, 1980.
Nicholson, Linda J., ed. *Feminism/Postmodernism.* New York: Routledge, 1990.
──────. "Feminism and the Politics of Postmodernism." In *Feminism and Postmodernism*, ed. Margaret Ferguson and Jennifer Wicke, 69–85. Durham, N.C.: Duke University Press, 1994.
Niebuhr, Richard R. "Pilgrims and Pioneers." *Parabola* 9, no. 3 (August 1984): 6–13.
Nobles, Wade W. "Extended Self: Rethinking the So-Called Negro Self-Concept." In *Black Psychology*, 3d ed., ed. Reginald L. Jones, 295–304. Berkeley, Calif.: Cobb & Henry, 1991.
Nouwen, Henri J. M. *Reaching Out.* Garden City, N.Y.: Image Books, 1975, 1986.
──────. *The Genesee Diary: Report from a Trappist Monastery.* Garden City, N.Y.: Image Books, 1981.
Ochs, Carol. *Women and Spirituality.* Totowa, N.J.: Rowman & Allanheld, 1983.
Ochse, Rhona. "Why There Were Relatively Few Eminent Women Creators." *Journal of Creative Behavior* 25, no. 4 (1991): 334–43.
──────. *Before the Gates of Excellence: The Determinants of Creative Genius.* Cambridge: Cambridge University Press, 1990.
Ogletree, Thomas W. *Hospitality to the Stranger.* Philadelphia: Fortress Press, 1985.
Olds, Linda E. *Metaphors of Interrelatedness: Towards a Systems Theory of Psychology.* Albany: State University of New York Press, 1992.
Palmer, Parker J. *The Company of Strangers.* New York: Crossroad, 1981.
──────. *The Courage to Teach: Exploring the Inner Landscape of a Teacher's Life.* San Francisco: Jossey-Bass Publishers, 1998.
Pamment, Margaret. "Path and Residence Metaphors in the Fourth Gospel." *Theology* 88, no. 722 (March 1985): 118–24.
Parabola 15, no. 4. "Hospitality." (November 1990): 1–127.
Parks, Sharon Daloz. *The Critical Years: The Young Adult Search for a Faith to Live By.* San Francisco: Harper and Row, 1986.
──────. "Home and Pilgrimage: Companion Metaphors for Personal and Social Transformation." *Soundings* 72, no. 2–3 (Summer/Fall 1989): 297–315.
Pennington, M. Basil. *Centering Prayer: Renewing an Ancient Christian Prayer Form.* Garden City, N.Y.: Image Books, 1982.
Peterson, Eugene H. "Rhythms of Grace." *Weavings* 8, no. 2 (March/April 1993): 14–19.
Pine, Fred. *Drive, Ego, Object, and Self: A Synthesis for Clinical Work.* New York: Basic Books, 1990.
Placher, William C. *The Domestication of Transcendence: How Modern Thinking about God Went Wrong.* Louisville: Westminster John Knox, 1996.
──────. *Narratives of a Vulnerable God: Christ, Theology, and Scripture.* Louisville: Westminster John Knox, 1994.
Porter, Natalie. "Supervision of Psychotherapists: Integrating Anti-Racist, Feminist, and Multicultural Perspectives." In *Bringing Cultural Diversity to Feminist Psychology*, ed. Hope Landrine, 163–75. Washington: American Psychological Association, 1995.
Post, Stephen G. "The Inadequacy of Selflessness: God's Suffering and the Theory of Love." *Journal of the American Academy of Religion* 56 (1988): 213–28.

Rabuzzi, Kathryn Allen. *The Sacred and the Feminine: Toward a Theology of Housework*. New York: Seabury Press, 1982.

———. "Women's Work and the Sense of Time in Women's Lives." In *Sacred Dimensions of Women's Experience*, ed. Elizabeth Dodson Gray, 153–65. Wellesley, Mass.: Roundtable Press, 1988.

Ragsdale, Katherine Hancock, ed. *Boundary Wars: Intimacy and Distance in Healing Relationships*. Cleveland, Ohio: Pilgrim Press, 1996.

Rizzuto, Ana-Maria. *The Birth of the Living God*. Chicago: University of Chicago Press, 1979.

Rogers, Carl. "Empathic: An Unappreciated Way of Being." *Counseling Psychologist* 5, no. 2 (1974): 2–10.

Roland, Alan. *In Search of Self in India and Japan: Toward a Cross-Cultural Psychology*. Princeton: Princeton University Press, 1988.

Rothbart, Daniel. *Explaining the Growth of Scientific Knowledge: Metaphors, Models and Meanings*. Lampeter, U.K.: Edwin Mellen Press, 1997.

Rouner, Leroy S., ed. *The Longing for Home*. Boston University Studies in Philosophy and Religion, no. 17. Notre Dame, Ind.: University of Notre Dame Press, 1997.

Ruddick, Sara. "Remarks on the Sexual Politics of Reason." In *Women and Moral Theory*, ed. Eva Feder Kittay and Diana T. Meyers, 237–60. Totowa, N.J.: Rowman & Littlefield, 1987.

———. *Maternal Thinking: Toward a Politics of Peace*. Boston: Beacon Press, 1989.

Russell, Letty M. *Church in the Round: Feminist Interpretation of the Church*. Louisville, Ky.: Westminster Press, 1993.

Saiving, Valerie. "The Human Situation: A Feminine View." In *Womanspirit Rising*, ed. Carol P. Christ and Judith Plaskow, 25–42. San Francisco: Harper & Row, 1979.

Samuels, Andrew. *The Plural Psyche: Personality, Morality, and the Father*. London: Routledge, 1989.

Sanders, Scott Russell. *Staying Put: Making a Home in a Restless World*. Boston: Beacon Press, 1993.

Saussy, Caroll. *God Images and Self-Esteem: Empowering Women in a Patriarchal Society*. Louisville, Ky.: Westminster/John Knox Press, 1991.

Schachtel, Ernest G. *Metamorphosis: On the Development of Affect, Perception, Attention, and Memory*. New York: Basic Books, 1984.

Schafer, R. "Generative Empathy in the Treatment Situation." *Psychoanalytic Quarterly* 28, no. 3 (1959): 342–73. Quoted in Ellen S. More, "Empathy as a Hermeneutic Practice." *Theoretical Medicine* 17 (1996): 243–54.

Schlauch, Chris R. *Faithful Companioning: How Pastoral Counseling Heals*. Minneapolis: Fortress Press, 1995.

Schweiker, William. "To Dwell On the Earth: Authority and Ecumenical Theology." In *Worldviews and Warrants: Plurality and Authority in Theology*, ed. Eilliam Schweiker and Per M. Anderson, 89–112. Lanham, Md.: University Press of America, 1987.

Sherburne, Donald W. *A Key to Whitehead's Process and Reality*. Chicago: University of Chicago Press, 1966.

Shriver, Donald W., Jr. "The Pain and Promise of Pluralism." *Christian Century* 97, no. 11 (26 March 1980): 345–50.

Signs 22, no.2 (Winter 1997): 341–402.

Simon, Robin W. "Gender, Multiple Roles, Role Meaning, and Mental Health." *Journal of Health and Social Behavior* 36 (June 1995): 182–94.

Smith, Archie, Jr. *The Relational Self: Ethics and Therapy from a Black Church Perspective.* Nashville: Abingdon, 1982.
Snyder-Ott, Joelynn. *Women and Creativity.* Millbrae, Calif.: Les Femmes Publishing, 1978.
Somerville, Diana. "Mary Catherine Bateson: Men Disadvantaged by Single Focus When Multiple Attention Is needed." *Boulder Daily Camera* (Boulder, Colo.), 14 September 1993, 1(B).
Southard, Naomi and Richard Payne. "Teaching the Introduction to Religions: Religious Pluralism in a Post-Colonial World." *Teaching Theology and Religion* 1, no. 1 (February 1998): 51–57.
Stein, Edith. *On the Problem of Empathy.* Trans. Waltraut Stein. Washington, D.C.: ICS Publications, 1989.
Stern, Daniel N. *The Interpersonal World of the Infant: A View from Psychoanalysis and Developmental Psychology.* New York: Basic Books, 1985.
──────. *Diary of a Baby.* New York: Basic Books, 1990.
Stiver, Irene P. *Work Inhibitions in Women.* Work in Progress, no. 3. Wellesley, Mass.: Stone Center, 1983.
Stone, Judith. "Creating the Possible." In *Sacred Dimensions of Women's Experience*, ed. Elizabeth Dodson Gray, 40–45. Wellesley, Mass.: Roundtable Press, 1988.
Storr, Anthony. "Individuation and the Creative Process." *Journal of Analytical Psychology* 28 (October 1983): 329–43.
Stoval, Lois H. Grace. "A Woman's Path to Power as a Sacred Process." In *Sacred Dimensions of Women's Experience*, ed. Elizabeth Dodson Gray, 23–31. Wellesley, Mass.: Roundtable Press, 1988.
Strayer, Janet. "Affective and Cognitive Perspectives on Empathy." In *Empathy and Its Development*, ed. Nancy Eisenberg and Janet Strayer, 218–44. Cambridge, Mass.: Cambridge University Press, 1987.
Suchocki, Marjorie Hewitt. "Openness and Mutuality in Process Thought and Feminist Action." In *Feminism and Process Thought*, ed. Sheila Greeve Davaney, 62–82. New York: Edwin Mellen Press, 1981.
──────. *God, Christ, Church.* New York: Crossroad, 1982.
──────. "Earthsong, Godsong: Women's Spirituality." *Theology Today* 45, no. 4 (January 1989): 392–402.
──────. *The Fall to Violence: Original Sin in Relational Theology.* New York: Continuum Publishing, 1995.
Surrey, Janet L. *The Self-In-Relation: A Theory of Women's Development.* Work in Progress, no. 13. Wellesley, Mass.: Stone Center, 1985.
──────. *Relationship and Empowerment.* Work in Progress, no. 30. Wellesley, Mass.: Stone Center, 1987.
Surrey, Janet L., Alexandra G. Kaplan, and Judith V. Jordan. *Empathy Revisited.* Work in Progress, no. 40. Wellesley, Mass.: Stone Center, 1990.
Tanner, Kathryn. "Social Theory Concerning the 'New Social Movements' and the Practice of Feminist Theology." In *Horizons in Feminist Theology: Identity, Tradition, and Norms*, ed. Rebecca S. Chopp and Sheila Greeve Davaney, 179–197. Minneapolis: Fortress Press, 1997.
Taylor, Mark Kline. *Remembering Esperanza: A Cultural-Political Theology for North American Praxis.* Maryknoll, N.Y.: Orbis Books, 1990.
Thandeka. "The Self Between Feminist Theory and Theology." In *Horizons in Feminist Theology: Identity, Tradition, and Norms*, ed. Rebecca S. Chopp and Sheila Greeve Davaney, 79–98. Minneapolis: Fortress Press, 1997.

Thistlethwaite, Susan Brooks. *Sex, Race, and God: Christian Feminism in Black and White*. New York: Crossroad, 1989.

———. "'I Am Become Death': God In the Nuclear Age." In *Lift Every Voice: Constructing Christian Theologies from the Underside*, ed. Susan Brooks Thistlethwaite and Mary Potter Engel, 95–110. San Francisco: Harper, 1990.

Thompson, Ross A. "Empathy and Emotional Understanding." In *Empathy and Its Development*, ed. Nancy Eisenberg and Janet Strayer, 119–45. Cambridge: Cambridge University Press, 1987.

Tillich, Paul. *Systematic Theology, Vol. 1*. Chicago: University of Chicago Press, 1951.

Tingey, Holly, Gary Kiger, and Pamela J. Riley. "Juggling Multiple Roles: Perceptions of Working Mothers." *Social Science Journal* 33, no. 2 (1996): 183–91.

Tinker, George. "Native Americans and the Land." In *Lift Every Voice: Constructing Christian Theologies from the Underside*, ed. Susan Brooks Thistlethwaite and Mary Potter Engel, 141–51. San Francisco: Harper, 1990.

Unterberger, Gail Lynn. *Through the Lens of Feminist Psychology and Feminist Theology: A Theoretical Model for Pastoral Counseling*. Ann Arbor, Mich.: University Microfilms International, 1990.

Van Wormer, Katherine. "Co-dependency: Implications for Women and Therapy." *Women and Therapy* 8, no. 4 (1989): 51–63.

Von Franz, Marie-Louise. *Patterns of Creativity Mirrored in Creation Myths*. Zurich: Spring Publications, 1978, 1975, 1972.

Waldron, Ingrid, and Jerry A. Jacobs. "Effects of Multiple Roles on Women's Health—Evidence from a National Longitudinal Study." *Women and Health* 15, no. 1 (1989): 3–19.

Walker, Alice. *In Search of Our Mothers' Gardens*. San Diego: Harcourt Brace Jovanovich, 1983.

Walker, Lenore E. A. "Foreword." In *Personality and Psychopathology: Feminist Reappraisals*, ed. Laura S. Brown and Mary Ballou, vii–x. New York: Guilford Press, 1992.

Wear, Delese, ed. *The Center of the Web: Women and Solitude*. Albany, N.Y.: State University of New York Press, 1993.

———. "A Reconnection to Self: Women and Solitude." In *The Center of the Web: Women and Solitude*, ed. Delese Wear, 3–11. Albany, N.Y.: State University of New York Press, 1993.

Weavings 8, no. 2. "And God Rested." (March/April 1993): 1–48.

Wells, Rosalie Ann. "Between Earth and Sky: Toward a Psychology of Homecoming." Ph.D. diss., University of Dallas, 1983.

Westhelle, Vitor. "Creation Motifs in the Search for a Vital Space: A Latin American Perspective." In *Lift Every Voice: Constructing Christian Theologies from the Underside*, ed. Susan Brooks Thistlethwaite and Mary Potter Engel, 128–40. San Francisco: Harper, 1990.

Westkott, Marcia C. "On the New Psychology of Women: A Cautionary View." *Feminist Issues* 10, no. 2 (Fall 1990): 3–18.

Whelehan, Imelda. *Modern Feminist Thought: From the Second Wave to "Post-Feminism."* New York: New York University Press, 1995.

Whitehead, Alfred North. *Science and the Modern World*. New York: Macmillan Company, 1925.

———. *Process and Reality*. Corrected edition, ed. David Ray Griffin and Donald W. Sherburne. New York: Macmillan Publishing, 1929; Free Press, 1978.

———. *Adventures of Ideas*. New York: Macmillan Company, 1933; Mentor Books, 1955.

———. *Modes of Thought*. New York: Macmillan Publishing, 1938; Free Press, 1968.

———. *Religion in the Making*. New York: Macmillan Company, 1926; Meridian Books, 1960.

Williams, Daniel Day. *The Spirit and the Forms of Love*. New York: Harper & Row, 1968; reprint, Lanham, Md.: University Press of America, 1981.

Williams, Delores. "Womanist Theology." In *Weaving the Visions: New Patterns in Feminist Spirituality*, ed. Judith Plaskow and Carol P. Christ, 179–86. San Francisco: Harper & Row, 1989.

Winnicott, D. W. *The Maturational Processes and the Facilitating Environment*. New York: International Universities Press, 1965.

Winter, Gibson. *Liberating Creation: Foundations of Religious Social Ethics*. New York: Crossroad, 1981.

Wolfman, Brunetta R. *Women and Their Many Roles*. Work in Progress, no. 7. Wellesley, Mass.: Stone Center, 1984.

Woolf, Virginia. *A Room of One's Own*. San Diego: Harcourt Brace Jovanovich, 1929.

Wright, Wendy M. *Sacred Dwelling: A Spirituality of Family Life*. New York: Crossroad, 1990.

INDEX

abide, 129, 131, 134
abstract, 4, 10-11, 18, 34-5, 40, 42, 85, 89, 116, 119, 153
abuse, 48, 107, 123
actual entity, 33–4, 42, 56–7, 60–8, 99, 101–5, 134
aesthetic, 11, 25, 40, 42, 58, 60, 78, 115
agape, 66, 80
agency, 4, 8, 17–9, 39, 48, 54, 63, 83–4, 98
ambiguity, 7, 26, 28, 30, 38, 53, 96–7, 104, 116, 145, 154
anger, 30, 41, 54, 92
autonomy, 2, 9–10, 18, 26, 47–8, 52, 64, 85–9, 123, 140, 155

Bateson, Mary Catherine, 95, 102, 114, 116, 117
beauty, ix, x, 18, 35, 42, 58, 65, 84, 91, 94, 100–8, 115, 125, 148, 149–50
boundary, x, 2, 19, 38, 52–6, 62, 66–9, 72–4, 87, 92, 94, 126, 130, 152
Brock, Rita Nakashima, x, 22, 39, 64, 66, 70, 73, 79, 80, 81
Brown, Delwin, 16, 19, 39, 76, 151, 157
Browning, Don S., 81, 121, 139

center, 52, 54, 61, 102, 107–11, 127–32, 136, 143, 149, 152
chaos, 21, 53, 67, 104, 135, 150, 156
Chodorow, Nancy J., 2, 75
clarity, x, xi, 7, 9–13, 17, 83–111, 116, 120–2, 130, 136, 143, 149, 152–3
Cobb, John B., Jr., 35, 37, 43, 64, 76, 79, 80, 81, 134, 140, 144

codependence. *See* enmeshment
compassion, 45–74, 104–6, 123, 143, 149
concrescence, 33–6, 42, 57–9, 61, 63, 65, 99–102, 105, 149
conflict, 2, 36, 50, 85, 98
consciousness, 20, 26, 28, 31, 43, 84, 100, 101, 115, 119
context, 3, 4, 8, 19–20, 28, 30, 33, 37–40, 47–9, 53, 61, 75, 83, 95–7, 125, 144, 147, 154
continuity, 6, 36, 47, 56, 125, 134–7, 142
contrast, ix, x, 11, 28, 38, 51–9, 67, 83, 98–101, 104, 107, 115–6, 121, 128, 130, 148–9
courage, 13, 31, 50, 52, 66, 69–72, 79, 85, 91, 126, 131, 137
creation spirituality, 22
creativity
    contextual, 10, 19–23, 29, 39, 101, 125, 138
    creative process, 23, 27–9, 31, 41–2, 45, 84, 134, 137, 148
    definition, 17

Daly, Mary, 11, 16, 22, 39
dance, 23, 138
decision, 20, 33, 101–3, 106, 108, 128, 134
differentiation, 48, 51, 52, 84, 85
diffuse, 85, 90–3, 99, 100
    See also fragmentation
divergent thinking, 26
dualism, 4, 10, 22, 42, 56, 58
dwelling, 119–39

ecology/ecofeminism, 36, 38, 116, 123, 127, 136, 141
empathy, 5, 31, 45–82, 92, 97, 100, 128, 136, 152–3
  defined, 7, 45
empirical theology, 10, 13, 103
enmeshment, 50–2, 59, 63–7, 77, 86–7, 90, 93, 99, 113, 154
epistemology, xi, 3, 13, 15, 58, 76, 88, 152
Eros, erotic, 22, 66, 128, 148
ex nihilo, 19, 43
external relations, 57

Fox, Matthew, 22, 23, 39, 40, 74, 81
fragmentation, xi, 7, 27, 85, 90, 95–9, 106–9, 149–50
Frankenberry, Nancy K., 4, 11, 14, 16, 40, 43, 103, 116
freedom, 9, 18, 37, 70, 89, 105, 108
Freud, Sigmund, 2, 40, 111, 154
fusion. *See* enmeshment

Gilligan, Carol, 2, 97, 115
God
  consequent nature, 35–6, 43, 65–8, 74, 103–5, 108, 117, 128, 148, 150
  omnipotence, 22, 66
  omniscience, 68
  primordial nature, 35–6, 42–3, 65, 80, 104–5, 108, 117, 149
Graham, Larry Kent, 39, 71, 81, 112, 115, 117

harmony, 11, 12, 23, 30, 52, 58–60, 71, 73, 103, 105, 108, 115, 139, 148
hearth, 125, 130, 143
Heidegger, Martin, 142
Heyward, Carter, 16, 22, 39, 64, 69, 71, 72, 79, 80, 81, 106, 117, 143, 145, 157
holding, 13, 46, 59–60, 67, 97, 103, 126, 129, 150
home, 71, 89, 115, 122–32, 141, 145
hooks, bell, 97, 115, 141
hope, 21, 24, 105, 108, 136
hospitality, 45, 80, 124, 126–8, 133, 135, 142, 150–3

identity, 2, 5, 7, 10, 17, 20, 35–7, 46–7, 50–2, 57–8, 66, 72, 83–6, 97–102, 109, 112, 122, 130-1, 139-43, 149-53
imagination, 17, 77, 134, 151
immanence, 57–8, 60, 65, 68, 74, 105–6, 110, 117
incarnation, 28, 69, 74, 80, 148
infancy, 88–90, 113, 149, 154
influence, 15, 48–9, 57–67, 74, 86, 93
initial aim, 34–5, 42, 65, 74, 104, 106, 149
intensity, 11, 48, 58– 60, 99, 100, 104, 107
intention, 69, 77, 84, 106, 109, 134
  See also agency
internal relations, 34, 57, 62, 65, 83, 136

Jung, Carl G., 27, 40, 41, 42
justice, 11–2, 21–2, 63, 68–9, 74, 78, 89, 107, 123, 137, 149

kaleidoscope, 90, 94, 95, 98, 119
Kohut, Heinz, 46, 75
Kristeva, Julia, 154, 158

lesbian, xi, 69, 86–7, 112
Levinas, Emmanuel, 130, 143
liberation theology, 21, 24, 70
limitation, 10, 19, 23, 29, 39, 54, 61–3, 67–68, 74–7, 80, 101, 104, 108, 143
Loomer, Bernard M., 13, 16, 59, 60, 67, 79, 80, 115, 128, 134, 144
Lorde, Audre, 22, 39, 53, 77

maturity, 1–3, 8, 53, 89, 123, 128, 133, 135–6
McCarthy, Marie, 53, 67, 77, 80, 81, 92, 113, 153, 157
McFague, Sallie, 8, 15, 38, 119, 121, 128, 139, 142, 143
Miller, Alice, 93, 114
Miller, Jean Baker, xii, 2, 14, 59, 61, 76, 77, 78, 79, 113, 114
Miller-McLemore, Bonnie, 41, 49, 76
monastic, 109–10, 132, 143
Morton, Nelle, 91, 113, 120, 121, 125, 131, 139, 141, 143

Index

novelty, x, 17, 20, 24, 34–5, 43, 59, 65, 134
   constructive, 34, 43, 101
   generative, 34, 42, 105

Ogletree, Thomas W., 75, 142
ontology, 9, 13, 19, 39, 62, 99, 151
openness, x, 26, 29–31, 38, 40, 45, 52, 56–60, 67, 70–4, 93, 97, 103–6, 124, 127, 148–9, 153
   expressive/revelatory, 45, 52, 63, 69, 74, 103, 148
   receptive, 45, 52, 60, 63–9, 74, 148
order, 18, 19, 21, 35, 58, 60, 121

Parks, Sharon Daloz, 41, 122
passive, 52, 55, 60, 71, 73, 94, 121, 137, 144
peace, 67, 108, 110, 136, 150
pilgrimage, 122, 150
power, 3, 19, 22, 39, 47, 49, 58–9, 64, 69, 79, 88, 93, 103, 112, 128–9
privacy, 54, 62, 68, 143, 152
progress, 17, 34–6, 88, 122–3, 128, 131–2, 150, 154

reality, xi, 4–5, 7–8, 10, 13, 21, 23, 31–7, 42, 52–3, 56–7, 62, 67, 69, 73, 74, 97, 99, 102–3, 110, 121, 123, 125, 130–5, 147–50
response/ability, 50, 71–4
resurrection, 70
revelation, 45, 52, 69–71, 132
   See also self-disclosure
risk. *See* courage
Rogers, Carl, 31, 46, 75
roles (social), multiple, xi, 5, 7, 30, 86, 87, 95–6, 101, 130, 150
Ruddick, Sara, 96, 112, 115
Russell, Letty M., 115, 127, 142

Sabbath, 133, 144
sacred space, 125
sacrifice, 21, 48, 49, 66, 73, 80, 111
satisfaction, 33–5, 50, 60, 99–104, 107, 110, 134–5, 148

self
   connective, 9
   definition of, 6
   embodied, 22, 127-8, 142
   separative, 88
self-disclosure, 45, 52, 55, 69, 80, 91, 94, 128, 136, 148
   See also revelation
self-in-relation, 47–50, 65, 71, 74, 77, 91
shame, 92
sin, xi, 20, 32, 71–4, 81, 107, 149
solitude, 30, 54, 63, 68, 110
stature. *See* "size"
Stein, Edith, 51, 77
stereotype, 30, 43, 52, 54, 87, 112, 125, 137, 138, 142
Stern, Daniel N., 89, 90, 94, 113
Stone Center, x, xii, 47, 48, 56, 58, 61, 74, 76, 85, 91, 93, 94, 157
stranger, 45, 75, 126, 128, 129, 142, 150, 152
subjective aim. *See* initial aim
suffering, 65, 69, 70, 80, 97, 111, 127, 144
surrender, 52, 53, 55, 66
systems theory, 86, 112

temenos. *See* holding
Tillich, Paul, 19, 39, 43
transcendence, 27, 52, 54, 63–4, 78, 105–6, 117, 148, 149
transition, 33–6, 57
triviality, 107, 134, 149
   See also fragmentation

unconscious, 26, 28, 40, 99
unity, 11, 33, 35, 57, 59, 61–2, 84, 94–5, 98–104, 127

vagueness, 18, 92, 98, 99, 100
value, 12, 25, 42, 56, 58–9, 102, 105, 107, 115–6, 148

web, of relationships, 7, 47, 50, 67, 71, 83, 103, 110, 119, 124, 130, 138
welcome, 67, 97, 126–8, 142–3, 152
Woolf, Virginia, 29, 41

HIEBERT LIBRARY

3 6877 00163 5670

BT
83.6
.H84
1998

DATE DUE

AG 8 '00			
SE 12 '00			
OC 10 '00			
NO 7 '00			
DE 05 '00			
JA 15 '04			

DEMCO 38-297